Philosophies and Cultures

FREDERICK C. COPLESTON,
S.J., F.B.A.

Professor Emeritus of
History of Philosophy in the
University of London

Oxford New York Toronto Melbourne
OXFORD UNIVERSITY PRESS
1980

31 734 *Oxford University Press, Walton Street, Oxford OX2 6DP*

OXFORD LONDON GLASGOW
NEW YORK TORONTO MELBOURNE WELLINGTON
KUALA LUMPUR SINGAPORE HONG KONG TOKYO
DELHI BOMBAY CALCUTTA MADRAS KARACHI
NAIROBI DAR ES SALAAM CAPE TOWN

British Library Cataloguing in Publication Data
Copleston, Frederick Charles
Philosophies and cultures
1. Philosophy, Comparative
I. Title
109 B799 79-41495
ISBN 0 19 213960 6

Printed in Hong Kong by Bright Sun Printing Press Co. Ltd.

Contents

Preface

This book is substantially the text of the first series of Martin D'Arcy lectures, given at Oxford in the Michaelmas term of 1978. Father Martin D'Arcy was Master of Campion Hall in the University of Oxford from 1933 to 1945. During his years at Oxford, both before and after his appointment as Master, he was a well-known and highly respected figure in University life. He also had a wide circle of friends outside Oxford, both in Great Britain and abroad, especially in the United States, a country to which he was deeply attached and where he spent happy periods in his later life. His books, a number of which were translated into foreign languages, made him known to a still wider circle. After his death in 1976, the then Master of Campion Hall, the Revd. B. Winterborn, S.J., conceived the idea of arranging for a series of memorial lectures to be given annually at Oxford. Realization of this project was made possible by the co-operation of British and foreign friends of Martin D'Arcy and of Campion Hall. The present writer was invited to give the first series of lectures.

It happens that the first Martin D'Arcy lecturer is an historian of philosophy. But it is not envisaged that the succeeding series should all deal with philosophical topics. The lecturers are likely to represent a variety of disciplines. Though, however, the lectures are supposed to be suitable for university audiences, they are not intended to be of such a specialized nature that they can be understood only by students in some limited academic area of study, such as philosophy, theology, physics, history or archaeology. They are intended for a wider audience. It is this aspect of the Martin D'Arcy lectures which encouraged me to venture into fields in which I am not, and at my age cannot hope to be, a specialist. However, some further remarks may be appropriate to explain why I have stuck my neck out by treating themes relating to Indian, Chinese and Islamic thought.

Having written a certain amount about the history of western philosophy, in recent years I have become interested in the study of comparative philosophy, in noting similarities and dissimilarities between western philosophy and the philosophies of other cultures, as well as in the question whether any recurrent patterns are discernible in the historical development of philosophical thought. This is a relatively new branch of study. There are, needless to say, specialists in such subjects as Indian, Chinese and Japanese thought, specialists who are thoroughly conversant with the relevant oriental language or languages. So far, however, few writers have risked embarking on more or less overall comparative surveys. This is perfectly understandable. For one thing, a person can hardly hope to acquire a real knowledge of all the relevant languages. For another thing, the literature in a particular field of study, such as Buddhist thought, may be so extensive that a scholar may very reasonably confine his attention to an even more limited area, such as Buddhism in Tibet or to a particular Buddhist school. At the same time in the modern world it is highly desirable that we should widen our horizons and acquire some knowledge of the ways of thought of other peoples, of cultures other than our own. Philosophy in a given country can become extremely parochial or provincial. Perhaps this is only to be expected, when philosophy has become a highly specialized discipline. Students are naturally not encouraged to dissipate their energies. We cannot, however, leave the task of increasing mutual understanding among peoples simply to politicians and traders. Philosophers are few in number, and, though there are exceptions, they do not generally influence the fortunes of peoples in a striking or dramatic manner. They have, however, a part to play in contributing to an enlarged awareness of the mentalities of other peoples. And there is room for works of a general character which do not claim to be the fruit of specialized knowledge but which can serve the purpose of illustrating different lines of thought. We are all human beings, to whatever culture we belong; and the philosophical traditions of different cultures can be seen as complementary expressions of the human mind, which should be taken into account in any world-wide dialogue.

The comparative study of the philosophies of different cultures implies certain presuppositions which give rise to problems of some importance. Reference is made to these presuppositions in the first chapter of this book, and something further is said in the Epilogue. The matter can, therefore, be passed over here. I wish, however, to make some remarks here about a possible objection to any claim that study of the philosophical traditions of non-western cultures is a worth-while procedure.

Any treatment of the historical development of philosophy in India will obviously cover, for example, the systems of the various Vedic schools. But the thought of the classical Indian schools became pretty well fossilized in the course of time, and in any case one not infrequently comes across modern Indian philosophers who have turned their backs on the past in favour of some western line of thought, such as the so-called analytic movement in the English-speaking world or French and German phenomenology. Similarly, any historical account of philosophy in China will have to refer to such worthies as Confucius and Mencius, to the Taoist sages, and to some Buddhist schools, as well as to Neo-Confucianism. Thought in mainland China, however, is not dominated by a philosophy of western origin. It can thus be argued that the idea of increasing mutual understanding among peoples by studying the classical philosophical traditions of oriental peoples is about as sensible as the idea of promoting understanding of the West through study of the fragments of Parmenides and Heraclitus or of the writings of Nicholas of Cusa. If we want to promote understanding among peoples, we have to look to the present, not to a past which has been or is being abandoned.

This line of argument obviously has some force. But it omits mention of an important point, namely that the classical philosophical tradition of a culture most probably expresses in specifiable ways attitudes and modes of thought which persist and which may very well mould and change whatever has been received from outside. For example, the Chinese had their own way of approaching and handling philosophical topics. Buddhism was to some extent adapted to Chinese traditions and attitudes, and there is no good reason to suppose that China will not imprint its own mentality and outlook on the Marxism which it has received from outside. In other words, while individual systems of philosophy come and go, the connected series of philosophies may very well express and reveal more lasting factors. We cannot simply detach past from present western thought and regard the former as being something purely external to the latter. In a real sense the West is its past. And the same holds good of the East. Confucius and Mencius lived a very long time ago. But it by no means follows that reflection on their ideas tells us nothing about more lasting features of the Chinese outlook or mentality. The recent anti-Confucius campaign can be misleading. The very fact that it occurred should be illuminating. What it illuminates is precisely the point which I have been trying to make.

Let me turn more directly to the structure of this book. As has already been stated, the book represents a series of lectures. When preparing the lectures, I had in mind the possibility that there would

probably be people who were interested in this or that particular theme
but who would not wish to hear all the lectures. I tried, therefore, as far
as was practicable, to cater for these members of the audience. The
result is that the chapters of the book may seem to deal with a variety of
themes which are related to one another only very loosely, falling
indeed within the general area of the comparative study of the
historical development of philosophical thought but treating of distinct
topics or issues within this area. Up to a point this is the case. But there
is rather more unity than may at first sight appear. Western philosophy
could not be excluded; but I felt that some general knowledge of it had
to be presupposed. Hence in the first chapter discussion is confined to
one particular theme relating to western philosophy, namely the
influence on it of extra-philosophical factors. It is indeed my conviction
that in any culture in which philosophy has developed, philosophical
thought has been influenced by a variety of non-philosophical factors.
But I thought that the point could be made most easily by confining
attention in the first instance to western philosophy. In the case,
however, of lectures delivered in a western university, especially to a
general audience, I did not think that a knowledge of the development
of philosophical thought in India and China could simply be presupposed. The second and third chapters, therefore, are devoted
respectively to fairly general surveys of Indian and Chinese thought,
and a chronological appendix has been added to the volume. These two
chapters are followed by comparative discussion of selected aspects of
western, Chinese and, in some cases, Islamic thought. Obviously, there
are plenty of other aspects which might have been discussed, but it was
necessary to select some and neglect others. It was also necessary to
pass over some cultures which would be relevant to any would-be
comprehensive comparative survey of philosophical traditions. Even
with a policy of selection, so much matter has been covered that, as I
am well aware, a philosopher is likely to find discussions of particular
issues sketchy and inadequate. To remedy this defect, however, one
would have had to write a different kind of book.

    As for the last two chapters, they treat of questions which are likely
to arise in the mind of any historian of philosophy, and they may give
the impression of being simply tacked on. This is not, however, quite
the case. There are specifiable connections between questions discussed
in these chapters and what goes before. For example, talk in the first
chapter about the influence of non-philosophical factors on western
philosophy gives rise to the question whether we should not subscribe
to historical or cultural relativism, a topic about which something is

said in the seventh chapter. Again, discussion of different approaches to and ways of handling similar philosophical problems in different cultures is connected with the question, also raised in the seventh chapter, whether we are entitled to speak of 'recurrent' philosophical problems and, if so, in what sense. Further, reference to the question whether any common recurrent pattern of development is discernible in these philosophies, and also to the question whether any laws can be formulated which relate to the historical development of philosophical thought and which enable us to predict is made in the final chapter of this book.

As for the conclusions at which I arrive, some, I think, emerge fairly clearly in the course of the text. In the Epilogue, however, I have tried to draw some threads together, and also to explain why in some cases the discussion of questions raised is, or seems to be, inconclusive. There is no need to say more about this matter at the moment.

When reference is made in the text or footnotes to a book which is also listed in the bibliography, the place of publication and the date are given only in the bibliography.

During the second semester of the academic year 1975–6 I had the pleasure of acting as a visiting professor in the Department of Philosophy of the State University of Hawaii at Honolulu. The student population, as indeed the general population of the islands, is ethnically mixed; and I found that the Department of Philosophy comprised professors and lecturers of different cultural origins, courses being offered on the philosophies of a variety of cultures. My visit of a few months contributed powerfully to reinforcing my conviction both that it is possible in principle to understand the ways of thought of people belonging to cultures other than one's own and that it is worth-while trying to do so. The factual judgement, that it is possible in principle to understand the philosophical thought of other cultures, and the value-judgement, that it is worth-while trying to do so, lie at the basis of this book. That is to say, they have inspired my mind. The book itself is simply a tentative contribution, and one of very limited scope, to what might be described, in modern jargon, as an ongoing enterprise.

It will be obvious to any readers of this book that it is not intended to provide religious uplift or to satisfy the needs of those who turn to the Orient for spiritual wisdom or mystical experience. It is not a handbook to esoteric Hindu spirituality, nor to the practice of Zen Buddhism, nor to Suffi mysticism. There are books of this kind, but this is not one of them. Reference is, of course, made to religious themes. It is not possible, for example, to discuss Indian philosophy as a whole without such reference. And the same goes for Islamic thought. This book, however, is intended to deal with philosophical topics. It is not a question of criticizing those who are attracted by oriental spirituality and mysticism. I can myself feel the fascination of the Upanishads. But I approach my selected themes as an historian of philosophy. And it should be remembered that there was a great deal of serious philosophical reflection in, say, India, arguments being employed which in many cases were similar to lines of thought advanced in western philosophy.

Needless to say, I have learned much both from the writings of others and from personal conversation with scholars who know a great deal more about non-western philosophies than I do. In many cases, however, I do not remember from what source or sources I derived this or that idea. I call to mind the limerick, which runs, unless my memory fails me:

> There was an old man of Khartoum,
> Who kept two sheep in a room.
> He said: They remind me
> Of one left behind me,
> I cannot remember of whom.

In any case, though I have occasionally referred to an authority, I am reluctant to attribute an idea to a definite person, when he or she might not be prepared to admit that I had understood correctly or had given the degree of weight to the idea which he or she would give it. It seems preferable that I should assume responsibility for what I have said.

Finally, let me refer to a well-known saying. 'East is East and West is West' is, verbally, a tautology. But if the additional statement 'and never the twain shall meet' is taken to mean that no mutual understanding is possible this side of the grave, the statement, if true, would not augur well for the future of humanity on earth. I hope that the statement is untrue.

I

Relations between Western Philosophy and some Extra-philosophical Factors

The Theme of the Chapter

The general title of this book is *Philosophies and Cultures*. There are, of course, a very considerable number of scholarly works dealing with the philosophical thought of this or that culture, Indian or Chinese, for example, or with individual thinkers such as Śaṁkara in India or Confucius in China. The comparative study of philosophical traditions, however, is a subject which is still, relatively speaking, in its infancy. And there is room perhaps for tentative contributions even by those who, like the present author, do not possess the ideal qualifications, linguistic qualifications, for instance. There is indeed the danger that one's intended contribution to the understanding of the thought of other cultures may in fact contribute to misunderstanding. But if one were unwilling to run any risks, one's activities would be severely limited.

There is in fact no intention of trying, in this book, to survey the whole field of the comparative study of philosophy. Even if the present author were competent to do so, the subject would be too wide and too complex for treatment here. Instead we confine our attention to certain selected themes, about which it is hoped that one can say something relevant, even if one is not a specialist in the thought of any non-western culture. These themes are indicated in the chapter titles. It should, however, be added that in the final chapter we consider the question whether a common recurrent pattern is discernible in the philosophies of those cultures in which philosophical thought is known to have developed. This theme is indicated by the word 'patterns' in the title of the eighth chapter.

One topic under discussion, as, for example, in the fourth, fifth and sixth chapters, is the different treatments of recognizably similar themes in the philosophies of different cultures. In regard to this topic I had better explain in advance that I am using the concept of similarity in a common-sense way. For instance, questions relating to the sources of human knowledge have been discussed in both western and Indian philosophy. And in view of the subject-matter the sets of questions are more similar to one another, in a specifiable way, than either is to, say, the question whether a proposition can be self-referring. In other words, in talking about similar themes or questions I do not intend to commit myself to the claim that precisely the same problems recur in the history of philosophy. To what extent, if any, we can speak of recurrent problems is a question to which reference will be made in the seventh chapter. Meanwhile all that I claim is that we can find recognizably similar themes in the philosophies of more than one culture. This seems to be simply an empirical fact. If it is asked 'what is the point of instituting such comparisons?' one possible answer is that in a given culture some aspect of a theme may have been emphasized which has been neglected or underestimated in the thought of another culture.

The topic selected for this chapter is 'relations between western philosophy and some extra-philosophical factors'. That is to say, examples of the historical conditioning of philosophical thought by extra-philosophical factors will be taken principally from western philosophy. Someone may, however, feel inclined to ask what is the point of studying the relations between philosophical thought and extra-philosophical factors? What is achieved by such study? One answer, I suppose, is that any branch of historical inquiry can have an intrinsic interest. If inquiry into the human past in general is justified, no special additional justification is required for a study of ways in which philosophical thought has been conditioned by various extra-philosophical factors. Another answer is that this line of study can contribute to overcoming a rather naïve dogmatism. For example, it can prompt us to think twice before accepting as final and definitive the view of the nature, function and scope of philosophy which happens to prevail in a given society at a given time. For if we understand how such views have been influenced in the past by a variety of extra-philo-sophical factors, we may be more ready to entertain the idea that our own view may express a limited perspective.

To avoid possible misunderstanding, it is desirable to make two points in advance. First, it is certainly not intended to suggest that philosophy is simply an ineffective reflection of extra-philosophical factors. For one thing, there can be internal connections between philosophical systems, and a philosopher's problems are often set by other philosophers. For another thing, philosophical ideas can exercise a real influence, through the choices and actions of those who accept these ideas. Marxism is an obvious example. Secondly, recognition of the historical conditioning of philosophical thought in specifiable ways does not entail the view that all truth is relative to some particular historical or cultural situation. As, however, I treat more specifically of historical relativism in the seventh chapter, we do not pursue the matter further here. Philosophers are naturally interested in questions of truth or falsity, and it is understandable if a philosopher is sensitive to any suggestion that such questions can be settled simply by reference to the historical conditioning of philosophical thought by extra-philosophical thought. But we are not concerned with propaganda in support of a relativist theory of truth. If it is said that the subject of this first chapter belongs more to the history of ideas or to cultural history than to the history of philosophy, this does not matter in this context.

Before, however, we approach this subject directly, something should be said about presuppositions.

Presuppositions of Comparative Philosophy

The project of comparing the philosophies of different cultures seems to make three presuppositions: that we know what philosophy is and can distinguish it from other disciplines; that we can identify distinct cultures; and that we can understand the thought of cultures other than our own. We cannot discuss these presuppositions at length. But a few brief remarks will serve to show that I am not blind to the fact that I am making certain presuppositions.

In regard to the nature of philosophy, I am not starting with a stipulative definition, stating what, in my opinion, philosophy ought to be or recommending one particular concept of philosophy when other concepts are possible. (Different conceptions of philosophy form part of the history of philosophy.) It may seem to amount to evasive action, but for present purposes let us understand by 'philosophy' all that can be understood as philosophy without obvious contravention of ordinary linguistic usage. To put the matter in another way, let us understand by philosophy all that is customarily counted as such in histories of philosophy. Let us not, for example, exclude early Chinese thought on the ground that it is conspicuously weak in what the western world would be likely to recognize as formal argumentation.

As for the identification of cultures, I admit that I am unable to provide precise criteria. Indeed, I doubt whether anyone is able to do so. It seems that an element of personal decision is unavoidable, and that any identification of distinct cultures is likely to be open to objections which are not purely captious. For example, are we to speak of western culture and western philosophy, or are we to divide western philosophy in the traditional manner? Again, are we to treat Islamic culture as one entity, or should we, for instance, consider the culture of Persia or Iran as a distinct entity? If we are to start at all, some decision has to be made. I intend, therefore, to treat as distinguishable entities western philosophy (excluding Islamic thought in the Middle Ages), the philosophical thought of the Islamic world, the philosophy of India, Chinese philosophy and the philosophy of Japan, though in fact we shall refer very little to Japan. (Philosophy in Japan was very largely dependent on Chinese thinkers. In the course of time, however, it naturally came to assume certain Japanese characteristics.)

Having said this, there are two further notes. In the first place, talk about distinguishable entities is not intended to imply that each entity is completely self-enclosed. For example, Islamic thought in the Middle Ages exercised a considerable influence on the thought of medieval Christendom. Again, Buddhism is a trans-cultural phenomenon, which passed from India to China and thence, by way of Korea in the first instance, to Japan, producing a number of philosophical schools in the countries in which it took root and spread. (Buddhism spread to other countries as well, of course, such as Ceylon, Thailand and Tibet. But we are concerned here simply with Buddhism as a link between India, China and Japan.) In the second place, if I do not count Jewish philosophy as a distinct entity, this should not be understood as implying any belittlement of the contribution made by thinkers of Jewish origin to philosophical thought. While there are certainly some philosophers who, in virtue of their presuppositions, can be classified as specifically Jewish thinkers, it would be quite unreasonable to extract philosophers such as Spinoza, Bergson and Husserl from the mainstream of western thought and put them in a separate compartment simply because they were of Jewish origin.

In regard to the third presupposition, namely that we can understand the thought of cultures other than our own, I adopt the commonsense position, namely that though there can sometimes be great difficulty in understanding the ways of thought and the reactions of people belonging to other cultural traditions, there can none the less be degrees of understanding and degrees of failure to understand. To be sure, it is possible to define 'understanding' in the context in such a way that it is true by definition that a cultural tradition cannot be understood by anyone belonging to another culture. If, for instance, understanding Buddhism were so defined that to understand it one had to be a Buddhist, it would follow that a non-Buddhist could not understand Buddhism. Again, it is possible to argue, for example, that where a westerner thinks that he understands an ancient Chinese text, what he actually understands is a mental construction of his own, not the mind of the Chinese writers. It seems that this argument, if pressed, would put paid to all historical understanding as ordinarily conceived. Some further reference to the topic of understanding is made in the epilogue to this book. For present purposes, however, I assume the common-sense view, that there can be degrees of understanding, that the distinction between understanding and failure to understand is not vacuous.

Extra-philosophical Factors

Historians of philosophy have sometimes been criticized for treating the historical development of philosophical thought as though it pursued an isolated path of its own and had little connection with extra-philosophical factors. Though some references are customarily made to the influence of such factors, they are generally reduced to a minimum. Emphasis is placed instead on philosophical issues and arguments and on the internal connections between philosophical systems and movements. To be sure, there have been some attempts to remedy this supposed defect. For example, the sub-title of Bertrand Russell's *A History of Western Philosophy* (1945) was 'Its connection with political and social circumstances from the earliest times to the present day'. Though, however, Russell did indeed refer to such circumstances, it can hardly be claimed that the programme indicated by the sub-title was fully carried out.

What count as extra-philosophical factors in this context? They include, of course, economic, social and political conditions, also religion and science. But they also include psychological factors. Thus historians of philosophy have occasionally been accused, for example by the Spanish writer Miguel de Unamuno, of treating the philosophers of the past as though they were simply minds or intellects, instead of seeing them as human beings of flesh and blood with desires, passions and personal interests which have influenced their philosophical thought.

As far as complaints against historians of philosophy are concerned, they seem to be of questionable validity. If an historian wishes to lay emphasis on the social and political background of philosophical thought, he is obviously entitled to do so. Generally speaking, however, it is desirable that he should pursue a policy of economy, concentrating his attention on philosophical problems, theories and arguments and on the internal connections between movements and systems, restricting discussion of extra-philosophical factors to the minimum required for understanding and not confusing the reader by attempting to provide a general account of man's social, political and intellectual life. As for psychological factors, while in the case of certain thinkers, such as Nietzsche and Kierkegaard, knowledge of the man can facilitate understanding of the spirit of his thought, the historian is well advised, in my opinion at any rate, to steer clear of amateur psycho-analysis. Besides, a psychological approach to the history of philosophy can easily give the impression that questions about the truth or falsity of theories, or about the validity or invalidity of arguments, can be settled by mentioning psychological factors which are believed to have influenced a philosopher's thought. This is something to be avoided. Discussion of the adequacy or inadequacy of Wittgenstein's picture-theory of the proposition as expounded in the *Tractatus* is not helped by speculation about Wittgenstein's sexual preferences. There is room, of course, for psychological studies of philosophers, when there are sufficient empirical data to warrant such studies. But they are best carried out by psychologists, provided that they know something about philosophy.[1] Again, talk about the influence of, say, economic life on the development of philosophy can be so impressionistic and vague that the historian of philosophy who values scholarly research and well-documented exegesis is understandably mistrustful of it.

At the same time philosophy obviously does not exist in a vacuum. It is subject to the influence of a variety of extra-philosophical factors, some cases of this influence being obvious enough. For example, philosophy in India was closely connected, in specifiable ways, with Indian religion. Again, philosophical thought in the Islamic world was strongly influenced, in a variety of ways, by the Muslim religion. This is indeed only what one would expect, given the fact that religion was the bond which united the Muslim peoples. Again, the background of early Chinese philosophy was formed by a situation of social and political unrest, which prompted philosophers such as the Confucianists, the Mohists and the Legalists to seek remedies for the ills of the time. Needless to say, in all such cases what is needed is not simply a very general assertion but a more specific account of the way or ways in which philosophy was influenced by extra-philosophical factors. But that there was such an influence seems to be clear enough.

We shall be considering Indian philosophy in the next chapter, Chinese philosophy in the subsequent chapter, while the fourth chapter will be devoted to discussion of some interrelations between philosophy and historic religions. In what remains of the present chapter I therefore propose to confine my attentions to western philosophy.

Greek Philosophy

When we turn to Greek philosophy, the most obvious example of the influence of extra-philosophical factors on philosophical thought is doubtless the relation between the Greek city-state organization and the political thought of Plato and Aristotle. The influence, however, of actual political society on the thought of philosophers who concern themselves with political theory is only to be expected. For unless a political philosopher proposes to confine himself to making statements which are so broad that they will apply to pretty well any civil society whatsoever, he naturally thinks in terms of the actual social organization of his time. It is existing society, existing within his horizon that is to say, which he takes as the subject of reflection, and possibly of recommendation. Indeed, if he is concerned with reform, what else can he do? Even if he thinks up an ideal state, his point of departure must be the actual state. And the former will reflect the latter in specifiable ways.

It is not, however, simply a case of Plato, Aristotle and the Greek *polis*. The political theorists of medieval Christendom naturally thought in terms of the relations between the feudal state (or in some cases the empire) and the Church, while Hegel thought in terms of the national state of his time and seemed incapable of widening his horizon beyond the dialectic of 'national spirits'. Karl Marx's horizon was, of course, wider, in the sense that he looked forward to a world-wide truly human society. But his thought was obviously profoundly influenced by his analysis of contemporary industrial society. It can hardly be denied that Marxian (the theory of Marx himself, that is to say, as distinct from later development) theory reflected, in specifiable ways, a certain phase of the industrial revolution. If it has subsequently been turned into a set of dogmas, this is another matter.

Nor is it a question only of the West. The Chinese philosopher who concerned himself with political theory and social reform naturally thought in terms of the Chinese social and political world of his time.

It may be said that even if the political philosopher takes the social and political organization of his milieu as his point of departure, there is no reason why he should not make statements which hold good in regard to any society which we would be prepared to describe as a political society. But I have no wish to deny this. I am simply citing some examples of the influence of extra-philosophical factors on philosophical thought. And political philosophy is an obvious source, inasmuch as there is a real sense in which it is more concrete and less abstract than some other branches of philosophy.

Some care must obviously be exercised in talking about extra-philosophical factors. Suppose that I were to refer to the intellectual ferment
at Athens in the fifth century BC as forming the background for Plato's
attempt to show that the human mind is capable of recognizing
objective values and absolute moral norms, as well as for his development, in outline at least, of a philosophical theology as a reply to
religious scepticism. If this contention were taken to imply that the
process of questioning which constituted the intellectual ferment was
an extra-philosophical factor, it could obviously be retorted that the
sort of radical questioning to which Plato refers in his dialogues was
itself philosophical. This seems to be true. At the same time it can be
argued that the questioning was intensified by a social factor, namely
by the Greeks' increased experience of the variety of human beliefs,
moral convictions and customs.

A further point. When we hear talk about the influence of extra-
philosophical factors on philosophical thought, we naturally tend to
think in the first place of actually existing factors. The Greek city-state
organization, in regard to its influence on the political theory of Plato
and Aristotle, is an obvious example. It must be added, however, that
the absence of a certain factor can also exercise an influence on
philosophy. I do not mean, of course, that a non-existent factor can
function as a causal agent. I mean that philosophy can be influenced in
a certain direction by a given situation because a certain factor is
lacking in this situation.

An example of this is provided by the way in which Greek philosophy
offered guidance for life and came increasingly to expound ways of life,
even in certain cases, a path to a religious goal. In ancient Greece
religion was cultic, not dogmatic, and there was no one universally
recognized teaching authority in the ethical and religious spheres.
Those who were not satisfied, for one reason or another, with myth and
with the ethical and religious traditions of the city-state, had to turn to
philosophy, even if it was only for a justification of scepticism. We
naturally tend to think of early Greek philosophy as expressing a
disinterested, though not of course uninterested, spirit of inquiry into
man's physical environment, into the real nature of the world about us,
a line of thought which was made possible by the relatively stable
urban civilization of the Greek cities of Ionia and southern Italy.
Though this point of view obviously represents a real aspect of early
Greek thought, we should not forget, for example, the religious
elements in the Pythagorean societies or the ethical implications of the
thought of Heraclitus. With Plato philosophy clearly becomes true

wisdom, a wisdom for life. And with the breakdown of the autonomous city-state organization and the appearance of first the Hellenistic and then the Roman Empires, we find increasing emphasis being placed on ethics and on ways to attain peace of soul and true happiness. To say this is not to deny, for example, that the Stoics developed logic, epistemology and cosmology. It is a question of the placing of emphasis in Hellenistic and Roman philosophy. In spite of the prevalence of what we might describe as popular philosophical preachers, it is certainly possible to exaggerate the extent to which individuals, in the post-Aristotelian ancient world, were cut adrift, so to speak, from their moorings and turned to philosophy for guidance in life. But it seems clear that the development of Stoicism, Epicureanism and Neoplatonism (even, to some extent, of scepticism) in Hellenistic and Roman society shows philosophy as meeting a need felt by the more intellectually minded citizens. After all, when some early Christian writers showed hostility to the philosophers, they were thinking mainly of philosophers as expounding ways of life, as untrustworthy guides.

This sort of situation was not confined to the Graeco-Roman world. In India, for example, the function of philosophy as a guide to life was even more marked. But this is a matter which will be treated later.

Religious Presuppositions of Medieval Thought

In medieval Christendom the situation was clearly very different from that in pre-Christian society. For guidance in life and for enlightenment about man's vocation in the world and his ultimate destiny, people looked to the Christian faith and to the teaching of the Church, rather than to philosophy as pursued in the medieval universities. St Augustine, living in the last days of the Roman Empire, had indeed described Christianity itself as the true philosophy or wisdom, for which Greek philosophy, especially the Platonic tradition, had been a preparation in the pagan world. But if we understand 'philosophy' in the sense in which, in medieval times, it came to be distinguished from what St Thomas Aquinas called 'sacred doctrine' (Christian theology), it is true to say that for guidance in life people looked to the Christian faith rather than to philosophy as taught, for example, at Paris or Oxford. There is indeed some evidence that in the course of the thirteenth century a naturalistic world-outlook was emerging in the faculty of arts at Paris. But even if this was the case, the movement was checked. And the critical thought of the fourteenth century restricted rather than extended the scope of philosophical knowledge. There were, of course, movements in the Middle Ages which expressed dissatisfaction with

the institutional Church, movements ranging from popular antinomian-
ism to an emphasis on mystical experience. But the members of such
groups looked for light to religious faith and experience rather than to
philosophy as expounded in the universities.

The point is that in medieval Christendom there were common
religious presuppositions which were not present in the ancient world
before the triumph of Christianity in the late Roman Empire, and that
this added cultural dimension had the effect of depriving philosophy of
its role as a guide for life and turning it into an academic discipline, or
set of disciplines, studied in universities as a preparation for theology.

Another way of putting the matter is to say that in medieval
Christendom theology was regarded as the chief science.[2] This statement naturally suggests that philosophical thought in the Middle Ages
was strongly influenced by theology. So it was, and naturally so,
inasmuch as most of the leading philosophers were or became professors
of theology. At the same time it will not do to represent philosophy in
medieval Christendom as being simply religious apologetics, the
business of which was to prove theological truths. For example,
Christians believed that the human soul did not perish at bodily death.
And a dim view would certainly have been taken of any philosopher
who claimed to have proved the impossibility of the soul's survival. It
does not follow, however, that the philosopher had to produce positive
proofs of the soul's survival. In the fourteenth century proofs offered by
previous thinkers were subjected to critical analysis, and there was a
tendency to represent belief in the soul's survival as a truth of faith
rather than as a demonstrated conclusion in philosophy.

This tendency was part of a general tendency to extend the range of
what could be known only by faith and to decrease the extent of what
could be philosophically proved. This was partly the result of a desire
on the part of some theologians to purify Christian faith from what they
regarded as the contamination of Graeco-Islamic metaphysics; but a
powerful contributing factor was a stricter idea of what constituted a
proof. In any case, the effect on philosophy was to transform it more
and more into critical analysis and sophisticated logical studies and so,
paradoxically perhaps, to make it more independent of theology.

Though commonly-held religious presuppositions were indeed an
important extra-philosophical factor which influenced philosophical
thought in the Middle ages, they were not the only one. One might
reflect, for example, on the influence exercised by the use of Latin as a
learned language on the treatment of problems relating to universal
terms, and indeed on other logical topics. Again, as has already been

remarked, political theory was clearly influenced by the actual social-political situation, which formed the empirical point of departure for reflection. The point is that if medieval philosophy tends to give the impression of being arid and remote from life, this is partly due to the fact that truths which were commonly regarded as being of supreme importance for human life were derived from another source.

Empirical Science and Modern Philosophy

In the Middle Ages theology, as we have noted, was regarded as the chief or supreme science, and study of it was the culminating stage in the educational programme. This is hardly the case in the modern world. The place of theology as the most prestigious branch of knowledge has been taken by empirical science. It is indeed true that the meaning attached to the word 'science' has undergone a change. But this change corresponds to and illustrates the growth in prestige of empirical science as a source of positive knowledge about the world. Whatever our own estimation of theology may be, it is obviously true that when people nowadays hear the word 'science', they tend to think at once of natural science and technology, unless the word is qualified by an epithet such as 'social'.

The development of the particular sciences has influenced philosophy in a variety of ways. Sometimes it has been a case of some science or sciences suggesting a paradigm of method. Thus whereas in the past some philosophers looked to mathematics for a paradigm of method, some of their successors have turned to empirical science. For example, some philosophers have proposed for metaphysics a method analogous to that of hypothesis, deduction and testing. It has been suggested that if a philosopher develops a view of reality on the basis of reflection on certain aspects of the world, he can then test his view by inquiring whether it is compatible with other aspects of the world or other aspects or fields of human experience. Again, sometimes it has been a case of the development of scientific knowledge suggesting problems to the philosopher's mind or at any rate providing a relevant factor in a problem. For instance, as every student of modern philosophy is aware, the classical or Newtonian physics is relevant to an understanding of the problematics of Immanuel Kant. Again, scientific theories can suggest themes for reflection, as in the case of Henri Bergson's philosophy of evolution. Further, science, once it has been sufficiently developed, can become the subject-matter of a new philosophical discipline, the philosophy of science. Then again, the growth of scientific knowledge can have, and has had, an influence on conceptions of the nature, function and scope of philosophy. It is this last mentioned form of influence with which we are concerned here.

If we bear in mind the wide meaning once given to the word 'philosophy' and then consider the process by which the particular sciences have developed as distinct disciplines, it is difficult to avoid the conclusion that these sciences have taken over one after another a number of areas once regarded as belonging to philosophy. To be sure, there is something left. For there are problems and themes which have been treated by philosophers in the past but which, by their very nature, cannot be handled by any of the particular sciences. The word 'God', for example, is not a scientific term, not at any rate if we mean by the word a transcendent reality. At the same time the development of the particular sciences and the growth of scientific knowledge can easily suggest that scientific method has progressively been substituted for philosophical speculation and *a priori* reasoning as the appropriate means of attaining positive knowledge of reality, and that if there are areas in which scientific method is inapplicable, they transcend the scope of human knowledge. In other words, such questions as the following arise. Has philosophy a field of its own? If so, what is it? If philosophy has no special field of its own, what is its function? What task or tasks remain for the philosopher to accomplish?

As we are all aware, a variety of answers to such questions has been given. For example, in the nineteenth century Auguste Comte maintained that the chief function of philosophy was to achieve a theoretical synthesis of the sciences; and, in the present century, members of the Vienna Circle made what was substantially the same point, though expressed in a different way, by calling for the construction of a common language for the sciences. Positivism of this kind, however, with its tendency to tie philosophy to inquiry into the logic of the sciences and, it can be argued, to elevate the language of science to the rank of the paradigm language, has been judged to be too narrow. As for what has been ascribed as therapeutic positivism, namely the contention that it is the philosopher's job to do his best to put himself out of business by dissolving the logical confusion out of which philosophical problems are supposed to arise, this concept of philosophy, though it may have had a certain vogue, was clearly not of such a kind as to commend itself to philosophers in general. Much more promising is the view of philosophy as a second-order discipline capable of being applied to a variety of first-order disciplines and activities. Philosophy is then seen as taking the form of philosophy of science, philosophy of history, philosophy of religion and so on. The philosopher is not, of course, conceived as competing with the practitioners of such disciplines or activities on their own levels, but rather as reflecting on problems which presuppose and arise out of these disciplines or activities as data. The philosopher of history, for example, is not conceived as providing us with a more exalted view of history than that offered by ordinary historians. He is concerned more with problems arising out of reflection on historiography, the problem of the nature of historical explanation, for instance. In one sense philosophy, as so viewed, does not have a field of its own, a section of reality, as it were, distinct from sections appropriate to other disciplines, but on the same level. In another sense philosophy obviously has a very broad field, and there is plenty for philosophers to do. If it is said that philosophy, as so conceived, is parasitic, this term is used not in a pejorative sense but to indicate that philosophy feeds off first-order disciplines and activities.

There are, however other ways of reacting to the development of the particular sciences. For example, it can be argued not so much that the nature of philosophy has changed as that the development of the particular sciences serves to purify philosophy, in the sense that it strips off accretions and helps to reveal the true nature of philosophical thought. According to the late Professor Karl Jaspers, for instance, the development of the particular sciences should help us to understand that philosophy is neither itself a particular science, alongside other scientific disciplines, nor a kind of super-science. It is not a science at all. It does not demonstrate the truth of certain theses, in the way in which what Kant described as dogmatic metaphysics tried to prove the truth of certain doctrines. Rather does it open the mind to the existential significance and importance of certain problems and illuminate the possibilities of human choice. Thus, according to Jaspers, if we objectify man and try to prove freedom, we are bound to fail. From the point of view of the spectator man is not free. As Kant put it, in the phenomenal order man is determined. At the same time the philosopher can illuminate the reality of freedom, by trying to speak from the point of view of the agent. (It can be argued that if one is going to speak at all, one cannot help taking an outside view. For example, if one talks about man, one objectifies him. If one accepts Jaspers' attitude, one has therefore to find a way of describing the function of philosophical language which takes account of this objection.) Again, philosophy cannot prove the existence of a transcendent reality, but it can open the mind to an unobjectifiable horizon of human experience and confront man with the choice between affirming or denying his relation to the divine reality.

This view of philosophy certainly has its difficulties. It can look very much like an attempt to say what, on the philosopher's own admission, cannot be said. None the less the point is that the philosophy of Karl Jaspers was influenced not only by the rise and development of the particular sciences but also by a cultural situation in which some people believe that there are problems which are of real importance for life but which cannot be solved by science, inasmuch as they are not scientific problems, but who at the same time lack confidence in the dogmatic teaching of religious bodies. For such people there is in modern western culture a need which cannot be satisfied by the particular sciences nor by institutional religion. In conversation with a Soviet philosopher I asked whether all students in his university had to study some philosophy. He replied that they did. Many of them, he admitted, were unsuited for any real philosophical reflection, but, as he put it, 'We think it important that they should have a framework for life'. Whether or not Marxism constitutes an acceptable framework for life, is irrelevant. The fact is that a need can be felt in our modern western culture which can have an influence on conceptions of philosophy and its function. Some people have felt driven to turn to the East for enlightenment. But this is not a phenomenon which need concern us at the moment.

If anyone asks what is my own view of the nature and function of philosophy, I can only reply that I mistrust restrictive definitions of philosophy. Obviously, philosophers have different views of what is worthwhile in philosophy, and they are perfectly entitled to express their convictions. In so far as any definitions which they offer can be interpreted as expressing evaluative judgements and as recommend-ations to concentrate on this or that approach or line of reflection, we can hardly claim that philosophers have no right to offer such definitions. What I mistrust are dogmatic assertions that this or that kind of philosophy is not philosophy at all. I do not wish to be understood as claiming, for example, that the kind of philosophy represented by the thought of Karl Jaspers is the only worthwhile kind of philosophy, and that someone who confines his attention to, say, critical philosophy of history is not doing philosophy. In any case, I have not been concerned with promoting the cause of any particular philosophical tradition or line of thought. I have simply been trying to illustrate, with the aid of some selected examples, the influence which can be exercised on philosophical thought by extra-philosophical factors. I have emphasized the influence of the development of the particular sciences, in regard to post-medieval philosophy. In the case of some philosophies, however, such as that of Karl Jaspers, we can see philosophy as responding to a felt need for a framework for life in a cultural situation in which the commonly accepted presuppositions of medieval Christendom can certainly not be taken for granted.

Philosophy in relation to Moral and Social-Political Problems

Mention of Karl Jaspers (and we might, of course, have mentioned other names too) may suggest that I am thinking simply of the revival of metaphysics of some form or another as a response to a felt need in modern western culture. Let me then introduce a rather different but complementary line of thought. It hardly needs saying that in our western society there are substantive moral issues about which there is fairly widespread uncertainty. A good many people believe either that the issues cannot be adequately settled by appeal to traditional ethical norms, even if these norms are of lasting validity, or that the norms themselves are questionable or obsolete. It is understandable, therefore, that some people should expect enlightenment from philosophy. Again, there are important social and political issues which have moral aspects and in regard to which people may expect philosophers to have something relevant to say. Obviously, no sensible person expects a philosopher, because he is a philosopher, to be able to solve problems in economics. But if philosophers refuse to say anything about substantive moral and social issues on the ground, for instance, that philosophy is concerned simply with meta-ethics and with the language of politics, they are then accused of being ivory-tower thinkers or of fiddling while Rome burns.

It is doubtless possible to argue that this kind of accusation is fair or unfair, justified or unjustified, in an *a priori* manner, by starting with a given concept of the nature of philosophy and pointing out the implications which are relevant to the point at issue. But I do not wish to proceed in this way. Instead I prefer to draw attention to the fact that philosophers are not unresponsive to the demand which I have mentioned. Among philosophers belonging to what is commonly described as the analytic movement there seems to be a markedly increased readiness to discuss substantive moral issues which ordinary people believe to be important. And it seems safe to say that philosophers are more open than they were not so long ago to John Dewey's ideas about the practical relevance of philosophical thought. The extent to which philosophers can solve our social and political problems is obviously limited. But they are able, for example, to point out the implications of the values professed by a society and to clarify the implications of emerging values. Again, as Dewey maintained, a political philosopher can criticize existing institutions in the light of man's changing needs and point out possible future developments to meet present needs. I do not mean to imply that only a professional philosopher can act in this sort of way. I am suggesting two things. First, philosophy can make a positive contribution, even if primarily through a clarification of issues, to discussion of substantive moral problems and of some social and political problems as well. Secondly, philosophers seem to be increasingly disposed to make such a contribution. We can thus see philosophy as responding to needs arising in a given historical situation.

It is indeed possible to conceive philosophy in such a way that it has little bearing on or relevance to practical issues. Bertrand Russell, as we all know, was a great campaigner on behalf of certain political issues, and he did not hesitate to express his judgements about substantive moral issues. At the same time he maintained that his writings on moral subjects (apart from his theory of the nature of the moral judgement) and his political writings were not, properly speaking, philosophical works, and that what he had to say on these subjects was in no way logically dependent on or deducible from his philosophy. Given his accounts of what he considered to be, strictly speaking, philosophy, this last contention was justified. (Russell was, of course, well aware that in terms of a less restrictive concept of philosophy his moral and political writings counted as philosophical.) Sharply opposed to this sort of concept of philosophy is that proposed by Karl Marx. It is certainly not my intention to pursue propaganda for Marxism. But it may be worth remarking that the Marxian view of philosophy and later ideas of the practical relevance of philosophical thought which have been inspired by Marx's thought are obviously responses to reflection on factors in the historical situation, in modern society. Socially orientated philosophy of this kind is clearly one more example of the influence of extra-philosophical factors on philosophical thought. In the feudal society of medieval Christendom learning developed under the auspices of the Church, the intellectually minded section of the population came predominantly from the ranks of the clergy, and this situation clearly influenced philosophical thought. In the post-medieval world creative thought tended to pass more and more out of the hands of the Church into those of representatives of the rising bourgeoisie and to reflect this development in a variety of ways. Later, with the industrial revolution the interests or alleged interests of the proletariat found expression in the writings of thinkers such as Marx and Engels, most of whom were of middle-class origin but whose thought was powerfully affected by the contemporary economic and social situation and who interpreted the past in the light of this situation.[3]

Concluding Remarks

A topic not yet discussed is evaluation of the influence of extra-philosophical factors on philosophical thought. Evaluative judgements in this field are apt to express particular philosophical positions. I do not mean to imply that there can be no such judgements which would be endorsed by philosophers in general. If, however, these are presupposed, there is room for a diversity of evaluative judgements which correspond to different philosophical stances. For example, Étienne Gilson, the eminent historian of medieval philosophy, maintained that philosophical thought in medieval Christendom benefited greatly from the stimulation provided by Christian theology. And he backed up his view by argument, by drawing attention to specific ways in which the influence of theology had been of benefit to the development of philosophical thought. Someone else, however, with a philosophical position different from that of Gilson, might argue that the influence of theology on medieval philosophy had been, in general, deleterious. It is not simply a question of taste. Discussion and argument are quite possible. But the arguments produced on either side are likely to express, to some extent, personal philosophical convictions. I have preferred to avoid expression of my own philosophical position and to focus attention on what seem to be historical facts. For instance, it seems to be an historical fact that the development of the particular sciences in the modern world has powerfully contributed to the emergence of restrictive concepts of the nature and functions of philosophy. [4] Whether one welcomes or disapproves of such restrictive concepts is another matter. If one values speculative metaphysics or the construction of comprehensive syntheses, one will obviously not regard as adequate any concept of philosophy which excludes speculative metaphysics. If one believes that comprehensive syntheses have little, if any, cognitive value and that their construction is a waste of time and intellectual ability, one will obviously take a different view. But the facts can be admitted by both parties.

The comment may be made that I have referred only to obvious facts. After all, who would wish to deny that in medieval Christendom philosophical thought was influenced by theology? And who would be prepared to assert that philosophy in the modern world has been in no way influenced by the development of empirical science? The facts are as plain as a pikestaff. It is surely possible to suggest much less obvious ways in which philosophical thought has been influenced by extra-philosophical factors.

Yes, it doubtless is possible. But one can easily move into a speculative area, in which it is difficult to substantiate one's assertions. For example, it has often been said (I have said it myself) that in the post-Aristotelian ancient world philosophy became a way of life and even a doctrine of salvation, as the old traditions, associated with the city-state organization, had broken down in the wider societies of the Hellenistic and Roman Empires. This statement, however, though it contains some truth, omits the obvious fact that with Socrates and Plato, and even before them with, say, the Pythagoreans, philosophy was already in some sense a guide to life. Again, I have heard it said, by a Marxist, that the medieval conception of the heavenly court, with its hierarchy of ranks of angels and saints, reflected the hierarchic structure of feudal society. This view of the matter may seem to serve as confirmation of the economic or materialist conception of history. It can be objected, however, that multiplication of intermediary beings between the One and the visible world was a favourite pastime with the Neoplatonists of the ancient world. The Marxist can retort, as I have heard one doing, that in the Middle Ages this conception of intermediary beings was, though already in existence, tailored to feudal society. But though this may be the case, to substantiate the assertion would require much more detailed investigation than would be possible here. Again, such questions as whether Kant's view of man reflected a bourgeois concept and to what extent German idealism in the first decades of the nineteenth century was an expression of the romantic movement would not be easily manageable in a single chapter. So I have kept to general examples of the influence of extra-philosophical factors on philosophical thought, even at the risk of labouring the obvious.

It seems worthwhile to raise some questions. It is not correct to say that there has been no science at all in the East, no interest in scientific studies. At the same time it is clear that modern western science and technology have spread to the East and in certain countries have become firmly implanted. We can safely assume, therefore, that in those countries which have ancient philosophical traditions the growth of a scientific outlook will have an influence on philosophical thought. Indeed, it is not simply a question of the future. In some cases there are already clear manifestations of these influences. The question arises, therefore, whether the ancient philosophical traditions should be considered as dead or obsolete or, if not, what changes they will have to undergo if they are to survive. We have reminded ourselves of ways in which the development of scientific knowledge has affected philosophy in the West. Are modern western conceptions of philosophy destined to supplant all other ideas? Or can the philosophical traditions of cultures other than our own still make a contribution to philosophy in general, perhaps by suggesting problems or approaches to problems which we have neglected or tended to pass over? Perhaps we are not in a position to answer all these questions. But we can bear them in mind when we are considering the philosophies of other cultures. It should not be simply taken for granted that other cultures have nothing to contribute to philosophical thought. In some ways western philosophy may well have advanced, in an evaluative sense of the word 'advance', but it is also possible that on the way elements of value have been forgotten or obscured, and that in one way or another reflection on non-western philosophical traditions can serve to remedy a certain myopia.

2

Features of Philosophy in India,
with Special Reference to
Theory of Knowledge

Some Mistaken Impressions of Indian Philosophy

It seems there is still a common impression that Indian philosophy took the form of ontological monism, at least among those who have not studied Indian philosophical thought as a whole but who have some acquaintance with religiously orientated philosophical speculation in the Hindu world. They tend to conceive Indian philosophy as teaching that the world of multiplicity, as a plurality of selves and things, is an illusory appearance of one reality, Brahman. The inner self, *ātman*, is indeed real, but it is conceived as one with Brahman or the Absolute, whereas the empirical self, conscious of its distinction from other selves, belongs to the sphere of appearance. The goal of life is liberation from the phenomenal world, from time and the cycle of rebirth, this liberation being achieved through realization of an already existing oneness with the unchanging ultimate reality, by the dissipation of ignorance.

This impression of Indian philosophy is certainly not devoid of any foundation. For it is based on the Advaita Vedānta, on the philosophy of Śaṁkara, who seems to have died about the year AD 820[1], and whose non-dualism or monism certainly became influential. At the same time the impression, as an impression of Indian philosophy as a whole, is inaccurate. The majority of the Indian philosophical schools maintained pluralist positions. Of the non-Vedic schools the materialists or Cārvāka (Lokāyata) philosophers were pluralists. So were the Jains. As for Buddhism, the Buddha avoided metaphysical pronouncements. But Hīnayāna Buddhism had its obviously pluralist schools, even if in Mahāyāna Buddhism there was a marked tendency to reintroduce the Absolute, sometimes conceived as 'Emptiness', the indescribable, the Ultimate Reality (*paramartha*). Of the schools which recognized or came to recognize the authority of the Vedas and are therefore known as Vedic schools, the Nyāya, Vaiśeṣika, Sāṁkhya, Yoga and Mīmāṁsā schools were all exponents of pluralism. For example, the Sāṁkhya school maintained that there was a plurality of souls or, more precisely,

pure subjects, even if it regarded physical things as evolutes of one substantial immanent cause, *Prakṛti*. Not even the Vedānta school can be
identified with monism. Thus in the eleventh century AD, after the time
of Śaṁkara, Rāmānuja defended what is sometimes described as
qualified non-dualism, a kind of panentheism, while in the thirteenth
century Madhva maintained the reality of the human subject of self
and of the things which in their interrelations form the physical world.
Śaṁkara may have been the most influential Vedānta thinker, and it
may be true to say that whereas in the West pluralism tended to
prevail, in India monism came to occupy the central position. But it is
none the less a mistake to identify classical Indian philosophy with
monism. There was much more variety than is allowed for by this
identification. Obviously common-sense pluralism was the original
Indian view, and pluralism continued to be the doctrine of the majority
of philosophical schools. Even in the Vedānta tradition pluralism came
to assert itself, largely no doubt under the influence of devotional
religion but also out of respect for ordinary experience.

Another not uncommon impression is that Indian philosophical
thought was and remained deeply religious, being practically identifi-
able with esoteric religion, whereas in the West philosophy has tended
to separate itself from religion and religious interests. This idea of
Indian philosophy is true in a certain sense. But it is important to
understand in what sense it is true. In a later chapter more will be said
about the relations between philosophy and religion. Here we are
concerned with the religious character of Indian philosophy in particular.

In the West we tend to associate religion with belief in the gods, in
the case, for example, of ancient Greece, or in God, in the sense of one
transcendent personal deity. This is not to imply that we simply
identify religion with such beliefs. Further, in modern times there have
been attempts to define religion in such a way that belief in a divine
reality is not included as an essential feature. There can be different
motives for such attempts. For example, it may be a case of wanting to
find a definition which is sufficiently wide to cover Buddhism and
possibly some attitudes which can reasonably be described as religious,
though these do not involve any explicit belief in a divine reality. But
there have also been some attempts to redefine religion, which are
based on the conviction that belief in God is not a living option for 'the
modern mind'. It seems clear, however, that in common estimation the
concept of religion includes belief in God.

If we adhere to this common idea of religion, we can hardly claim that Indian philosophy as a whole was religious. The materialist school was obviously atheistic. But so too was Jainism. And in its original form Buddhism did not include any belief in God. (It is very difficult, if not impossible, to obtain certain knowledge of 'original Buddhism'. But it seems clear that the Buddha abstained from metaphysical pronouncements.) Of the Vedic schools the Nyāya school can be described as theistic (that is to say, it, like Vaiśesika, came to adopt theism), while the Sāṁkhya-Yoga school recognized a relatively supreme being, Iśvara. In the Mīmāmsā school emphasis on the sacrificial rites doubtless once presupposed belief in the Vedic deities; but in the course of time the deities seem to have become heroic types or personified ideals, belief in their actual existence being more or less a matter of indifference, even if with Kumārila the idea of a supreme being came to the fore. As for the Vedānta tradition, it included various points of view. For Śaṁkara the concept of a personal God belonged to the phenomenal world, in the sense that it represented the way in which impersonal or supra-personal Brahman appeared to the devout religious consciousness. The thought of Rāmānuja, however, and especially of Madhva, was much closer to theism. In general we can say that in the Vedic schools belief in a personal God became prominent when the philosophy in question became associated with devotional religion, with the *bhakti* movement, of which the supreme literary expression was the *Gītā*.

In spite, however, of the ambivalent attitude of Indian philosophy as a whole to belief in the existence of God or of divine beings, there is certainly a sense in which it can reasonably be described as religiously orientated. For apart from the materialist school (which regarded mind or soul as epiphenomenal and had no place for a doctrine of final liberation), philosophical thought was or became orientated to the liberation of the human spirit from the effects of evil actions and from the wheel of rebirth, to enlightenment and to what might be called salvation. For example, though Jain philosophy was atheistic, it can hardly be described as irreligious. Quite apart from the fact that Jainism as a religion came to find room for some Hindu deities, the Jain thinkers envisaged the purified soul as joining the company of the Jain sages in their state of complete knowledge and of unending peace and happiness. If we exclude the early materialist school, we can say that all schools, both Vedic and non-Vedic, offered ways of life leading to enlightenment and liberation. The schools thus tended to be more than groups of people who studied and developed (or conserved) this or that philosophical tradition. For they also aimed at initiating disciples into a way of life leading to enlightenment and liberation. To be sure, the philosophical schools as such could not exercise a widespread popular appeal or take the place of popular religion. Their doctrines were often too abstruse for this. The thought of, for instance, Nāgārjuna, the chief representative of the so-called Middle Way school of Mahāyāna Buddhism, was far too difficult to be appreciated by the populace. In the course of time there arose Buddhist sects, such as the Jōdo sect in Japan, which emphasized faith in the eternal Buddha as the means of gaining entry to paradise. But the more popular the appeal exercised by a sect, the less was the philosophical, or at any rate the metaphysical, content of its doctrines. In any case we are concerned here with philosophy, not with popular religion. The restricted appeal of philosophical theory does not, however, invalidate the claim that, generally speaking, the schools, both Vedic and non-Vedic, offered theories which formed the basis for a way of life aiming at enlightenment and liberation.

Mention of an orientation of thought to spiritual enlightenment and liberation can easily suggest to the western mind that the schools were really religious sects, and that no serious philosophical reflection can be expected from them. This idea, however, is erroneous. Obviously, the orientation in question formed a general background or context, and for the understanding of any given system as a whole we have to see discussions of particular issues or topics in their general setting. But it by no means follows that such discussions are not examples of serious philosophical reflection.

It can be objected that it is not simply a question of a religious interest or orientation of thought. For there is also the influence of sacred texts to consider. After all, certain schools are called Vedic because they accepted or came to accept, as the case may be, the authority of the *Vedas*, while of the non-Vedic schools the Buddhists and the Jains had their own sacred texts. If philosophers base their doctrines on the authority of sacred texts, should not these doctrines be described as theological doctrines rather than as philosophical theories?

The extent to which the Vedic schools were dependent on scriptural authority can easily be exaggerated. For example, the Vaiśesika doctrine seems to have originated independently, though the school later accepted the authority of the *Vedas*. Further, even if the Nyāya school, with which Vaiśesika came to be associated, was more closely linked with reflection on the sacred texts, the logical system which it developed was obviously not derived from these texts. Again, it must be remembered that the *Vedas* (including the *Vedānta*) contained different lines of thought and even incompatible ideas, and that there was no authority external to the schools themselves which could decide between rival doctrines and interpretations. The Sāṁkhya philosophers insisted on the need for rational argument to discriminate between sound and unsound appeals to the sacred writings. If any thesis contradicted the principles of logic, it could not express a truth imparted to or grasped by the ancient sages and enshrined in the Vedic literature. Any claim to truth must have rational support. It is indeed true that the Mīmāṁsā and Vedānta schools laid emphasis on the authority of the Veda, which they regarded as eternal. (The *Veda*, that is to say, had no author. We cannot discuss here the precise meaning given to this contention.) But their basic lines of interpretation were very different. The Mīmāṁsā thinkers concentrated on the early Vedic literature, especially the Brāhmanas, and they emphasized the ritual and moral injunctions. In their view the sacred texts were orientated to action, and *prima facie* existential and descriptive statements were given pragmatic interpretations, whenever possible. In other words, the sacred texts, according to the Mīmāṁsā school, told people what they should do rather than what they should believe about reality. The Vedānta school, however, with its great emphasis on knowledge, maintained that the sacred writings provided knowledge which the human mind could not obtain through perception and inference. At the same time there were considerable differences in accounts of what the knowledge was. For example, according to Śaṁkara, the knowledge provided could be summed up in the famous statement of the *Chāndogya* Upanishad 'That thou art', whereas for Madhva, the expounder of the Dvaita or 'dualist' Vedānta, the *Veda* imparted knowledge of the existence and attributes of Brahman, in the sense of a personal God. Obviously, the different interpretations had to be supported by argument. In any case, the fact that the Mīmāṁsā and Vedānta thinkers laid emphasis on the authority of the sacred texts does not entail the conclusion that they pursued no genuine philosophical reflection. To be sure, Madhva was inclined to finish a polemical discussion by saying that the idea which he rejected was contrary to the Veda and to perception or contrary to tradition and experience. But much of what he has to say about, for instance, the nature of the self and about knowledge is established independently of appeals to authority, even if he is at pains to show that his conclusions do not contradict the sacred texts.

The only really convincing way of showing that Indian philosophers did pursue serious philosophical reflection is obviously to cite some examples of it. And by way of illustration I refer to certain topics in

Indian theory of knowledge. I am aware that I lay myself open to the accusation of isolating certain questions and considering them apart from their context or background, and perhaps also to the charge of trying to make Indian philosophy appear respectable by selecting themes which are likely to be acceptable in the eyes of those who have little use for talk about the Absolute. But this is a risk which I am prepared to run. In any case it is an undeniable fact that knowledge was a prominent theme for discussion in Indian philosophy. The schools provided a sort of esoteric wisdom or knowledge, and topics such as the sources of knowledge and the criteria of truth were naturally of importance to Indian thinkers. The Chinese were much more concerned with conduct and with the practical bearing of theory. The Indians, though they had of course their ethical theories, were much more inclined to abstract thought and laid great emphasis on what we might describe as the intellectual ascent of the mind to knowledge of reality.

Sources of Knowledge recognized by Indian Schools
From an early time the Indian philosophers reflected on the sources of knowledge, formulated their positions, and criticized the views with which they disagreed. In the first place all schools accepted sense-perception as a source of knowledge. This may indeed seem to be patently untrue of the Advaita Vedānta philosophy of Śaṁkara and his followers. Perception presents us with a plurality of objects. How then, it may be asked, can perception possibly be regarded as a source of knowledge, if plurality is believed to belong to the sphere of appearance, and if reality is believed to be one being, Brahman, which is declared to be imperceptible? On the assumption that these beliefs are true, are we not compelled to hold that sense-perception is a source of error rather than of knowledge?

These questions are understandable. We have, however, to bear in mind the fact that though, for Śaṁkara, the empirical world, the world of multiplicity, was appearance in relation to Brahman, it was none the less real enough on the level of practical life and of what we would call scientific knowledge. If perception implies a distinction between perceiver and perceived, subject and object, and if ultimate reality transcends the subject-object distinction, perception must obviously belong to the sphere of appearance, to the level on which the One appears as the Many. But to say that the empirical world is appearance is not the same thing as saying that it is nothing. There is such a thing as empirical knowledge. And it presupposes perception as a source of knowledge.

The statement that all Indian schools recognized sense-perception as a source of knowledge should not be understood as implying that they all gave the same account of perception. Consider, for example, Hīnayāna Buddhism. One school, the Sautrāntika, maintained a causal theory of perception, according to which what we directly perceive is an impression caused by the object. This impression represents the object, and the existence of the extramental object is inferred. In other words, the Sautrāntikas defended a representative theory of perception. The Vaibhāsikas or Sarvastivādins, however, were not prepared to accept this theory. What, they asked, was the ground for inferring the existence of any extramental object at all? If there is no direct perception, how can we distinguish, justifiably that is to say, between mental states or impressions which are caused by extramental objects and those which are not? If to infer the existence of extramental objects is justified, must not direct perception be pre-supposed, so that we can distinguish between cases in which the inference is justified and cases in which it is not justified?

The question was rendered more complex by the fact that these schools accepted the doctrine of 'momentariness' (a development of Buddhist phenomenalism), according to which the continued existence of subject and object is reducible to successive vanishing 'moments'. Given this doctrine, acceptance of a theory of direct perception presumably commits us to regarding perception as a relation between two simultaneous vanishing moments, one in the life of the subject, the other in the life of the extramental thing. Otherwise it seems that what is perceived must be a relic, as it were, of a moment which no longer exists. And then we have a representative theory of perception. It is perhaps not surprising that problems arising out of the theory of momentariness pushed some Hīnayāna Buddhists in the direction of reintroducing the concept of substance. But we cannot discuss the matter here.

It has been stated above that all Indian schools accepted sense-perception as a source of knowledge. This is true. It should be added, however, that most schools did not understand by perception simply sense-perception but included non-sensory perception. They thus allowed for the intuitive apprehension of the self and its states and of other spiritual realities. (This statement refers to Vedic schools and Jainism. The Buddhists rejected the concept of *ātman*.) The materialists, however, did not accept the idea of spiritual realities and recognized only sense-perception.

To claim that perception is a source of knowledge is obviously not the same thing as to claim that it is the only source of knowledge. Most Indian schools accepted inference too, and also testimony. The materialists, however, the Cārvākas or Lokāyatas, are said to have rejected inference and to have accepted only sense-perception. The trouble is that for information about the materialist school we have to rely mainly on reports by critics. (The school was of ancient origin, going back to pre-Buddhist times. But its texts have perished. Though the school pretty well faded out as a school, it does not necessarily follow, of course, that a materialist outlook did not survive.) It is thus very difficult to know precisely how we should understand the materialists' rejection of inference. Jain and other Indian logicians objected that if a Cārvāka philosopher were challenged to defend his view of sense-perception as being the only source of knowledge, and if he were unwilling to have recourse to sheer dogmatism, he would have to offer a reason, a procedure which would be tantamount to using inference as a source of knowledge. This line of objection implies that Cārvāka rejection of inference was total. It has been conjectured, however, that the materialists did not so much reject inference outright as argue that inductive inference could not give the sort of certainty which perception can give. If, for example, we infer from the occurrence of x the occurrence of unperceived event y, we do so on the basis of a general conviction about the relation between x's and y's. But perception does not reveal universal connections. Hence we take a risk when we infer y from x; and we cannot be said to know the truth of our conclusion, unless we can confirm it by actually perceiving the occurrence of y. However this may be, it seems clear that the Cārvākas recognized only sense-perception as a source of certain knowledge. As has already been said, other schools accepted inference too. And logical theory was developed by the Nyāya school and also by the Buddhist logicians.

A word must be said about testimony as a source of knowledge. Testimony has an obvious practical importance in human life. If, however, we were challenged to defend our acceptance of testimony, we would have to have recourse to inference. It is natural, therefore, that the Cārvāka philosophers, rejecting inference as a source of certain knowledge, should reject testimony too. There is, however, another side to the matter. One reason why a number of schools accepted testimony as a distinct source of knowledge was their reliance on sacred texts as expressing a wisdom imparted to sages in ancient times. It is obvious, for example, that the Vedānta doctrine of Brahman was derived from the Upanishads. As Brahman was there represented as not only imperceptible to the senses but also as transcending discursive thought, the testimony of the sacred texts could be confirmed only by non-sensory perception, an intuitive grasp of reality, and, negatively, by showing that other views of reality were self-contradictory and untenable. Testimony came first, as it were. We can therefore understand why a number of schools accepted it as a distinct source of knowledge.

We have mentioned perception, inference and testimony as allegedly distinct sources of knowledge. In point of fact theories about this matter were more complex than this threefold division suggests. For example, the Jains regarded what they called 'recognition' as a distinct kind of knowledge. This referred both to recognition of similarity (as when *A* is seen to be similar to *B*) and to recognition of identity (as when Tom, a grown man, is recognized as being the same person as Tom when he was a child). We might indeed wish to reduce recognition in this sense to perception and memory. The Jain philosophers, however, while admitting that perception and memory were presupposed, regarded the act of recognition as something over and above them. Again, Kumārila, leader of one of the sub-schools of the Mīmāmsā tradition, admitted three sources of knowledge in addition to perception, testimony and inference. One of the additional sources of knowledge was 'non-apprehension', the apprehension, that is to say, of negative facts. Suppose that I am looking for a book on my shelves. The book is a perceptible object. Given therefore the fulfilment of certain conditions, such as the presence of sufficient light, the book should be visible, if it is on any of my shelves. In spite, however, of a thorough search I do not see it. Its non-existence on the shelves, its non-presence or absence that is to say, is grasped by non-apprehension.

Obviously, in the case of an object such as a book perception might reveal its presence elsewhere. Further, if I know that the book exists and I do not find it on my shelves, I can legitimately presume that it is somewhere else, lent to a friend perhaps. But if the existence of an alleged object cannot be known by any of the five other *pramānas*, (sources of knowledge), its absolute non-existence is known by non-apprehension.

Prabhākara, leader of another Mīmāmsā sub-school, refused to recognize non-apprehension as a distinct source of knowledge. In his view our knowledge of the non-presence or of the non-existence of *x* could be explained in terms of perception and inference. I see, for example, books *a*, *b* and *c* on a shelf, and I infer that book *d* is not there. To this Kumārila replied that before we could infer the absence of book *d* from the shelf, we would have to perceive the presence of books *a*, *b* and *c* as negatively qualified, as not including the presence of book *d*. But it is only present objects which can affect a sense-organ and cause perception. Hence non-apprehension is required to grasp the negative fact of book *d*'s non-presence.

It is not intended to suggest that Kumārila was right in postulating non-apprehension as a distinct and irreducible source of knowledge. We are simply considering some features of Indian philosophy. In the first place, it seems clear that discussion of knowledge by the Indian philosophers showed a high degree of sophistication, which appears also in their discussion of some other topics. In the second place, some of the questions discussed can be isolated and treated by themselves. The question whether perception is direct or indirect is a case in point. But, in the third place, it cannot be justifiably claimed that the metaphysical and religious background makes no difference at all to Indian theories of knowledge and our understanding of them. Reference was made above to non-sensory perception, the postulation of which allowed not only for perception of mental states or introspection but also for the intuitive apprehension implied by the idea of enlightenment. Reference has also been made to the acceptance by the majority of schools of testimony as a distinct *pramāna* or source of knowledge. As has already been noted, reliance on testimony plays an important role in human life in any case, quite apart from any religious considerations. (It does not follow, of course, that we have to regard testimony as an irreducible source of knowledge.) At the same time the attitudes of schools other than the materialist school to sacred texts helps to explain the prominence given to testimony as a source of knowledge. Attitudes differed considerably. In Japanese Zen Buddhism, for example, we can find a marked tendency to play down the role of sacred texts and to emphasize personal experience. But we are concerned with India here.

Truth and Falsity: Knowledge and Error
The relations between particular lines of philosophical inquiry and reflection on the one hand and, on the other, the general orientation of Indian philosophy (apart from materialism) to enlightenment and liberation can be further illustrated by reference to the problem of error. Whatever the sources of or ways of arriving at knowledge may be, it is obviously natural to ask, how can we be sure that what we believe to be knowledge is actually what we believe it to be? Error, after all, is a fairly common phenomenon. How then are we to distinguish between truth and falsity?

In considering such questions the Indian philosophers tended to concentrate on knowledge of perceptible objects. Given this approach, we would naturally expect to find an emphasis on empirical testing as a means of determining the truth or falsity of statements. This emphasis was a marked feature of the Nyāya-Vaiśeṣika school. Suppose that I claim to know that a certain substance is water. If the substance is found to have the effects characteristic of water, such as quenching thirst, my claim is validated. That is to say, the statement that a particular substance is water is verified. If, however, the relevant expectations are not fulfilled, my claim is invalidated, and the conclusion can be drawn that I was in error, that I took the substance to be what it was not. The error was subjective, that is to say, the misrepresentation was in my mind. Falsity should be predicated of the judgement or statement, not of the thing. For this was simply what it was, even if I misrepresented it.

The Nyāya-Vaiśeṣika philosophers tended to speak as though all assumed knowledge needed to be validated in this sort of way. It could, therefore, be objected that they themselves postulated eternal imperceptible atoms which became perceptible only at a certain level of combination, and that the existence of imperceptible atoms could not be proved by empirical verification. But the existence of the atoms was, of course, inferred[2] and, as we have seen, the Nyāyā-Vaiśesika-school accepted inference as a source of knowledge. Further, it has already been mentioned that when the Indian philosophers discussed error, they tended to concentrate their attention on knowledge of perceptible objects. Anyway, the Nyāya-Vaiśeṣika school emphasized the need for empirical testing of claims to knowledge, though how much testing was required before a statement could be regarded as verified was left obscure. The approach was a common-sense approach. If an object claimed to be an apple behaved, so to speak, as an apple and not as a ball painted to look like an apple, what more could be required to substantiate the claim that it was really an apple?

It is obviously true that when doubt arises about the truth of a statement relating to a perceptible object, we have recourse to empirical testing, if it is possible to do so and if we think it worthwhile. If someone tells us that an object at Madame Tussaud's is a policeman, and if we doubt the truth of the statement, we can look more closely, speak to the object, feel it, and so on. At the same time, if the claim to hear the truth of a statement has to be validated by showing that another statement is true, and the truth of this other statement has to be validated by showing that yet another statement is true, it seems that we are involved in an infinite regress, unless there are cases in which knowledge is self-authenticating or, if preferred, that truth manifests itself. This is in fact what some Indian schools, such as Mīmāmsā, maintained. To be sure, they were accustomed to claim simply that knowledge is self-authenticating. As, however, they had no intention of denying that error occurs, their claim seems to have meant in practice that the presumption that what seems to be knowledge is knowledge stands, unless there is serious ground for doubt. At any rate this seems to be the case when it is a question of claiming, for example, that this object is a snake. If it were a question of seeing that q follows logically from p, the claim that truth manifests itself would presumably mean that we simply see that p implies q. Let us, however, concentrate on knowledge considered as a cognitive relation between a perceiving subject and a perceptible object, an object of sense-perception that is to say.

For schools such as Mīmāmsā grounds for serious doubt about claims to knowledge in the sense just mentioned can be of two kinds. In the first place, we may have reason to suppose that there is some defect in the means of obtaining knowledge or in a condition for obtaining it. For example, if my eyesight is known to be defective, this is clearly a reason for doubting the truth of my claim to have seem someone in a place where it is unlikely that he or she would be at the time in question. In the second place, if a claim to know something is incompatible with already established knowledge, this too is a serious reason for doubting the validity of the claim. And when such doubt arises, claims to knowledge have to be subjected to testing.

The schools mentioned above, Nyāya-Vaiśesika and Mīmāmsā, were both exponents of pluralism. Knowledge, therefore, considered as a relation between perceiver and perceived, was not regarded as belonging simply to the phenomenal sphere. And the schools can be said to have accepted a correspondence theory of truth. As we have seen, the Nyāya-Vaiśesika school emphasized the need for validating claims to knowledge by practical verification, by ascertaining whether the alleged knowledge 'worked'. It does not necessarily follow, however, that truth could be defined as what works. Empirical verification was looked upon as a test of truth-claims rather than as the nature of truth. Similarly, though the Mīmāmsā school insisted that a truth-claim made on behalf of p was rendered doubtful if p conflicted with already established knowledge,[3] coherence was used as a test of truth rather than as a definition of it. If by the term 'knowledge' we understand mainly knowledge of perceptible objects, the natural way of regarding truth is as correspondence between a statement and the state of affairs which the statement purports to represent.

When, however, we turn to the philosophy of Śaṁkara, the Advaita Vedānta, we are faced by a different situation. The plurality of selves and of things, the whole world of multiplicity, is regarded as appearance, as not being really real. Knowledge, however, as we ordinarily conceive it, implies a distinction between subject and object, knower and known. Even in self-consciousness there is a distinction between the self as subject and the self as object. Does it not follow, therefore, that knowledge belongs to the sphere of appearance? And in this case, it may be asked, how can Śaṁkara justifiably claim to know that empirical reality is the appearance of Brahman? For the knowledge by which he claims to know it is itself appearance. Must not the whole non-dualist philosophy be simply phenomenal, a dream?

In the first place, it is important to understand that when Śaṁkara describes the world of plurality as the appearance of Brahman, he does not mean to imply that it is precisely on the same level as what we call a dream, still less that it is nothing. The world of ordinary waking experience can be likened to a dream when it is contrasted with the Absolute in itself, but it is real enough in comparison with the world of dreams, in the usual sense of dreams. For one thing, the world of our waking hours is a public world, whereas the world of my dreams is a private world, even if the dream-images are representations of objects which exist in the public world.

Within the framework, therefore, of this public world the distinctions between truth and falsity, knowledge and error, are meaningful. Śaṁkara can thus treat, for example, of error in a quite straightforward and ordinary manner. When discussing erroneous perception, he distinguishes between datum and interpretation, or between the thing and our judgement about it, ascribing error to the interpretation or judgement. If, for instance, we believe that a coiled rope is a snake or that the stick partially immersed in water is actually bent, it is our judgement which is erroneous, not the rope or the stick. Further, in both cases the error is corrigible. Erroneous perception is shown to be erroneous when it is contradicted by other experiences. Thus our judgement that the stick is bent is contradicted by our feeling the stick and discovering that it is not bent. Truth in fine is manifested by absence of contradiction. Śaṁkara accepts the idea of truth as self-manifesting, but he admits that the truth can be veiled. In the case of an erroneous judgement of perception, experience which contradicts the judgement serves to unveil the truth. The rope which seemed to be a snake is now seen to be what it is, a rope. The judgement that it is a rope is not itself contradicted by any other experience.

It would obviously be a mistake to conclude from talk about absence of contradiction that for Śaṁkara the highest level of knowledge was comprehensive knowledge of reality as a coherent system. For he did not regard reality, in the full sense of the word, as a system. The concept of a system involves the idea of interrelated entities. But for Śaṁkara ultimate reality was Brahman, transcending plurality and relations. This consideration, however, does not affect the fact that within the framework of reference of empirical reality, the phenomenal world, Śaṁkara recognizes the validity of distinctions between knowledge and error, truth and falsity. Further, it is obviously possible to isolate some of his theories, such as his analysis of erroneous perception, and evalute it without any mention of the Absolute, Brahman.

At the same time it is true that the subject-object distinction belongs, for Śaṁkara, to the phenomenal world, the sphere of appearance. In so far, therefore, as knowledge implies or involves this distinction, it too belongs to the phenomenal world, together with the empirical self. It follows from this that our knowledge of the Absolute, at any rate in so far as it is expressed, is at best inadequate. For talk about Brahman objectifies Brahman as an object of knowledge, as something about which to talk; and Brahman as object for a subject is, so to speak, less than Brahman. Talk about the Absolute is bound to misrepresent it. Indeed, it seems that Brahman belongs to the sphere of the inexpressible.

This line of thought would not worry Śaṁkara in the least. As he maintains that Brahman transcends discursive thought, he is obviously quite prepared to admit that our concepts of Brahman are inadequate, and that talk about the Absolute is misleading, unless perhaps we understand its inherent inadequacy. We can none the less still ask, with what justification does Śaṁkara claim to know that there is an Absolute to talk about, even if inadequately? By definition, Brahman is imperceptible. It cannot, therefore, be apprehended by sense-perception.[4] Further, as Brahman is said to transcend thought, discursive thinking that is to say, it is difficult to see how the existence of Brahman can be proved by inference. How then is the existence and nature of Brahman supposed to be known?

The Advaitins were one of the schools which recognized testimony as a distinct source of knowledge. And they appealed to the *Vedānta* as witness to the existence of Brahman, the oneness of the inner self with Brahman, and the phenomenal character of the empirical world.[5] It hardly needs saying that an appeal to scriptural authority would not bear any weight with philosophers such as the materialists, who did not recognize the authority of sacred texts. Quite apart, however, from this consideration, the Vedic literature as a whole contained a number of conflicting doctrines. So some reason was required for maintaining that the teaching of the *Vedānta*, as expressed in the passages to which the Advaitins appealed, must prevail. Here the Advaitins could apply their general principle that a statement can stand when it is not contradicted, truth being manifested by the absence of contradiction. In their view the statement relating to the metaphenomenal Brahman in the sacred texts was not contradicted by any experience.

This, however, had to be argued. For the pluralist would obviously claim that monism was in fact contradicted by experience. In reply the Advaitin tried to show that the theories of the pluralist schools were untenable. For example, the philosophers of the Sāmkhya-Yoga school postulated a plurality of eternal selves or spirits in addition to the primal substance, *Prakṛti*, of which all material entities were evolutes. In man spirit and matter were combined. According to Śaṁkara, however, the relation between spirit and matter had never been explained. In fact, it could not be understood. And the conclusion to be drawn was that reality could not be predicated of both spirit and matter, not at any rate in the same sense. For Śaṁkara, needless to say, it was spirit which was real, matter being phenomenal. Again, though the subject-object distinction in consciousness worked all right for practical purposes and for scientific knowledge, the relation between the two factors was philosophically unintelligible. Insoluble difficulties arise, whether we describe the relation in terms of contact or of inherence. We thus have to conclude that empirical consciousness, involving the subject-object distinction, is phenomenal, not fully real. In fine, the Advāitins argued that it was pluralism, not monism, which gave rise to antimonies or contradictions. The Advaita philosophy left the phenomenal world intact, so to speak, at its own level, the level of appearance, while the doctrine of the Absolute, transcending distinctions and relations, was free from the difficulties which arose if distinctions were assumed to be fully real.

A more positive approach to non-dualism was made by way of reflection on the self. In a real sense the self is, for Śaṁkara, the key to reality. The existence of the self is, he insists, indubitable. For any expression of doubt implies the doubter's existence.[6] But it does not necessarily follow that the nature of the self is known. The empirical ego, which is conscious of itself as distinct from other selves, is, according to Śaṁkara, phenomenal. To say this, however, is to say that it is the appearance of something. It is the appearance of the self as metaphenomenal, as *ātman*, which is presupposed by empirical consciousness but eludes objectification.[7] *Ātman* transcends individuation, except, of course, on the level of phenomenal reality, as, that is to say the empirical self. This means that it is one with the universal *Ātman*, the ultimate reality or Brahman. This oneness cannot be expressed in language, except in a way which is inevitably distorting. It can be grasped only by an intuitive apprehension in which the subject-object distinction disappears. This is enlightenment.

If we were discussing the metaphysics of Śaṁkara with a view to critical evaluation, we would obviously have to pay attention to problems which arise in regard to the relation between appearance and reality, problems similar to those which arise in the case of the absolute idealism of F. H. Bradley. In the present context, however, we are concerned simply with the relation between Śaṁkara's metaphysics and his theory of knowledge. My contention is, in effect, that a theory of degrees of reality demands a theory of degrees of knowledge and truth.[8] If we assume that ultimate reality is a seamless One, transcending distinctions and relations, it obviously cannot be apprehended by a form of knowledge which involves the subject-object distinction. Knowledge in this sense must belong to the sphere of appearance. If the Absolute can in fact be known, it must be by an intuitive apprehension which transcends the subject-object distinction. I must indeed confess to a serious doubt whether the term 'knowledge' retains any meaning, if it is used in this way. However this may be, if we embrace the metaphysical theory that reality is a One transcending distinction and relations, and, if we wish also to maintain that the One can be known by acquaintance, we shall have to postulate an intuitive apprehension in which subject and object are one, and we shall have to assign knowledge, in so far as it involves the subject-object distinction, to a lower level, inferior to the level of true enlightenment. In this sense our metaphysics will influence our theory of knowledge.

We can note in passing that on the level of an intuitive apprehension of ultimate reality, in which subject and object are one, error is impossible. There can be no question, for example, of the subject mistaking the object for something else or attributing to it a characteristic which it does not possess. But does truth also disappear, together with error? The idea of truth as correspondence is clearly inapplicable. If the idea of truth is applicable at all at this level, truth must presumably coincide and be identical with reality itself. It is difficult even to say that reality knows itself as true, in the sense of transcending all contradictions. For to speak in this way is to reintroduce the subject-object distinction.

Theory of Knowledge and Metaphysics

Having used the philosophy of Śaṁkara to illustrate the influence of metaphysics on theory of knowledge, I now wish to stigmatize this procedure as one-sided or misleading. Consider the thought of Madhva, an exponent of the Dvaita Vedānta. It is not unreasonable to see his theistic metaphysics as influencing his theory of knowledge, in the sense that it favours the idea of knowledge as involving a distinction between knower and known. But we might equally well see his insistence on the subject-object distinction in knowledge as influencing his metaphysics by militating against the monism which in fact he rejected. Again, suppose that we agree with the Jain thinkers that the idea of experience which is not the experience of anything is meaningless, and that knowledge is necessarily knowledge of something, whether of the self or of the other than self. In this case we are likely to support a pluralistic ontology. In other words, if ontology can influence theory of knowledge, so can theory of knowledge influence ontological theory. And I conclude that it is preferable to speak of the correlation of disciplines or of inter-relations between them than to harp on a particular point, namely the influence of metaphysics on epistemology. For the matter of that, though a reasonable case can be made out for claiming that Śaṁkara's theory of knowledge was influenced in specifiable ways by his metaphysics, it is none the less clear that in the Upanishads he found not only the concept of the Absolute, Brahman, but also, correlated with it, the idea of an intuitive apprehension of Brahman, which transcends the subject–object distinction. He did not first work out his metaphysics and then develop a theory of knowledge under his influence. The two were closely interrelated.

Such interrelations can be found in all the systems of Indian philosophy. Needless to say, we can also find what are or seem to be inconsistencies and juxtaposed doctrines which do not appear to fit together. For example, there is some difficulty in seeing how Buddhist rejection of the concept of *ātman* in favour of a phenomenalistic analysis of the self can be successfully reconciled with the theory of trans-migration, which was accepted by the Buddhists.[9] By and large, however, the philosophies of the Indian schools constitute a variety of systems, in which ethics, psychology, theory of knowledge and cos-mology or metaphysics are interrelated. Further, though there is a variety of systems, they are all united (with the exception of Cārvāka) in a common basic orientation to enlightenment and liberation.

On both counts Indian philosophy may seem to many western minds to be old-fashioned, a monument from the past, having only an historical interest. That is to say, the construction of world-views may seem to be an enterprise which has been wisely discarded, as being of dubious cognitive value, while the orientation of most Indian philosophies to enlightenment and liberation and their expositions of ways of life are out of tune with the sort of philosophizing to which most of us are accustomed nowadays. Further, though the Indian philosophies certainly comprised ethical teaching, relating to conduct in this world, they may tend to give the overall impression of directing people's attention away from social issues to an other-worldly goal, an impression which is obviously intensified if we fix our attention on Buddhist talk about attainment of the state of Nirvāna or on Śaṁkara's ideal of realization of oneness with the Absolute. Even if we recognize, as we should, that the leading Indian philosophers pursued serious philosophical reflection, we may none the less be inclined to think that their philosophies have little to offer to us today. Nor is it only a question of 'we'. For some modern Indian philosophers tend to think in much the same way.

There is, however, another point of view. It is natural enough to look for some synthesis of, say, the scientific outlook and the aesthetic and religious aspects of human experience. And though there is certainly much in Indian philosophical thought, as indeed in past western philosophy, which is primarily of historical interest, the philosophies of India can none the less have a stimulative value, by pointing to the possibility of renewed attempts at synthesis. As for the orientation to enlightenment and liberation, we are all aware that a number of westerners have looked to India for spiritual guidance and wisdom. Whether they can find it there is another question. But the search is presumably the expression of a felt need. And those who think on these lines will doubtless sympathize with the hope expressed by the late Professor S. Radhakrishnan, one-time President of India, that the Indian philosophical tradition, which had become static, would be given fresh life and creatively developed. What Radhakrishnan had in mind was neither an appeal to sacred texts nor the literal revival of this or that Indian system but a renewal of what we can describe, in a broad sense, as an ethical-religious orientation of thought in the light of modern scientific knowledge and theory and of contemporary social needs. This desired renewal was contrasted with the policy of repudiating the heritage of Indian thought in the conviction that the future of free India lay simply and solely in the adoption of western science and of Anglo-American philosophy. Whether or not the hopes expressed by Radhakrishnan will be fulfilled is obviously not a question which can be answered in advance. In any case, if the study of Greek and medieval logic is worth while, so is the study of the analytic and logical tradition in Indian philosophy.

3

Some Characteristics of
Chinese Philosophy

In what Sense was Chinese Philosophy This-worldly?
Among the broad generalizations which have been made about
philosophy in China, one is the assertion that Chinese philosophy was
more this-worldly and less metaphysical than Indian thought. If we ask
in what sense philosophy in China was this-worldly, we may be told
that it was primarily humanistic, centring round man, man in his
moral life and in his social relations.

On hearing or reading a generalization of this kind, the critical mind
is apt to think at once of objections, or at any rate of qualifications. For
example, in regard to the generalization which has just been mentioned,
it might be objected that Indian philosophy was also centred round
man, round the thought of the goal of human life and of the way to
attain it. To be sure, philosophy in India included a conspicuous
amount of cosmological and metaphysical speculation. But was
philosophy in China devoid of metaphysics? Did not Taoism expound a
theory of ultimate reality, the indescribable source of the myriad
things? Did not some of the Buddhist schools pursue pretty abstruse
metaphysical speculation? And do we not find in the Neo-Confucianism
of the Sung and Ming periods theories relating to the Great Ultimate
and to the 'principles' or dynamic forms of things?

By their very nature broad generalizations omit a great deal. They are
apt to be impressionistic. It does not necessarily follow, however, that
the general impressions which they represent are devoid of any
foundation in fact. For example, though it is true in a sense that Indian
philosophy centred round man, it was orientated, apart from the
materialist school, to the idea of liberation from the phenomenal world
of time and rebirth. In this sense Indian philosophy can reasonably be
described as other-worldly. Chinese philosophers, however, generally
showed remarkably little concern with the after life, even when they
accepted the idea, which was by no means always the case. It is true that
Taoism as a religion came to show a preoccupation with the idea of
immortality.[1] But Taoist sages such as Chuang Tzu were primarily

concerned with the free development of the individual in this world, not with life in another world. As for Buddhism, which entered China from India during the first century AD,[2] its teaching was, of course, orientated to enlightenment and to the attainment of Nirvāna. But it is worth remarking that Ch'an Buddhism, which was a Chinese creation and the parent of Japanese Zen, laid emphasis on the possibility of enlightenment in the midst of a person's daily and socially useful occupations. Moreover, the Absolute of Ch'an Buddhism was not a transcendent reality, ontologically distinct from this world. It was the phenomenal world, the inside, so to speak, of the phenomenal world, as seen by the enlightened mind. We can also mention that Chinese philosophers were inclined to lay stress on the intimate relation between theory and practice, practice meaning primarily moral action.

If we understand the term 'this-worldly' as implying an absence of ethical ideals, the description of philosophy in China as this-worldly would be quite unjustified. But if we understand the term as implying a predominant concern with this world and with man's life in it, the assertion that philosophy in China was, by and large, more this-worldly or more down to earth than philosophy in India seems to be reasonable enough, provided at any rate that we make some distinction between philosophy and popular religion, whether Taoist or Buddhist, and that we allow for a number of qualifications. It must be added, however, that the assertion is intended to be purely descriptive, not evaluative. We are not concerned here with preferences.

Perhaps the matter might be expressed in the following somewhat provocative way. Suppose that India were to accept Marxism-Leninism as the official philosophy. Indian Marxists would doubtless refer to the ancient materialist tradition in Indian thought, represented by the early Cārvāka school. None the less, adoption of Marxism-Leninism would be generally regarded, and rightly, as involving a radical repudiation of the spirit of the classical philosophical tradition of the country. In the case of China the situation, it seems, is rather different. To be sure, Marxism, a western philosophy by origin, is opposed in a variety of ways not only to Taoism and Buddhism but also to Confucianism. For one thing, Confucianism was or became an instrument of conservatism, whereas the triumph of Communism, bringing with it the imposition of Marxism-Leninism, meant a break with the past. In spite, however, of all differences between them, Confucianism, for centuries the official philosophy of imperial China,[3] and Marxism, the official philosophy of contemporary China,[4] obviously possess a common central theme, namely man in his social relations. In this sense the change from the old Chinese philosophical tradition to Marxism involved a less striking break with the past than would have been the case if the traditional philosophy of India had been suddenly supplanted by this-worldly Marxism.

It is not intended to imply that there are no ways in which Chinese philosophy is likely to appear strange and alien to minds accustomed to western philosophical thought. As one can easily see for oneself, early Chinese philosophy, of the period, that is to say, in which the best known Chinese thinkers lived, was predominantly aphoristic and illustrative, ideas being suggested or conveyed by stories or anecdotes rather than stated in an abstract manner.[5] Moreover, even when ideas were stated abstractly, sustained argument to support them tended to be conspicuous by its absence. In early times there was indeed the small School of Names, the members of which are customarily described as logicians and who are known for their paradoxical assertions, such as Kung-sun Lung's statement that a white horse is not a horse[6] and Hui Shih's statement that one goes to the state of Yüeh and arrives there yesterday. These dialecticians, however, did not produce any explicit logical theory such as Aristotle developed in the West or the Nyāya logicians in India. Later on, Indian logic, imported into China, remained pretty well a possession of Buddhist monks. In modern times Professor Fung Yu-lan, author of a well-known history of Chinese philosophy, recognized the lack of serious study and development of logic in China and called for the use of western logical analysis as an instrument in the reconstruction and updating of Chinese thought.[7] We have indeed to allow for the different ways of thinking of different peoples. It is not intended to suggest either that Chinese philosophy does not deserve to be called philosophy or that it possesses no logical structure at all. The fact remains, however, that if we are looking for serious studies in logic, we have to turn to India rather than to China.

Early Chinese Philosophy and Social Reform
In the last chapter of this book reference will be made to the general thesis of Alois Dempf that the philosophy of any culture presupposes a cultural crisis, which it tries to overcome. To a certain extent early Chinese philosophy can reasonably be regarded as providing support for this thesis. About the year 1112 BC the Shang dynasty was overthrown. The Chou rulers had perforce to delegate a great deal of authority to land-owning lords or nobles, some of whom had miniature

courts of their own. Early in the eighth century BC a party of feudal lords killed the Chou monarch, and his successors, the eastern Chou kings, were reduced pretty well to the status of puppets, while the feudal lords contested for land and power. This period of turmoil lasted from about 771 BC until 221 BC, when China was more or less unified under the Ch'in Emperor; and it formed the background for the lives of such sages as Confucius (551–479 BC), Mo Tzu (c.479–438 BC) and Mencius (c.370–c.290 BC), who were largely concerned with the reform of society through moral education and development. The tradition that there was an older contemporary of Confucius called Lao Tzu, who was the author of the work known as the *Lao Tzu* or *Tao te Ching*, has been called in question; but early Taoism belonged to the period of which we are speaking, even if the *Lao Tzu* is an anthology.

It would be a mistake to think of all the early Chinese philosophies as being concerned exclusively with moral and social reform. The School of Names, mentioned above, seems to have been remarkably unconcerned.[8] And the Yin-Yang theorists were primarily occupied with cosmological themes, with the ultimate principles of cosmic change and with the 'five agents' or derivative active elements,[9] though their speculation was extended to include a theory of historical cycles and the idea of balance or harmony in society. In any case Confucianism, Mohism and Taoism had as their background a period of unrest, which gave rise to problems which these philosophies, in their several ways, sought to solve.[10] The same can be said of the legalist movement, to which further reference will be made presently.

It does not follow, however, that the ideas of Confucius and of the Taoist sages can justifiably be regarded as conceived simply in response to a contemporary period of political disunity and unrest. In the period of the Shang dynasty, as was later stated in the *Book of Rites*, great attention was paid to honouring and serving spiritual beings, including the personal national deity. Spiritual beings were conceived as causing natural events, whether beneficial or calamitous, and as intervening in the affairs of men. Their approval and assistance was constantly sought. During the succeeding Chou period, however, a change of attitude showed itself. Spiritual beings, though still honoured, came to be regarded as providing moral examples rather than as intervening actively in human affairs, and Heaven (*T'ien*), the supreme lord of all, was looked on as being, in some ill-defined sense, the source of ethical standards. An illustration of the shift of emphasis is provided by the justification offered by the Chou dynasty for its usurpation of power, namely that because of its virtue it had received from Heaven the mandate to rule, which the previous dynasty had forfeited because of its lack of virtue. This implied that moral virtue was the criterion of worth and the factor which won the favour of Heaven, rather than birth or rites performed in honour of spiritual beings. Again, in the *Book of Odes* administrators were exhorted to cultivate virtue and to keep in harmony with the mandate of Heaven rather than to spend their time thinking about their ancestors.[11] The extent of the shift of emphasis from reliance on spiritual beings and on the spirits of ancestors to reliance on human effort and the cultivation of virtue as the means of winning the favour of Heaven can doubtless be exaggerated. At the same time Confucius can be regarded as having made this growing ethical humanism explicit, by representing the moral life as the foundation of social unity, whether in the family or in the state. As for Taoism, its doctrine of ultimate reality, the nameless One, was obviously not simply a response to a contemporary situation of social unrest.[12]

In the judgement of Confucius the reform which was needed was primarily moral reform. The stability and harmony of society, whether that of the family or of a large group, depended on the moral qualities of the individuals composing the society in question. Confucius is often described as a conservative. So he was, in specifiable ways. He tended to look back, in the sense that he appealed to the moral example of legendary sage-emperors, to a golden past, that he valued tradition and the observance of ancient customs and rites, and that he thought in terms of the hierarchic structure of feudal society. For Confucius, the family was the basic society, a person's primary social obligations were determined by his or her position in the family, as father or mother or eldest son, for example, and benevolence or love, a great Confucian virtue, was envisaged as being practised first and foremost in the family and then as widening out to cover, for instance, one's attitude to the ruler. It has been suggested[13] that this emphasis on family ties and on the primacy of obligations within the family circle reflected the position of the family in the agricultural life of China. Indeed, in a real sense the ideal state was for Confucius the family writ large. In his view, the emperor was under an obligation to set a good moral example and to facilitate and promote the moral education of the citizens. Virtue could not be implanted by coercion. The less coercion and force needed to be used, the better. The emperor or king had to have his administrators and judges, of course, but his first job was to honour Heaven by leading his subjects through moral example.

This point of view obviously implied two things. First, human beings are capable of responding to moral example and education. Confucius may not have asserted as explicitly as Mencius was to do, that man is good by nature; but Mencius' interpretation was doubtless justified. Confucius was well aware, of course, that man could become bad, but he regarded human beings as born not only with the capacity to distinguish between good and evil, right and wrong, but also with positive inclinations to virtue.[14] Hsün Tzu, who was active in the third century BC, maintained that man was by nature bad or prone to evil.[15] Man could become good, but, without self-control and the requisite moral education, he was naturally subject to self-centred desire, such as desires for sensual pleasure and for one's own profit to the exclusion of others. In recognizing the force of desire Hsün Tzu was showing, one can say, a realistic attitude; and later on there was a good deal of discussion about the nature of desire. But the emphasis laid by Confucius and Mencius on the innate dispositions of man to the acquisition of moral virtues clearly fitted in with their view of the morally educative function of government.

The second implication of Confucius' point of view is that moral standards are not purely conventional, that they are recognized by man rather than determined by him. In point of fact ethical norms and values had for Confucius a metaphysical basis. He regarded them as emanating, in some vague sense, from Heaven, though not as arbitrarily determined by the will of a personal deity.[16] It has been said that Confucius, having accepted traditional moral ideals, read them back into the universe, and then derived them from Heaven. However this may be, he certainly thought of the morally good man and of the well-ordered society as being in harmony with the universe or with Heaven.

The Mohists, followers of Mo Tzu,[17] constituted an important school in ancient times, up to about the beginning of the Han dynasty (206 BC). As far as the need for moral reform, considered abstractly, was concerned, they were in agreement with Confucius and his disciples. At the same time there was sharp opposition between the two schools. For example, the Mohists proclaimed the ideal of universal love without preference or discrimination. This idea was strongly attacked by Mencius, on the ground, for instance, that it was unnatural and subversive of good order to claim that one should love other people's parents as much as one's own. Again, the Mohists were more overtly religious than the Confucianists, insisting on belief in spiritual beings[18] and emphasizing the idea of acting rightly because it was the will of the Lord of Heaven. Further, whereas the Confucianists stressed the idea of doing what was right because it was right, the Mohists expounded a sort of utilitarianism, at any rate as a means of persuading people to practise benevolence or love. For example, if everyone practised universal love, this would eliminate war and benefit society, and what benefits all benefits each. Show love, and you will be loved; do harm to others, and they will do harm to you. In spite, however, of all differences between them, Confucianists and Mohists were at one in emphasizing moral reform rather than legislation and coercion. Both groups were ethical idealists, but the Confucianists were more practically minded. And it was Confucius, not Mo Tzu, who became the great educator of China.

A very different point of view from that of Confucius was presented by the Taoist sages. In their judgement Confucian ethics could not possibly be an effective instrument for remedying the social situation. It appealed to moral precepts and judgements of value as absolutes, when they were really conventional in character, and it failed to go to the root of the matter, to the basic cause of social evils. The basic cause of strife, whether between individuals or societies, was, for the Taoists, desire or, more precisely, the multiplication and growth of desires. To be sure, there were certain basic desires, corresponding to basic needs, which could not be eliminated without eliminating the human race, the desire for food, for example. But desires for more than the basic necessities of life, the desire, for instance, to accumulate land or wealth, the desire to be top dog, even the desire for great learning, led to rivalry, discontent, competition, strife and unrest. So did the urge to interfere with other people, to regulate their lives for them, an urge which the Taoists saw as a prominent feature of Confucianism. The more people abandoned inordinate and self-multiplying desires, the less need would there be for moral rules, which were conventions established to ameliorate a situation which could be avoided in a more fundamental manner. As for governmental activity, the less there was of it, the better. Apart from ensuring that there were sufficient basic necessities, such as food, the ruler should pursue a policy of inaction. Paradoxically, he should act by non-acting – that is to say, government would act beneficially by avoiding any course of action which hindered or prevented the free development of people's natures.

These ideas were given a metaphysical foundation. They were represented, that is to say, as following from metaphysical premises. The ultimate reality, the *Tao*,[19] the nameless mother of all things,[20] could not properly be said to act; yet from it all things flowed. It acts spontaneously because it is what it is, not intentionally nor with artificial contrivance. This spontaneous activity according to nature can be seen both in inanimate and in animate things, such as trees and animals. The ideal for the human individual is also one of spontaneous activity according to his or her nature. Man would then be at one with the rest of nature. Indeed, in the omnipresent *Tao* all things are unified and in a real sense one. The ideal for man is to realize this unity in himself, to live in harmony with the universe. If life is a feature of the phenomenal world, so is death. And the wise man simply accepts it. At death he returns to that out of which he came.

Confucianism and Taoism were clearly opposed in important respects. They were both, however, together with Mohism, opposed by the so-called Legalists, who were simply concerned with the efficient running of the state. In the view of the Legalist school the social and political situation could not be remedied by moral exhortation and good example. Still less could it be remedied by people simply following their natures. It could be remedied only by the rule of law, backed by sanctions. The Legalists thus laid emphasis on the concepts of political power, the rule of law, and the use of punishment for infringement of the law. The hard-headed are likely to feel that the Legalists' ideas were more practical than those of the Confucianists and Taoists, especially the latter. Unfortunately for their reputation, the Legalists were instrumental in establishing the oppressive Ch'in régime; and they encouraged the régime in an attempt, symbolized by the 'burning of books' in 213 BC, to ban all teaching other than their own. When the Ch'in régime was overthrown in 206 BC, the Legalists were blamed, not without reason, for its harsh rule. And that was to all intents and purposes the end of the Legalist school, though, somewhat ironically, after Confucianism had become the official state philosophy and study of Confucian Classics was required for entry to the civil service, some critics of Confucianism accused it of expounding Confucian ideals but having recourse to Legalist policies in practice.

So far early Chinese philosophy, apart from the School of Names and the Yin-Yang cosmology, has been related to the social disunity and unrest created by the disintegration of the feudal system and the loss of effective central power. That is to say, we have been thinking in terms of offering various remedies for the social situation. But I have also indicated how there was much more to Confucianism and Taoism, from a philosophical point of view, than responses to contemporary social problems. In Confucianism we are presented with a theory of human nature, an ethical humanism, while in Taoism we find a theory of ultimate reality. In both cases there is the idea of living in harmony with Heaven or with the universe, though in Confucianism the emphasis is on man as a social being, while in Taoism the emphasis is more on the free development of the individual, the microcosm, so to speak, of the macrocosm, the universe considered as one.

Taoism, Buddhism and the Development of Neo-Confucianism

Let us now consider a few points concerning the later development of such philosophical ideas. Confucianism was elevated to the rank of state philosophy in 136 BC under the Emperor Wu of the Han dynasty. Both Confucianism and Taoism had been opposed to the ideas of the Legalists; but Confucianism, as a system of social ethics which emphasized social obligations, the institutions of family and state, and the guiding roles of heads of families and rulers, and which promoted the observance of traditional rites and ceremonies, was clearly more suitable than Taoism to provide a framework of thought for members of the imperial civil service. In the course of time the practice was established of requiring all aspirants to the civil service to study and pass examinations in the Confucian Classics. In other words, Confucianism was regarded as a bulwark of Chinese social traditions and as providing the desirable moral outlook for the imperial administration.

The Confucianism, however, which became the official philosophy of China was not quite the same as that of Confucius and Mencius. For it had absorbed into itself the Yin-Yang cosmology. Thus the Confucianist Tung Chung-shu, who was instrumental in bringing about adoption of Confucianism as the officially favoured philosophy and who was himself a minister for a time, expounded an analysis of man in terms of the theory of two cosmic principles, one passive (*yin*), the other active (*yang*). According to this analysis, desire and feeling corresponded to or exemplified the passive element, while the nature, the seat of human-heartedness, corresponded to or exemplified the active element.[21] Further, just as Heaven restricted the operation of the cosmic passive principle, so that it would not interfere, for example, with the coming of spring and summer (corresponding to the active principle), so in man the desires and feelings should be weakened and restricted, not allowed to run riot. Only in this way could harmony be secured in man, corresponding to harmony in the universe. This required education, which had two aspects. The people should look to the ruler to complete their education, in order that the potential good in them might be actualized, while the ruler's duty was to obey the will of Heaven and promote the moral education of the citizens. In the social relations between father and son, elder brother and younger brother, ruler and subjects, the first member of each pair represented *Yang*, while the second member represented *Yin*, the active principle.

Though some of these ideas are obviously likely to seem quaint to the modern mind, they express a felt need in Confucianism for a cosmological background to its ethical humanism. It is doubtless true that to some extent a cosmological or metaphysical background was always present, being implied by the notions of the mandate of Heaven and of the sage being in harmony with the universe. But absorption of the Yin-Yang cosmology provided a more explicit cosmological structure. It is understandable that some Confucianists regarded such ideas as undesirable accretions. But the tendency to develop cosmological speculation was later intensified in Neo-Confucianism.

It hardly needs saying that an official philosophy, enjoying governmental patronage, tends to become fossilized or to degenerate into an arid scholasticism. After all, its function as a state ideology is to preserve the established order rather than to pursue radical questioning. Provided, therefore, that other ways of thought are not stifled or proscribed, the link between a particular philosophy and the political régime may well stimulate other ways of thought to take on a fresh lease of life. An example of this is the development of Neo-Taoism in China.

There was, however, another reason for the development of Neo-Taoism. In the last years of the Han dynasty China became divided, and after the collapse of the dynasty in AD 220 there was a period of unrest, warfare and corruption, the political situation being accompanied by economic deterioration. This state of affairs encouraged interest in a philosophy, namely Taoism, which was associated with a policy of withdrawal or standing aloof from political life. (After the period of the northern and southern dynasties the empire was reunited in 589 under the Sui dynasty.)

It was not, however, simply a question of escapism, of seeking a refuge from the troubles of the time. While the Confucianists were inclined to regard certain institutions as willed by Heaven[22] and the corresponding system of social ethics as perennially valid, the Neo-Taoists, or some of them at any rate, while taking over elements of Confucian ethics, emphasized the conventional character of custom and even moral rules and maintained that institutions and customs which had been useful at one time could become outdated and hindrances rather than helps to the free development of man's potentialities. This point of view was in harmony with the original Taoist refusal to attribute conventional human values to reality in general, and it meant that Neo-Taoist thought could be an instrument for criticizing the existing social and political state of affairs.

While some Neo-Taoists emphasized the life of feeling and impulse in what we might describe, for want of a better word, as a romantic spirit, others laid more stress on philosophical speculation; and it was these latter who were responsible for what is known as the 'dark learning', obscure metaphysics that is to say. A prominent feature of this dark learning was the concept of the One, ultimate reality, as not-being.[23] This concept, however, could be understood in two ways. On the one hand, to describe the *Tao* as not-being might be equivalent to saying that it was not a determinate being, with these characteristics rather than those, though it was the mother or source of all determinate things. In this case, if finite and changing things were regarded as transformations of the One, a distinction was required between the *Tao* in itself, as indescribable 'substance', and the *Tao* as 'function', as manifesting itself in the phenomenal world. (The substance-function distinction was to become important in Chinese philosophy. As applied to the One, it bears some resemblance to the distinction between *Natura naturans* and *Natura naturata*. But it came to be applied to determinate things as well.) On the other hand, the description of the *Tao* as not-being could be understood literally. In this case the objection could obviously be raised that not-being cannot be the source or cause of anything. Thus we find Kuo Hsiang, who died in AD 312, maintaining that terms such as 'universe' and '*Tao*' were simply names for all things taken together, the things, that is to say, which, as interrelated, form the world (cf. Note 23). These things, according to Kuo Hsiang, did not emanate from anything beyond them. Perhaps we can describe this view as representing a naturalistic tendency in Taoist thought.

Given metaphysical speculation of this kind, it is not surprising if the interest of Taoist scholars was aroused by the doctrines of Mahāyāna Buddhism which, as already noted, began to establish itself in China during the first century AD. For example, the Taoist concept of not-being invited comparison with the Buddhist concept of emptiness (*sūnyatā*). In the earlier days of the life of Buddhism in China there was a good deal of discussion, especially in southern China, between Taoist and Buddhist scholars, and Buddhist philosophers were influenced by Taoist ideas. The Buddhist Three-Treatise school, the Chinese continuation of the Middle Doctrine school of Nāgārjuna in India, has, with the dialectic of negation, an obvious affinity with Taoism. And Ch'an Buddhism, a Chinese creation, reflected some Taoist ideas, such as the inexpressible nature of the Absolute. Again, there was some similarity between the Ch'an idea of the presence of the Buddha-mind or Buddha-nature in all animate things and the Taoist theory of the immanence of the One in all beings. It is certainly not my intention to endorse the Taoist legend that the Buddha was a disciple of Lao Tzu, nor to suggest that Buddhism in China was a form of Taoism in disguise. While, however, Taoist scholars took some interest in Buddhist thought, Buddhist philosophers, in the process of Buddhism's self-adaptation to the Chinese cultural environment, were influenced by Taoism. Sometimes it was more a question of using Taoist language for Buddhist ideas. But sometimes it was a question of incorporating Taoist ideas. Ch'an (Zen) Buddhism obviously makes use of Buddhist terms, such as 'Buddha-nature' or 'Buddha-mind'. In some respects, however, affinities with Taoism are so noticeable that one may well have the impression of being confronted by Taoism expressed in Buddhist language.

We have been referring, of course, to Taoism and Buddhism on the level of philosophical thought. Buddhism was a religion; it adapted itself in a variety of ways to its new environment, and it developed forms of devotional religion, such as Pure Land Buddhism, which were capable of exercising a popular appeal which abstruse metaphysics obviously could not exercise. There was also organized Taoist religion. And on the level of religion Taoism and Buddhism were opposed. The chief critics of Buddhism were, as one might expect, the Confucianists. In the fifth and sixth centuries AD Confucianist critics accused Buddhism of being a foreign importation unsuited for the Chinese people, of weakening family relationships by promoting its monastic ideal, of failing to show the proper attitude towards the state, and of teaching false doctrines such as that of reincarnation, while the monks were charged with being social parasites. When, however, the northern emperor issued drastic decrees against Buddhism in 446, he had been persuaded to do so, it is said, by a Confucianist and a Taoist, each of which wished to safeguard the interests of his own group. Again, when in 845 a large number of Buddhist monasteries and temples were destroyed and their lands confiscated, the repressive measures taken by the political authorities seem to have been instigated not only by Confucianist bureaucrats but also by representatives of Taoist religion. All this, however, does not alter the fact that Taoist philosophy had an influence on Buddhist thought. In other words, on the level of philosophical thought, there were syncretistic tendencies.

The interest in cosmological and metaphysical theory, which found expression in Neo-Taoism and in some schools of Mahāyāna Buddhism, came to find expression in Confucianism as well. It was indeed natural that Confucianists should reassert Confucian ideas in opposition to those of Taoism and Buddhism. For example, Han Yü, who lived under the T'ang dynasty, which had reasserted the status of Confucianism as the official state philosophy (he died in 824), expounded what he considered to be the right interpretation of the Confucian concepts of human nature and virtue, maintaining that in contemporary thought the genuine Confucian concepts had become confused with Buddhist and Taoist theories. He also argued that Taoism and Buddhism turned people's minds away from their obligations as members of families and citizens of the state, and that they advocated what amounted pretty well to annihilation of the personality. None the less, syncretistic tendencies manifested themselves even in Confucianism. The new speculative thought was represented as a kind of esoteric wisdom going back to Confucius, if not further (the T'ien-t'ai and Ch'an Buddhist schools postulated an esoteric teaching of the Buddha, transmitted through a succession of disciples. It is possible that the analogous idea in Confucianism was an adaptation of the Ch'an tradition.); but there can be no doubt that in point of fact Taoist and Buddhist thought exercised a positive influence on Confucianism. The result of the systematic combination of a variety of ideas was Neo-Confucianism, which developed in the eleventh and twelfth centuries and which continued to dominate philosophical thought in China, though under the Ch'ing or Manchu dynasty (1644–1912) there was a critical reaction against the metaphysical ideas of the Neo-Confucianism of the Sung and Ming periods, a reaction which might perhaps be described as a kind of 'back to Confucius and Mencius' movement.

It is not possible to do more here than to illustrate briefly two tendencies in the Neo-Confucian movement. (The two tendencies are customarily derived from the two Ch'eng brothers in the eleventh century. But their ideas too had some antecedents.) One of these tendencies or lines of thought, represented by the influential philosopher Chu Hsi (1130–1200), is commonly described as rationalistic Neo-Confucianism. According to Chu Hsi, every thing has its 'principle', all particular principles being united in the Great Ultimate, which is described as the principle of heaven and earth and the myriad things. The Great Ultimate, corresponding to the One of Taoism, is also said to be Mind, though Mind in this sense does not involve consciousness.[24] It can thus be said that while Principle is one, its manifestations are many. Particular principles do not exist apart from matter or material force. Without principle material force would be nothing definite, while without matter principle would not be the principle of anything. The general process of production, integration and disintegration of things in the world presupposes both principle and material force. But the relation of material force to the Great Ultimate or Principle of Nature is not explained clearly.

Chu Hsi's theory of principle and material force naturally brings to mind Aristotle's theory of form and matter, though some writers prefer to see a resemblance to Plato's thought. However this may be, in the rationalistic Neo-Confucianism which dominated in the period of the Sung dynasty emphasis was laid on the investigation of principles, in the sense of the principles of things. It is not a case of Chu Hsi having neglected ethics. The concept of principle included moral principles. But sufficient stress was laid on the objective study of the principles or forms of things to have stimulated a turning to scientific knowledge, even if this result did not in fact occur.[25]

In what is sometimes called the idealistic tendency in Neo-Confucianism, which flourished more under the Ming dynasty, emphasis was laid more on the mind's insight into itself, especially into innate moral principles. According to Wang Yang-ming (1472–1529), investigation into the specific principles of external things tends to disperse the attention of the mind and make it restless, whereas peace and tranquillity are attained if the mind seeks its highest good within itself, especially by grasping and practising the principles of *jen* (humanity or human-heartedness).

We may add that Wang Fu-chih, whose life (1619–92) spanned the transition between the Ming and Manchu periods, while accepting the concepts of principle, material force, substance and function, rejected any theory of abstract entities such as the Great Ultimate, the Way or *Tao*, and the Principle of Nature. The world, he asserted, consists only of concrete things. We can indeed distinguish between principle and material force, but they never exist apart. Taoist talk about Not-Being is folly. A dog is not a rabbit, but there is no entity called Not-Being. Nor does the absolute Emptiness of Buddhism refer to any reality. Nor does the Neo-Confucian Great Ultimate or Principle of Nature, unless it is understood simply as a global way of referring to the principles of concrete things.

Sufficient has been said here to indicate how inaccurate it would be to assert that the Chinese philosophers had no interest in cosmological and metaphysical themes. Even in Confucianism, which is sometimes depicted as being simply an ethical system, a need was felt for a world-view to serve as a background for the ethical theory. This was natural enough. For Confucianism centred round the theme of human nature, and human beings are obviously members of a greater whole. Moreover, from early days there was the conviction that the Confucian sage was in harmony with Heaven, with the universe as a whole, in a manner analogous to that in which the Taoist wise man was thought to be in harmony with Nature and with ultimate reality, the *Tao*. The development of Neo-Confucian metaphysics can be seen as an attempt to make this concept of harmony more explicit.

At the same time the development of cosmological and metaphysical speculation within Confucianism was balanced by reassertions of the primacy of the ethical and by recalls to the spirit of Confucius and Mencius. It was further balanced from time to time by a down-to-earth criticism of metaphysical abstractions, as represented, for example, by the naturalism of Wang Ch'ung in the first century AD and, in the seventeenth century, by the materialism of Wang Fu-Chih. But throughout philosophy in China remained a way of life. Ideas of how life should be lived naturally differed. We have referred to the sharp attacks by Confucianists on what they considered to be Buddhist (and also Taoist) escapism. But we have also noted that in Chinese Buddhism, as distinct from Buddhism in China,[26] emphasis came to be placed on enlightenment in the midst of daily life. One reason why Ch'an Buddhism survived the repressive measures of AD 845 was perhaps that the Ch'an monks were by no means social parasites but did a good deal of socially useful work.

Theory and Practice: Knowledge and Action

In the foregoing section I have tended to represent cosmological and metaphysical speculation in China as an attempt to provide ethical doctrines with a wide background or framework. This picture is open to a number of objections. For example, it can be objected that cosmological speculation goes back to a very early time in Chinese thought, its remote origins being probably connected with the practice of divination. It can also be objected that the picture which I have painted does not do justice to those Chinese thinkers who had a genuine interest in cosmological themes for their own sake. This picture, however, at least draws attention to the primacy of the ethical in Chinese thought. Ethics, however, were orientated to practice. Confucianists, Taoists and Buddhists were all concerned with what they severally considered to be the desirable kind of life for man. It is not surprising, therefore, if we find in Chinese philosophy a recurring emphasis on the close connection between knowledge and action.

It is clear enough that Confucius regarded ethical knowledge as issuing in moral self-cultivation and action. For example, the rulers should know the mandate of Heaven or the Way in order to govern the state according to this knowledge. For explicit statements, however, of the relation between knowledge and action we have to look to a later period. Thus Chu Hsi, the twelfth century Neo-Confucianist, wrote that knowledge and action require one another. From the point of view of order, from the temporal point of view that is to say, knowledge comes first; but from the point of view of importance action occupies the first place. We must know before we can act; but if someone has knowledge but has not yet acted according to his knowledge, his knowledge is shallow or superficial. For in action experience is gained which alters the quality of the knowledge. What is already known should be acted upon, and further knowledge should be sought with a view to further action.

This point of view was even more strongly expressed by Wang Yang-ming (1472–1529), who held various administrative posts, though he had his enemies and consequently suffered some troubles. In his view it was not simply a question of saying that one must have knowledge before one can act, and that knowledge should lead to action. This is indeed true, but it is compatible with claiming that knowledge and action are distinct things, whereas for Wang Yang-ming they form a unity. Action is the completion of knowledge, and without action what seems to be knowledge is not really knowledge. We tend to think, for example, that a son can know his obligations towards his parents and yet neglect to perform these obligations, and that, therefore, knowledge and action must be distinct, even if the former should lead to the latter. In reality, however, the son's 'knowledge' is not really knowledge. For if it were, it would be completed in action. This doctrine may remind us of Josiah Royce's interpretation of ideas as inchoate action, the beginning of action.

The primary context of Wang Yang-ming's theory of the unity of knowledge and action is, as we would expect in the case of a Confucianist, an ethical one. At the same time the theory is expressed in a quite general way, without any explicit restriction to the ethical sphere. Some of the statements made by Wang Yang-ming are open to question. Consider, for example, his statement that one can know what pain is only after one has experienced it. If knowing what pain is means knowing pain by acquaintance, by experience, the assertion is tautological. If, however, we were to understand knowing what pain is as referring to scientific knowledge of the nature of pain, the truth of the assertion might perhaps be questioned. In any case it is clear that 'knowledge' and 'action' are understood in pretty wide senses. Knowledge seems to include not only knowledge that but also knowledge by acquaintance, and action seems to include such activities as feeling. According to Wang Yang-ming when one perceives a bad smell (knows it), one immediately dislikes it (acts). One does not first have the knowledge and then make up one's mind to dislike it. In other words, the thesis of the unity of knowledge and action is a quite general one. It was also given a general application by the Confucianist Yen Yüan (1635–1704), who asserted, for example, that ability to read musical scores and discuss them does not entail the conclusion that the person knows music. To have a real knowledge of music the person must be able to play the scores.

The theory of the unity of knowledge and action seems to give rise to some difficulties, unless, of course, knowledge and action are given meanings which make the theory necessarily true. At the same time the theory illustrates the practically-minded bent of so much Chinese thought. When in his essay *On Practice* Mao Tse-Tung referred to the pattern of discovering truth through practice, of verifying this truth by practice, and of advancing to a higher level of practice and knowledge, he was doubtless speaking in Marxist-Leninist terms; but some of the things which he said might have come from Confucianist thinkers such as Chu Hsi.

Chinese Philosophy and Science

It is at any rate not unreasonable to argue that Chinese philosophical thought was not, generally speaking, of such a kind as to stimulate a lively and sustained interest in natural science. We have indeed noted above that the rationalistic school of Neo-Confucianism, as represented by Chu Hsi, emphasized inquiry into the principles of things, and that this idea could have encouraged scientific inquiry. But we have also seen that, within the Neo-Confucian movement, there was a reassertion of the primary importance of inquiry into moral principles. There certainly emerged from time to time a naturalistic tendency in Confucianism; but, in general, Confucianists were preoccupied with human nature and with moral values and, in certain periods, with textual scholarship. One might perhaps have expected that Taoism, with its emphasis on nature, would have encouraged the development of natural science, but Taoist interest in nature, when not meta-physical, tended to be more aesthetic than scientific. As for Buddhism, its spirit and the orientation of its thought was hardly conducive to focusing attention on natural science. As we have indicated, there was indeed cosmological speculation in Chinese philosophy, going back to very ancient times in the form of the Yin-Yang school. But, generally speaking, emphasis tended to be placed on human life and the way to lead it.

One might indeed argue in another way and maintain that the idea of a great harmony between Heaven and Earth, between man and nature, was eminently suited to encourage scientific inquiry. But interest was centred more in the mirroring of this harmony in human society and on the human being's integration into the harmony through the correspondence of his or her life with the Way, whether this term, the Way, was understood in the Confucian or in the Taoist manner.

It is, however, one thing to argue that Chinese philosophy, being primarily orientated to the right ordering of human life and society, was not of such a kind as to stimulate a lively and sustained interest in natural science, and it is quite another thing to assert that Chinese philosophy was responsible for the absence of science in the culture of imperial China. For it is untrue to say that science was absent. On the contrary, the Chinese pursued, for example, astronomical and medical studies; they made technological progress; and their inventions often anticipated by a very considerable time analogous inventions in Europe.[27] It is indeed true that in modern times the West drew ahead of imperial China in the scientific field, a fact which came to be understood by the Chinese themselves, even if they thought that the West had little of value to offer except science and technology. But the point is that the West drew ahead of a level of scientific knowledge which was already there in China, a level which once surpassed the level hitherto attained in Europe.

When Chinese science is mentioned, reference is usually made to the inventions of printing, gunpowder, the compass, the clock[28] and so on. This perhaps suggests that science in ancient China reveals the practical orientation and sense of the concrete in the Chinese mind. The Chinese were strong in medicine and technology. It is true that they also pursued astronomical studies and made noteworthy obser-vations; but for a long time observation and registration of astro-nomical phenomena were regarded as relevant to divining the fortunes of the state. This idea was natural enough, given the idea of the great harmony of the universe, but it manifests a practical interest.

This should not be taken to imply that the Chinese had no general physical theories. They had. But though they had some empirical basis, they were arrived at more or less intuitively, and Chinese scientists had little idea of deductive argumentation from hypothetical premises and the systematic testing of conclusions. Deductive logic was not one of their strong points, whether in philosophy or in science. For a very long time China was ahead of Europe in various scientific fields, but in the end it had to appropriate western logic and western scientific method.

What is being suggested is, of course, that it is much more a case of certain characteristics showing themselves in both Chinese philosophy and Chinese science than of philosophy inhibiting the development of natural science. That is to say, both philosophy and science manifested a practical turn of mind, a feeling for the concrete, and a lack of interest in theoretical deduction. We have already noted that Fung Yu-lan, who stood in the Confucian tradition until he turned to Marxism, recognized the need for enriching philosophical thought in China by an appropriation of western logic. In the field of natural science it was not a question of taking over a body of scientific knowledge to fill a vacuum (for there was no such vacuum) but rather of appropriating modern scientific method.

The Typical Chinese View of the World

Perhaps we can fittingly conclude this chapter by drawing attention to the fact that the typical Chinese view of the world was that of a constantly changing totality. Taoist talk about the ultimate reality as nameless and indescribable and Neo-Confucianist talk about the Great Ultimate can be misleading. For such talk tends to suggest the idea of a transcendent reality beyond this world, a reality which is in itself unchanging. We can indeed find the idea of an unchanging Absolute in Indian philosophy, the ultimate reality to which the inner self can be said to return, even if it is actually always one with the reality and separated from it only by the veil of ignorance. In Chinese metaphysics, however, the myriad things are the transformations of the One. There is only one world. And it was in this one world that the Chinese thinkers were interested. In a real sense Being was for them Becoming. Obviously, for those who believe in a transcendent God or in the unchanging Brahman of the Advaita Vedānta the typical Chinese view of the world leaves something to be desired. But, equally obviously, there are those who find the Chinese view congenial, the view of one changing, self-transforming universe, in which harmony is preserved in the midst of the dynamic process. Personal beliefs and preferences apart, however, there can be little doubt that, as was asserted at the beginning of this chapter, there is a sense in which Chinese philosophical thought was more this-worldly than Indian philosophy, provided, of course, that we do not understand the term 'this-worldly' as implying an absence of moral ideals.

4

Interrelations between Philosophy
and the Historic Religions

The Concept of Religion

By an 'historic religion' I understand a religion which has existed or exists as a social and cultural phenomenon. To put the matter in another way, by an historic religion I mean a religion which already exists as an historical datum when the philosopher starts to reflect about religion. It can thus be distinguished from a religion which is invented by a philosopher, comprising, for example, those beliefs which, in the philosopher's opinion, would be accepted by human beings, if they were all rational, according to the philosopher's criterion of rationality. The concept of 'natural religion', as proposed by some philosophers of the eighteenth-century Enlightenment, seems to me to constitute an example.

It must be admitted that it is difficult to make absolutely clear-cut distinctions of this sort. Auguste Comte invented a religion, the religion of Humanity. Inasmuch as it was adopted by the members of a kind of positivist church, one might, I suppose, speak of it as an historical social phenomenon. But it hardly enjoyed a flourishing life. It obviously represented some eccentric ideas of the famous positivist philosopher and was incapable of winning the adherence even of most of those who accepted the general line of thought expressed in Comte's philosophy. The very limited existence of a positivist church does not seem to me to deprive the distinction mentioned above of validity and usefulness.

In the present context we are concerned only with those historic religions which existed in cultures in which there was a recognizable philosophical tradition, and in which there could, therefore, be interrelations between philosophy and religion.

There are indeed cases in which there can be differences of opinion about the propriety of describing *x* as a religion. For example, some writers have maintained that Buddhism is an ethical system rather than a religion. If the reason for making this judgement is that Buddhism does not include belief in a personal transcendent God, the judgement presupposes a definition of religion in which theism, as exemplified in Judaism, Christianity and Islam, is taken as paradigmatic. Though it is open to anyone to adopt such a definition if he wishes, the fact remains that on some broader definitions of religion which have been proposed, Buddhism is certainly a religion. Besides, how could we describe Pure Land Buddhism, in which those who invoke the name of the Amitābha Buddha are represented as being admitted to the western paradise through the saving grace of the Buddha, as anything else but a religion? Some writers make a distinction between Buddhism as religion and Buddhism as philosophy. (In Pure Land Buddhism in Japan special stress was laid on salvation by faith alone.) But though a rough distinction of this kind can doubtless be made, and indeed has to be made if we wish to discuss Buddhist philosophy, it must be remembered that the thought of the Buddhist schools arose within and not outside Buddhism. Though the abstruse speculation of some Buddhist sects or schools could certainly not be appreciated by most of the adherents of Buddhism as a popular religion, the schools did not lose sight of the Buddhist view of the ultimate goal of human life.

It can be safely assumed that most people regard Buddhism as a religion. In the case of Confucianism the situation is rather different. To be sure, Confucianism can be said to have occupied in China much of the field which in the West has been occupied by religion and law. Further, there were several attempts to convert Confucianism into a religion. They were not, however, successful. And though on some very broad definitions of religion Confucianism may count as a religion, many people would think it misleading to describe the official ideology or ethical and social doctrine of imperial China in this way.

If, then, one adopts a definition based on the selection of a certain religion or group of religions as a paradigm, one will find oneself either excluding from the class of religions something which is generally called a religion or regarding it as defective on the ground that it lacks this or that characteristic mentioned in or implied by the definition. If, however, one adopts a very broad definition, framed to cover everything which is commonly described as religion, one may find that it will also cover some phenomena which most people would hesitate to recognize as religious. Broad definitions, however, can serve the useful purpose of shaking firmly entrenched conventional ideas and of enabling us to see religious attitudes where we may not have seen them before. But to avoid becoming involved in prolonged discussion of such topics, attention here is confined to certain aspects of the relations between philosophy on the one hand and Hinduism, Buddhism, Islam and Christianity on the other.

Philosophy and Religion in Hindu Thought

Religion, like art, is older than philosophy. It is hardly necessary to say that I have no intention of denying that philosophy existed before this or that world-religion came into existence. Greek philosophy, for example, preceded the birth and growth of Christianity, not to speak of Islam. What I mean is that in given cultures, such as those of Greece, India, China and Japan, religion existed before anything which we would ordinarily recognize as philosophy.

Let us consider India. The early Vedic poems obviously express polytheism, though now one deity, now another (such as Varuna or Indra) comes to the fore and is described in terms borrowed, so to speak, from other deities. Further, in the *Rig-Veda* the wise man is said to call the one divinity by many names.[1] In the Upanishads, however, the earlier of which seem to have been composed from about 800–400 BC,[2] the concept of one ultimate reality becomes prominent. It is not so much a case of the gods and goddesses disappearing altogether as of the concept of a reality which transcends the Many (including the deities) coming to the fore. The Vedānta school arose out of reflection on the Upanishads, and it is with this school that we are concerned here. We are hardly in a position to determine any precise date at which the school arose. Its most famous philosopher, Śaṁkara, seems to have lived from about 788 until about 820, but he had his predecessors. Anyway, the question of dates has little relevance here.

In his valuable work *Early Buddhist Theory of Knowledge* Professor K. N. Jayatilleke refers to the 'metaphysicians' of the early Upanishads as rationalists, in the sense that they 'derived their knowledge from reasoning and speculation without any claims to extrasensory perception.[3] This may indeed be true. But it seems to me unlikely. Even if there is no explicit claim by the writers in question that their doctrine of the ultimate reality was based on non-sensory perception, argument is not much in evidence. The doctrine of Brahman is stated rather than argued, and it seems to be probable, though I could not prove it, that the doctrine was in fact partially based on some form of Yogic concentration of mind or inward-turning contemplation.[4] Anyway, though the doctrine of Brahman can, of course, be described as metaphysical, the philosopher who believes that argument is essential to philosophy is likely to regard the Upanishads as religious texts of a mystical nature rather than as philosophical works in the sense in which Kant's first *Critique* is a philosophical work. While, therefore, we certainly find philosophy in the Vedānta school, it is perfectly reasonable, in my opinion, to represent the school's reflection on the Upanishads as reflection arising out of a religious matrix or background.

In the Upanishads we can find two lines of thought in regard to the ultimate reality, Brahman. In one line of thought, emphasis is laid on the already existing unity of the inner self of the human being with the Absolute, and Brahman is represented as suprapersonal. In the other line of thought, emphasis is laid more on a religious attitude of love and devotion to a divine reality conceived as personal. It is not intended to imply that these lines of thought are clearly distinguished and developed in the sacred texts. But they can be discerned by the reflective mind. It is not surprising, therefore, that within the Vedānta school as a whole there emerged different sub-schools corresponding to the different lines of thought discernible in the Upanishads. Thus in the non-dualist or Advaita Vedānta, of which Śaṁkara is the best known exponent, emphasis was laid upon the thesis that from the point of view of the higher level of knowledge there is only one true reality, Brahman or the Absolute, with which the abiding self in the human being, *ātman*, is one.[5] Brahman, for the Advaita Vedānta, is suprapersonal. To be sure, for the ordinary level of consciousness Brahman appears as personal, as Saguna-Brahman, but what so appears is Nirguna-Brahman, the suprapersonal Absolute. In this philosophy stress must obviously be laid on knowledge. For one thing, the unity of man's inner self with Brahman is not so much something to be achieved as something to be recognized as already existing, though hidden behind the veils of ignorance. For another thing, as far as the level of ordinary everyday practical life and knowledge is concerned, the Many are real enough; it is only on a higher level of knowledge that the Many are seen as appearances which veil the One. As with Spinoza, therefore, a theory of degrees of knowledge is of great importance.[6]

When we turn to the 'dualist' or Dvaita Vedānta, of which Madhva (in the thirteenth century) was a leading representative, we find the more theistic line of thought in the Upanishads coming to the fore. Emphasis is laid on loving devotion to and service of God, an emphasis which implies a distinction between the human spirit and God. There is, to borrow a phrase from modern theology, an I-Thou relationship. In the Dvaita Vedānta the devotional aspect of Hindu religion, the *bhakti* movement, comes, as it were, to explicit self-consciousness.

Though, however, the philosophy of Madhva certainly has its roots in religion, it is none the less philosophy. Madhva appeals not only to the sacred texts but also to experience, our experience of plurality, and argues that it is nonsense to talk about a form of knowledge which transcends the subject-object relationship. Just as for the modern phenomenologist consciousness is essentially consciousness *of*, so for Madhva knowledge is essentially knowledge *of*. It implies a distinction between knower and known, and we cannot speak intelligibly of a knowledge which transcends this distinction. Madhva was strongly opposed to the Advaitins and he accused them, somewhat unfairly,[7] of destroying religion. Even if, however, his attacks on other thinkers were sometimes intemperate in tone,[8] he certainly made some good points against monism.

Advaita and Dvaita were sharply opposed. There was another line of thought, within the Vedānta tradition, which is generally described as qualified non-dualism and which was expounded by Rāmānuja, who lived in the twelfth century and, therefore, came after Śaṁkara and before Madhva. On the one hand the thought of Rāmānuja represented a religious reaction against the monism of the Advaita school. That is to say, he stood for the religious tradition of worship and devotion and, therefore, maintained that there must be some distinction between the human spirit and Brahman, conceived as personal. For if there were no distinction, worship and loving devotion to God would make no sense. On the other hand Rāmānuja had no intention of dismissing those passages of the Upanishads in which the oneness of the human spirit with Brahman was clearly asserted. His task as a philosopher was, therefore, to find a way of reconciling these two points of view. In his endeavour to perform this task he made use of the analogy of the relationship between soul and body. On the one hand we cannot simply identify soul and body, admitting no distinction. On the other hand we cannot regard them as two entirely separate entities. Without the soul the human body is not a human body. And its actions are directed by the soul. Analogously, the world of sentient and non-sentient beings can be regarded as the body of God, the body of which God is the efficient and material cause. In this case it would seem to follow that changes in creatures are changes in God, and that if a creature moves, God moves. Rāmānuja maintained, however, that God in himself, in his essential nature, does not change. He is changeable only in the body which proceeds from him and depends on him as its soul. Some such distinction as that between *Natura naturans* and *Natura naturata* in the philosophy of Spinoza is obviously required.[9]

Vedānta philosophy is a clear example of philosophical reflection arising out of the matrix of religion and remaining within religion. It is for this reason that I have chosen it as an example of one type of relationship between philosophy and religion. As was noted in the second chapter of this book, there is a sense in which all the Vedic schools were religiously orientated. But in the case of certain schools their remote origins are obscure. And some features, such as the Nyāya logic and Vaiśesika atomism, were certainly not derived simply from reflection on the sacred texts. We can indeed say that the Mīmāmsā school arose out of the matrix of religion and remained within religion. But the Vedānta school is the most famous and the most influential.[10] For those with only a smattering of knowledge of classical Indian thought it tends to represent Indian philosophy in general.

Buddhist Thought and Religion

According to Dr Edward Conze, a specialist in Buddhist studies, 'Buddhism is an Eastern form of spirituality'.[11] The emphasis in original Buddhism was certainly on a way of life, leading to an ideal goal. If one wishes to call it a 'philosophy of life', it was a very simplified one. It rejected the ritualism of previous Indian religion, and it passed over in silence mythology and all speculation about ultimate reality. Stress was placed on recognizing the omnipresence of suffering and its cause in desire, on overcoming desire and on attaining inner peace and tranquillity, with the goal of attaining Nirvāna. As far as I am aware, there is no solid evidence that the Buddha ever denied that there is a metaphenomenal reality. He seems, however, to have steered clear of such topics, partly because he considered that the relevant questions were unanswerable, partly because he believed that such speculation was irrelevant to the main task of attaining detachment, inner peace and the right attitude to others. It is, of course, extremely hazardous for anyone to claim that he has certain knowledge of original Buddhism, but it is clear enough that the Buddha's message was simple, as far as understanding was concerned (practice is obviously a different matter) and that metaphysical speculation did not form part of it.[12]

Even the relatively simple message of early Buddhism inevitably gave rise to questions in reflective minds. For example, all things were looked on as phenomenal. That is to say, they were not self-sufficient. There existence was caused and depended constantly on conditions; and they were transient, being in a constant state of change. This was interpreted to mean that in no thing is there an unchanging substance or core. The self is no exception. In other words, the theory of *ātman*, an inner unchanging self, was rejected. The self consisted of a succession of states. The question then arose whether each state had duration. In other words, the general idea of the impermanence of things (all things change and are transient) prompted a philosophical or logical analysis of the idea, the theory of momentariness, of momentary states, was developed in Hīnayāna Buddhism. This theory obviously gave rise to problems in explaining the sense of continuing personal identity. And such problems were not diminished by the Sautrāntika school's rejection of the idea of any static element in the life, so to speak, of a mental state. For if each successive moment was a vanishing moment, how could it cause the following state? It had, so to speak, no time to cause anything. How could memory be accounted for? It is not surprising that in the course of time there arose a tendency, represented in Indian Buddhism by the Pudgalavādins, to reintroduce the idea of a permanent self. It was not, however, simply a question of memory. Buddhism taught that the human being was affected by good or evil actions. If, however, the self was reducible to successive momentary states, who or what was the agent of good or evil actions? Hīnayāna Buddhism as a whole tries to resist any approximation to the Hindu conception of *ātman*. But we are concerned here simply with an illustration of the way in which philosophical questions inevitably arose within Buddhism as a way of life.

The doctrine of no-self also gave rise to difficulties in regard to belief in transmigration, which for Buddhists had an ethical significance, in the sense that the law of cause and effect meant that one's good and evil actions inevitably had their effects in time and determined the nature of one's next life. On the theory of no-self is it possible to speak of 'one's next life'? Who or what passes from one embodiment to another, enabling us to speak of 'reincarnation' or 'transmigration'? If nothing passes but there is simply a 'karmanic' connection, analogous to the way in which one ball, striking another ball, determines the direction in which the second ball moves, how is this causal connection to be explained in the case of transmigration, when there is nothing comparable to the contact between the two balls? It is no wonder that when Buddhism had been introduced to China, the Chinese found difficulty in seeing how transmigration made any sense without the idea of a soul. Given the theory of no-self, how would it be possible, even in principle, to remember past lives?[13]

As for the doctrine of Nirvāna, it was doubtless possible to leave the nature of Nirvāna undetermined, to insist on acquiring those moral qualities which could be developed by one's own efforts, and to hold out the prospect of complete peace and absence of suffering without saying anything further, on the ground that it was impossible to know what, if anything, lay beyond the phenomenal world. At the same time it was natural that the reflective mind should raise questions. What was meant by Nirvāna? Was it equivalent to extinction or annihilation? Or should it be taken as implying that the self would become one with the ultimate reality? If so, what was the nature of this reality? Should it be described as the Void or Emptiness, as the Mādhyamika school (Three-Treatises school in China) described it? Or as Pure Mind or Pure Consciousness, as the Yogācāra school of Mahāyāna Buddhism described it? Again, however Nirvāna might be described, whether as oneness with the Void or with Pure Consciousness or, as in Ch'an (Zen) Buddhism, with the Buddha-mind or Buddha-nature, what was the relation of the ultimate reality, the Absolute, to the phenomenal world? Dōgen (1200–53), the Japanese Buddhist teacher who introduced the Sōtō sect of Zen Buddhism into Japan, identified Being and Becoming. There was for him, as for Zen Buddhism in general, one world, the One appearing in the Many.[14]

The Buddhist thinkers, especially in Mahāyāna Buddhism, pursued some pretty abstruse speculation, which was far too abstract for the general run of Buddhists. Pure Land Buddhism suited them much better. And Zen Buddhism was able to appeal to a wider circle than, say the Three-Treatises school, inasmuch as emphasis was laid on 'meditation' (*zazen*)[15] rather than on study of texts or on philosophy. At the same time even the abstruse speculation of some schools arose within Buddhism, largely out of reflection on basic Buddhist doctrines. It is thus a mistake, in my opinion, to regard Buddhist philosophy as a superfluous accretion to a simple rule of life. It arose quite naturally within Buddhism. Further, the people whom we describe as Buddhist philosophers were also religious teachers. Dōgen, for example, was first and foremost a religious teacher.

What has been said above should be sufficient to show that the Buddhist thinkers were by no means blind to the theoretical difficulties arising out of reflection on basic Buddhist ideas. Perhaps one may add the following rather striking example. In Mahāyāna Buddhism the holy man who could enter Nirvāna but who postponed his entry in order to save others was known as a *bodhisattva*. If, however, the self is reduced by analysis to successive vanishing moments, the question arises, whom is there to save? Again, on this view of the self, who attains enlightenment? Some Buddhist thinkers did not hesitate to say that there is nobody to save. In fact there are no saviour and no saved. Similarly, nobody is enlightened. Such statements may seem to be not only paradoxical but also incompatible with Buddhist beliefs about human destiny. Presumably, however, conclusions were being drawn from the conception of the world as phenomenal. The distinction between saviour and saved is phenomenal. So is the distinction between the enlightened and the non-enlightened. All phenomena are 'empty', and in the end there is only Emptiness or the Void. Once more the question becomes acute, whether Emptiness is to be understood as Not-being in a literal sense or in the sense of an Absolute which is void for us, inasmuch as it transcends our thought and language.

We have briefly considered the Vedānta tradition and Buddhist philosophy as examples of religion giving rise to philosophy through the instrumentality of reflection. The fact, however, that they have been considered separately should not be taken to imply that they were completely heterogeneous. There is in fact an obvious similarity between some forms of Mahāyāna Buddhism and the philosophy of Śaṁkara. Further, Śaṁkara, like the Buddhist Nāgārjuna before him, criticized some Buddhist ideas of causality (though we cannot here discuss the extent to which Śaṁkara may have been influenced by Nāgārjuna's Middle-way philosophy; in any case Śaṁkara did not adopt Nāgārjuna's characteristic dialectical method).

Islam and Philosophy

To the immediate disciples of Mohammed (*c.* AD 570–632), the prophet's message doubtless seemed extremely simple; there is one God, and Mohammed is his prophet. (Mohammed was regarded as the last and greatest of the prophets, but not as the only one. Mohammed himself recognized Moses, for example, as a prophet.) For many people, I suppose, this simplicity has been one main attraction of Islam. None the less there were at any rate some questions to which meditation on the Koran gave rise in the reflective mind. For example, people are called on to obey the will of Allah, and there are frequent references in the sacred text to rewards and punishments in the after-life. One would, therefore, naturally assume that human beings are free to obey or disobey, and that those who receive punishment after death are punished for having done what they could have refrained from doing. At the same time there are passages in the Koran which seems to imply a doctrine of divine predestination. For instance, it is stated several times that evildoers are led astray by God.[16] When therefore Muslims began to reflect seriously on the implications of what was said in the Koran, they very naturally raised and discussed the question of human freedom. Another question which arose was whether moral precepts could be known without revelation. If all human beings were subject to divine judgement, whether or not they were acquainted with the Koran and its teaching, or with preceding revelation, must it not be possible for them to discover by the use of reason the principles of conduct, observance of which was required for salvation? Or were things so arranged by Allah that those who had not the benefit of revealed knowledge were doomed to hell?

These questions were, of course, raised and discussed in a theological setting, different groups of theologians giving different answers. The development of philosophical thought on a wider scale was the result of the contact of Islam with other cultures, either through literature or through the spread of Islam outside the Arab world. Thus, in the course of its development in Persia, Islamic thought was in contact not only with Zoroastrian ideas but also with Indian philosophy. It is, of course, difficult to assess the extent to which Muslim thinkers were actually influenced by the religious and philosophical ideas of already existing cultures, but it is only to be expected that on the intellectual level the conquerors would be affected by the thought of the cultured peoples whose lands they ruled, even though they were intent on maintaining the religion of Islam.

As far as the West is concerned, the most significant contact was with Greek philosophy and science through the medium of literature. Works by Aristotle and other Greek philosophers, as well as writings in the fields of mathematics and medicine, had been translated from Greek into Syriac by Christian scholars at Nestorian and Monophysite schools in the Middle East. This work was little interfered with by the Arab conquerors. Indeed, when the Abbassid dynasty came to power at Baghdad, the rulers welcomed Christian scholars, and the work of translation from Syriac into Arabic was begun, though some translations into Arabic were made directly from Greek texts. A regular school of translators, a 'House of Wisdom', was established at Baghdad during the reign of the Caliph Al-Mamun-al-Rashid (813–33). As might be expected, the Caliph favoured the Mu'tazilites, the more liberal group of theologians. So did his two successors. The resulting knowledge of Greek philosophy and science formed a basis for the development of Islamic thought in the Middle Ages. As far as categories of thought and models of argument were concerned, the new knowledge affected Islamic intellectual life on a wide scale. Al-Kindī (*c*.800–*c*.866) made a signal contribution to providing the Arabs with a philosophical terminology.

It is not possible to recount here the history of Islamic philosophy in the Middle Ages. What I wish to do is to draw attention to the relationship between philosophy, as represented by such thinkers as Al-Fārābi (*c*.875–*c*.950), Avicenna (Abu Ibn Sīnā, 980–1037), and Averroes (*c*.1126–*c*.1198), and the Muslim religion. These philosophers naturally differed somewhat in their ideas. For example, while the first two, Al-Fārābi and Avicenna, have been described either as 'neo-platonising Aristotelians' or as 'Islamic Neoplatonists',[17] Averroes, the great commentator on Aristotle, was concerned with presenting what he believed to be the genuine thought of the Greek philosopher. We can, however, see in Islamic philosophy during the Middle Ages a growing tendency to regard philosophy as providing the highest degree of penetration of the truth which was available to man in this life. It was not a case of denying the Muslim religion but rather of distinguishing between different levels of understanding the truth. This idea was clearly expressed by Averroes. The minds of most people, he believed, are governed by their lives of sense-perception to such an extent that they can hardly conceive supersensible reality as such. The truth has to be presented to them in imaginative form, and the only forms of argument which they can appreciate and which can move them to action are rhetorical or persuasive arguments. The needs of such people are admirably catered for by the Koran; for example, by its pictorial representations of the after life. In the second place there are people who can grasp dialectical arguments, leading to probable conclusions. Their needs too are met by the Koran, provided that it is interpreted in the light of theological reasoning. Thirdly, there are those who are capable of understanding logical demonstrations and of grasping truth in a conceptual form, as found in philosophy. The Koran caters for them too, but indirectly, by providing material for philosophical penetration.[18]

What we have just been saying stands in need of qualification. For example, Avicenna, besides trying to reconcile his philosophy with the Muslim faith, wrote on mystical spirituality; and he exercised a lasting influence on Islamic thought. It is understandable, however, that Islamic philosophy in the Middle Ages aroused suspicion in the minds of orthodox theologians, who tended to regard it as an insidious betrayal of the Muslim faith to rationalism.[19] From one point of view, it may be possible to regard Islamic philosophy in the Middle Ages as part of the process of Islam coming to reflective self-consciousness, of Muslim faith seeking understanding of itself. From another point of view, however, it may well appear, as it appeared to the more conservative theologians, as a progressive substitution of Greek philosophy for the simple faith preached by Mohammed. In this case one might expect either that philosophy would be suppressed or that it would take a separate road and assert its autonomy.

There is, however, an important factor to consider, which we have not yet discussed. Islam can be considered as emphasizing in an unambiguous way the divine transcendence. God can, and should, be obeyed. But any idea of being or becoming one with God threatens belief in the divine transcendence. There have been and still are Muslims who think in this way and who regard mysticism as unorthodox.[20] At the same time a tradition of mystical spirituality goes back a very long way in Islam, and there are at any rate some passages in the Koran to which mystics can appeal, such as the statement that God is closer to man 'than the vein of his neck'.[21] Islamic mysticism found expression in poetry, as with Rūmi (d.1273), but it also found expression in Islamic philosophy in Persia. Avicenna, who wrote on the stages of the soul's ascent to God, was a Persian by birth. So was his critic Al-Ghazālī, who was himself a mystic. In Persia Suhrawardī (1155–91) developed a metaphysics of light in which the world was represented as the divine theophany. In the course of time various lines of thought, such as the illuminationism of Suhrawardī, the theosophical ideas of Ibn 'Arabī (1165–1240)[22] and Sufi mystical spirituality tended to come together in the movement of Islamic gnosis or wisdom, of which the foremost exponent was Mullā Sadrā (1571–1640). But Islamic thought in Persia did not consist simply of a doctrine of mysticism. There was a strong philosophical element, largely inspired, whether by way of development or of criticism, by the philosophy of Avicenna. Mullā Sadrā, for example, reflecting critically on what had been said by predecessors such as Avicenna, Suhrwardī and Ibn 'Arabī, developed a metaphysical theory of the unity of being, in the sense of existence. In this metaphysics God was conceived as absolute Being or Existence, hidden and unknowable in himself but unfolding and manifesting himself as the source of all finite existents, which, in their relation to the divine reality were conceived as analogous to written letters on a page or the waves of the sea. That is to say, the letters and the waves are distinguishable, but the letters are nothing but ink and the waves nothing but water. Ultimately there is only the divine Absolute. In the nineteenth century Mullā Sadrā's theory of the unity of being was expounded in a more analytic and scholastic manner by Sabzawārī.

The point is this. Al-Fārābi, unlike his successor Avicenna, looked askance at mysticism, and he clearly believed that philosophy was the highest form of knowledge available to man.[23] This was obviously not the sort of view which was likely to win acceptance in the minds of conservative Muslim theologians, since it made philosophy the judge of the truth expressed in revelation. In the lines of thought, however, which culminated in Persian gnosis or wisdom, philosophical thought was closely associated with religion, not so much with exoteric Muslim religion as with the esoteric mystical spirituality of Islam. For example, Mullā Sadrā maintained that the unity of being could be apprehended only through illumination or mystical intuition; and Sabzawārī, who was a mystic as well as a philosopher, took much the same point of view. Philosophy then tends to become a conceptual explication of what is apprehended by spiritual illumination. This kind of philosophy is obviously not acceptable to everyone. And the question arises whether it can survive in Islam in view of western influences. One can, however, point out that the basic unifying factor between Muslim peoples is religion. And if philosophy in Islam were to become entirely divorced from religion,[24] this would certainly affect religious belief.

Modern Western Philosophy and Religion

What has been said so far in this chapter lies open to the charge of being one-sided or unduly selective. For example, attention was paid to the Vedānta school, as it provides an obvious example of philosophical reflection growing out of a religious matrix. Other interests, however, are discernible in Indian philosophy considered as a whole. We can easily find exemplifications of a 'disinterested' curiosity in the nature of the physical universe.

This is doubtless true, and it applies, though in a different way, to Greek philosophy. That is to say, it is possible to emphasize the scientific spirit of Greek thought to such an extent that its religious affiliations and the religiously orientated direction of phases of Greek philosophy are belittled or even passed over in silence. The view that in Greece European philosophical thought was non-religious, that it later passed under the domination of Christian theology, and that after the Middle Ages it regained its autonomy constitutes an over-simplification of the situation.

It is undoubtedly true that in medieval Christendom philosophy was influenced in specifiable ways by Christian belief and theology. Something was said about this subject in the first chapter of this book. It is also true that in the post-medieval world philosophy has become progressively more separate from theology and from religious interests. To a certain extent this separation began within the medieval period itself. In the first place philosophy was assigned a position and functions of its own, as by St Thomas Aquinas. In the second place, in the late Middle Ages there was a marked tendency to restrict the scope of philosophy in the area in which it came nearest to the field of theology, and so, in effect, to make philosophy more autonomous.[25] It was, however, in the post-medieval world that philosophy clearly asserted its independence of theology, as can be seen not only in the great world-views, such as that of Spinoza, but also in the philosophy of the Enlightenment.

This separation made possible the development of philosophy of religion as a discipline in which religion was looked on, as it were, from the outside. I do not mean that all modern philosophers stood outside religion. This would be clearly untrue. What I mean is that it was the separation of philosophy from theological presuppositions which made it possible to treat religion in general as a cultural and social phenomenon about which the philosopher reflected, as he might reflect about science or about aesthetic experience and art.

It was probably natural enough that the growth of this external approach should, at first, find expression in markedly negative criticism, directly primarily, though not exclusively, to criticism of truth-claims made on behalf of religious beliefs. This critical attitude was characteristic of much of the philosophy of the Enlightenment, particularly of the French Enlightenment. It was sometimes accompanied by criticism of the social effects of religion. But in the controversy of the time discussion of truth-claims was the more prominent feature.

This preoccupation with truth-claims, which was largely determined by the emphasis placed on belief in the Christian religion, can still, of course, be found. We can doubtless all think of examples. After all, if a philosopher wishes to criticize religion, the easiest thing for him to do is to examine arguments offered on behalf of religious beliefs and the logical coherence or incoherence of the beliefs in questions. Discussion of the social effects of religion inevitably involves judgements of value; and if it is a question of discussing, for instance, the value of a 'religious dimension in life', the philosopher may feel quite at sea. What counts as a 'religious dimension'? By far the easiest policy is to stick to discussion of truth-claims.

To the religiously-minded person, however, it may well seem that the philosopher who is constantly harping on truth-claims and on the logical coherence or incoherence of doctrines is circling round religion from outside, sniping at it but never really understanding it or coming to grips with its significance in human life. To a certain extent, I think, this was felt by Hegel. In the first place he saw clearly the great cultural importance of religion. In the second place he extended his field of vision to include the religious life of cultures other than his own. And in the third place he tried to give a phenomenology of religious experience. He was by no means blind to the shortcomings of the approach to religion characteristic of the philosophers of the eighteenth-century Enlightenment.

At the same time Hegel was obviously concerned with interpreting religion in terms of the principles of absolute idealism. His lectures on the philosophy of religion, remarkable though they may be, are clearly part of the system. Religion was looked at from the point of view of an absolute idealist, and the result was that Hegel proposed a theory of the relation of religious thought to philosophy which may well remind us of the theory proposed by Averroes in the Middle Ages.

If we turn to the modern theory of autonomous language-games, we can see that there is a real sense in which it allows religion to be itself. Religion is not made to fit any metaphysical world-view. Further, it is understood that each form of religious language, Christian, Buddhist or whatever, expresses a form of life, in which it is rooted. Again, so far from the philosopher being considered competent to judge all religion from the outside, it is contended that a given language-game can be understood only by those who participate in the form of life in which it is rooted and which it expresses.[26] This contention can be seen as expressing an understanding of religion's being based on religious experience of some kind.

The present writer has his reservations about the language-games theory, if the language-games are conceived as completely autonomous, in a sense which implies that the person who does not participate in the relevant form of life and actually use the corresponding language can have no understanding of it, and in the sense that there are no criteria which are applicable, so to speak, across the board. For one thing, can we justifiably make a sharp distinction between those who stand within religion and those who stand outside? We have to allow for all sorts of degrees. For another thing, if in a given religion statements are made which purport to be statements of fact, of what is the case, it seems to me quite legitimate to ask whether they conform to any conditions which there may be for the meaningfulness of factual statements. Further, if we postulate completely autonomous language-games, we seem to imply that there can be a language which is both public and private at the same time, public in the sense that it is understood and used by members of a group or society, private in the sense that it cannot be understood by the outsider. There could indeed be a language which was not in fact understood except by members of a certain group. It is not logically impossible for the Chinese language to be in fact known and understood only by Chinese. But it is with intelligibility in principle that we are concerned here. One can, of course, make it true by definition that, for example, nobody but a Christian can understand Christianity. To do this one only has to attach such a meaning to 'understand Christianity' that it follows necessarily that the non-Christian, by the very fact that he is not a committed believer, is incapable of understanding the language of the Christian religion. If, however, one does not adopt this policy, the natural view to take is that there can be degrees of understanding, and of misunderstanding. To be sure, if there were someone who was entirely devoid of any religious sense whatsoever, there would be a sense in which religious language would be as meaningless for him as the language of morals would be for someone who was entirely devoid of any moral sense. Both persons could learn to use the relevant words correctly according to whatever recognized rules there might be, but there would none the less be a sense in which it would be true to say that for the person in question the relevant language had no meaning. But there are certainly people who do not commit themselves to any definite religious beliefs but who are not devoid of a religious sense. It seems to me that they can perfectly well understand sufficiently to participate in critical discussion of, for example, beliefs which they themselves hesitate to accept.[27]

What this amounts to is an expression of serious doubt about any form of the language-games theory which attempts to make religious language immune from any external criticism whatsoever, on the ground that such criticism is bound to be based on misunderstanding, so that the believer and the non-believer are necessarily at cross purposes. Apart from this claim, which seems exaggerated, the language-games theory has a use. And it provides a point of departure for the last section of this chapter.

Concluding Comments

In *Philosophical Investigations* Wittgenstein remarks that 'new types of language, new language-games, as we may say, come into existence and others become obsolete and get forgotten'.[28] This statement might be applied, I suppose, to past religions which are to all intents and purposes obsolete and are forgotten except by scholars investigating the history of religion. In the course of human history new religions have come into existence, supplanting old ones, though often, of course, borrowing features from their predecessors. A very natural question to raise is whether religious language as a whole is becoming obsolete, inasmuch as it no longer responds to any human need. The rise of science has obviously tended to drive out the language of magic, and good reasons can be given for this development. Can good reasons be given for claiming that a like fate awaits the language of religion? This is what some people think. Other people, however, think that there are good reasons why religious language, in some form or other, should persist. Even if they are unwilling to predict what form or forms it will take, they believe that it is likely to survive all attempts to suppress it, inasmuch as it has firm roots in the human being, considered in his or her relations to reality.

The theory of language-games, taken by itself, cannot deal with this sort of question. It can say, as Wittgenstein said, that language-games come into existence and become obsolete; but if it is a question simply of describing language, we are confined within the limits of a sort of linguistic positivism. At any rate we try to preserve, whether success-fully or not, an attitude of metaphysical neutrality. At the same time the theory of language-games obviously provides a basis for going somewhat further. All language-games are played by human beings; they are forms of human language. And all 'forms of life', in which the language-games are said to be rooted, are forms of human life. That is to say, all 'forms of life', with the corresponding language-games, are rooted in human nature, in its potentialities and in its needs. If it is important to see a language-game as expressing a certain form of life, it is also important to see these forms of life as expressive of and in relation to human nature. In my opinion, therefore, the concept of language-games leads on naturally to the concept of a philosophical anthropology. Inasmuch, however, as man does not exist in a void, thought about the human person is likely to lead on to thought about the world in which we live or about reality in general. This is not meant to imply, of course, that a philosopher is not entitled to specialize, to confine his attention to a narrowly circumscribed area. I am not claiming, for example, that all those who reflect on the implications of ordinary language should take to general metaphysics. What I mean is that there is a natural progression of thought in the direction of synthesis.

Criticism of religion nowadays often takes the form of social criticism, of the social effects of religion, that is to say. This line of criticism is commonly associated with the name of Marx, but it goes back very much further. That it should become more widespread in the modern world is understandable. For one thing, if one wishes to criticize Buddhism or Hinduism, criticism on social grounds seems to be much more apposite than criticism of truth-claims.[29] Anyway, the point is that discussion of such criticism cannot be conducted simply in terms of a theory of language-games. Reference to a theory of the human being, to a philosophical anthropology, is required.

In the development of any such philosophical anthropology, or of a wider synthesis, reflection on the philosophical traditions of cultures other than one's own seems to be highly desirable. For these traditions reflect various aspects of human experience, including religious experience, which should be borne in mind in working towards any overall view of human nature. If a philosopher tries (and it is, in my opinion, desirable that some should try) to work out a synoptic view[30] of the various types of human experience, as expressed in various kinds of language-games, he should not lose sight of the fact that the cultural society or civilization to which he belongs is not the only one.

5

The Psychophysical Constitution of
the Human Person: Different Approaches

Common Phenomena as the Basis for Reflection on Human Nature
The relation between mind and body has been a prominent theme for discussion in western philosophy. It was discussed, for example, by Aristotle, Descartes, Bergson, and Gilbert Ryle. To be sure, approaches and formulations of questions have differed. With Aristotle, for example, discussion of the relation between a mental operation such as thinking and bodily organs arose in the context of a general inquiry into the difference between the living and the non-living. The approach can be described as biological. But mental operations are clearly expressions of life; and if we assume with Aristotle that life is due to a principle of life, an organizing entelechy, the 'soul' or *psyche*, the question of the relation between the principle of intellectual life in man and the human body and its organs arises as part of the general question of the relation between soul and body. If, however, we assume with Descartes that substances can be divided into bodies, characterized by extension, and minds, characterized by thought, the problem of the relation between mind and body obviously becomes a problem on its own and ceases to be simply one element in a more general theme. The same holds good if it is a question not of presupposing the Cartesian theory of substances but rather of leaving inquiry into life to the biologists. In this case some questions treated by Aristotle are likely to be regarded as themes for consideration by physiologists and psychologists, the attention of philosophers being focused more on conceptual analysis and questions relating to language. In one form or another, however, the mind-body problem has been a recurrent problem in western philosophy. Even if we wish to maintain that one should speak of distinct problems rather than of one recurrent problem, we must at any rate admit the existence of recognizable similarities between these problems, which enable us to treat them as a group of related questions.

It would be surprising, however, if discussion of the psychophysical constitution of man were confined to western philosophy. For there are obvious facts, advertence to which naturally gives rise to such discussion, facts which occur in all cultures. A dead man does not walk about or eat or talk, and the dead body normally disintegrates. On the face of it something either departs at death or perishes, leaving the body lifeless. Again, while activities such as walking, playing a game or digging are publicly observable, we naturally think of such phenomena as thought and emotive reactions as private, in the sense that they are not observable from outside, unless we either choose to express them in language or in some other way or betray ourselves, so to speak, by facial expression or gesture. By saying this I am not trying to settle philosophical problems about privacy; I am simply drawing attention to appearances, to what we might perhaps describe as surface phenomena. The point is simply that such phenomena are not confined to any particular human society, and we might, therefore, expect that questions relating to 'soul' and body, or to mind and body, or to mental and physical operations, would be raised in the philosophies of more than one of the cultures in which philosophical thought has developed.

Such questions are not, however, raised and discussed in isolation from any context or from any presuppositions or general direction of interest. It is, therefore, natural that recognizably similar questions should be approached in different ways in different philosophical traditions, and that different aspects should be emphasized. It is proposed to illustrate such differences by referring to some features of discussion of the psychophysical constitution of the human being in different philosophical traditions. And we begin with India.

The Self in Indian Philosophy

It is natural to think of Indian psychological theory as being dependent on belief in the possibility and desirability of human liberation from the phenomenal world. That is to say, if the attainability of liberation is presupposed, it follows that there must be something in man which can experience liberation. It can hardly be the visible and tangible body, as this clearly belongs to the phenomenal world. There must be something in the human being which survives death; and this something must be the real self, if talk about this or that human being achieving complete liberation is to have any real meaning. It is also natural to think of belief in transmigration, the process of successive rebirths from which the human being is set free at final liberation, as demanding belief in a permanent substantial self, the *ātman*, the continued existence of which makes it possible to identify the self of a later terrestrial life with the self of an earlier life.

While, however, there are certainly connections between the psychological theories of the Vedic schools and their metaphysical and religious ideas, the foregoing impression of Indian psychology or philosophical anthropology is inaccurate and open to serious objection. For one thing, the views of the materialists and of the Buddhists are entirely neglected. For another thing, though the doctrine of transmigration came to be generally accepted (except by the materialists), it was not a matter of common belief in early times. Besides, different schools offered arguments in support of their psychological theories, and we cannot take it simply for granted that these arguments were no more than rationalizations of a desire to support a preconceived metaphysical or religious doctrine.

As we have had occasion to note, for knowledge of the views and arguments of the materialists, the Cārvāka or Lokāyata school, we have to rely mainly on reports by their critics. It is clear, however, that the materialists denied the existence in the human being of a substantial and spiritual soul, mainly on the ground that its existence could not be empirically confirmed. In the first place, a spiritual soul could not be seen. One can draw a sword out of its scabbard and say, 'This is a sword'; but one cannot draw a soul out of a body and say, 'This is a soul'. In the second place, even if it is claimed that the existence of the soul can be inferred, the validity of the inference cannot be confirmed by observation. In other words, the materialists believed that to be or to exist is to be a possible object of sense-perception. And it was on this basis that they interpreted phrases, such as 'my body', which seem to support the theory of man as consisting of body and soul or spirit. 'My body' should be understood as meaning 'the body which is I'. The pronoun 'I' should be understood as referring to the living body, not to something other than the body.

Some materialists seem to have maintained that soul and body are the same thing, in the sense that there is only the body. They argued that there was no evidence whatsoever to support the view that at death a soul rose, as it were, out of the body. Other materialists, however, seem to have defended a rather more sophisticated point of view, maintaining in effect that consciousness was an epiphenomenon or by-product of the organization of matter. They allowed that in some sense there was an empirical self or ego which could not be identified simply with the tangible body, but they denied that there was any sufficient reason for supposing that the empirical self or consciousness was a substantial entity which survived death.

The materialists were dogmatists, in the sense that they held a definite doctrine which excluded belief in an immortal soul and which determined the way of interpreting phrases and statements which appeared, at first sight at any rate, to conflict with the materialist point of view. It seems, however, that in the pre-Buddhist period there were sceptics who cast doubt on the possibility of knowledge (which the materialists did not do) and who suspended judgement. The Katha Upanishad teaches the doctrine of *ātman*; but we can perhaps find in it a reference to a sceptical attitude when the boy, Nachiketas, says to his father, 'When a man dies, this doubt arises: some say "he is", while some say "he is not". The boy wants to hear the truth, but he is aware of the conflict of opinions which was the chief ground for scepticism.

The Buddhists were not, of couse, materialists. They did not identify mental and physical operations. Indeed, in the course of time there arose, within Mahāyāna Buddhism, the idealist Yogācāra school, associated with the name of Vasubandhu, for which there was consciousness only and which was faced with the task of explaining the rise of empirical consciousness, the distinction between waking and sleeping, and phenomena such as error. Though, however, the Buddhists were not materialists, they did not accept the theory of a permanent substantial self, *ātman*. Whether the Buddha himself categorically denied the existence of *ātman* or whether he simply suspended judgement about the existence or non-existence of a permanent subject of changing states it is difficult to say. But his followers at any rate gave a phenomenalistic analysis of the self. For them, there was a continuity of changing mental states but no permanent unchanging self to which these states could be attributed. The Buddhist philosophers argued that to think that there must be a permanent self is to be misled by language, by believing, wrongly, that to the pronoun 'I' there must correspond an unchanging substance. To be sure, Buddhist phenomenalist analysis of the self, especially when it took the form of the doctrine of momentariness, gave rise to difficulties; and it is not surprising that some Buddhist thinkers, the Pudgalavādins, postulated what they called 'the person' to provide continuity and a centre to which successive changing states could be ascribed. In general, however, the Buddhists were opposed both to materialist identification of the soul or mind with the body and to the theory of *ātman*.

It seems to me difficult to reconcile what is known as the doctrine of 'no-self' with Buddhist acceptance of belief in transmigration. If we suppose that in one terrestrial life *x* is a human being and in the next terrestrial life a lion, the two bodies are obviously different. What then provides the continuity entitling us to claim that *x* is the subject of both lives? Further, if *x* attains liberation from the succession of rebirth and enters Nirvāna, and if entry into Nirvāna is not interpreted as complete annihilation but as a permanent state, it is natural to ask, a state of what?

The reason why the doctrine of transmigration became so widely accepted was its link with belief in *karma*, in the causal effects of good and evil actions. Nobody could attain liberation until the effects of evil actions had worked themselves out and the soul had become purified. If, therefore, evil actions had not produced their full effects in one life, they would do so in another life or in other lives. The Buddhists doubtless thought that the *ātman* theory was incompatible with belief in *karma*, inasmuch as a permanent unchanging self would remain unaffected by good or evil actions. Even if, however, they could present a good case for rejecting the *ātman* theory, to give reasons for rejecting someone else's theory is not quite the same thing as to answer objections against one's own theory. The Buddhist can, of course, maintain that in the case of a single life the succession of causally linked mental states provides sufficient ground for talk about the same person. But in what sense is there continuity between the succession of states in the life of Tom Smith and the succession of states forming the mental life of John Brown or of an animal? It is not a case of all Buddhist thinkers being blind to such problems. But it is difficult to see how the problems can be satisfactorily solved. It was supposed that in rare cases a person could recollect his or her past lives. But how is this possible, if we once assume a phenomenalistic analysis of the self?

It is indeed possible to reply that Buddhist thinkers were concerned not so much with the truth or falsity of theories and with logical consistency as with the pragmatic value of theories. On the one hand, they wanted to help people to grasp the 'emptiness' or non-substantial character of all phenomena, and the doctrine of non-self was a powerful means to attain this end. On the other hand, they wanted people to understand their moral responsibility and the need for purification if the goal of life were to be attained, and the doctrine of transmigration served this purpose. Whether the two theories were logically consistent did not really matter from the Buddhist point of view. Nāgārjuna maintained that no statement is true without qualification. If we say 'it is', we must add 'and it is not'. If we say 'it is not', we must add 'and it is'. We should also add 'it neither is nor is not'. Though, however, this line of reply may express the point of view of Buddhist thinkers and their willingness to live with apparent contradictions, it is unlikely to appear completely satisfactory to the western mind, with its preoccupation with logical consistency.

As for the Vedic schools, it has already been mentioned that the majority of them professed pluralism. In the present context this means that the Vedic schools, apart from the Advaita Vedānta regarded the existence of a plurality of selves as an ultimate truth. I say 'ultimate truth' for the following reason. The Advaita Vedānta did not deny that on the level of phenomenal reality and experience there was a plurality of selves, of centres of consciousness. What it denied was that this plurality was a feature of ultimate reality. Ultimately, all selves were one with Brahman. The other Vedic schools did not regard plurality as something which is ultimately transcended.

A variety of arguments were given by the Vedic schools to prove the existence of non-material selves. For example, the Nyāya-Vaiśesika philosophers argued that the existence of the self can be known as the common subject of experiences such as those of pleasure and pain. When I say 'I am pleased', I am aware of myself as the subject of the experience of pleasure; and when I say 'I am in pain', I am aware of myself as the subject of the experience of pain. But the subject in both cases is the same. I can say, 'I was in pain but now I am experiencing pleasure'. To account for this element of continuity in the experience of different feelings and desires, it is necessary to assert the existence of a continuing self. Again, whereas the senses apprehend different kinds of objects or different aspects of an object, sense-data are co-ordinated in one total experience; and we must, therefore, postulate the existence of a soul which is not itself a sense. Memory too bears witness to the existence of a permanent self. So does human purposive activity. As for the plurality of souls or selves, this can be proved, for example, by the diversity of experiences. My pain is not your pain. You can desire something, while I do not desire it. And we can have different ideas.

In the Sāṁkhya-Yoga tradition emphasis was laid on the subject-object distinction in consciousness. The existence of an object of consciousness implies the existence of a subject of consciousness, which is not itself object. This subject is the *purusha*. But we cannot reasonably assert the existence of only one subject. For if we do, we cannot explain the obvious differences which exist between individuals as centres of consciousness and subjects of experience.

The Mīmāṁsā philosophers laid much more emphasis on the sacred texts than, say, the Nyāya philosophers, and they were inclined to argue that Vedic talk about reward and punishment after death implied the existence of selves or souls distinct from bodies. No doubt this was the case. But it was an argument based on scriptural authority, a line of thought to which the Nyāya school paid little attention. The Mīmāṃsā school, however, supported the view that there was a plurality of selves by arguing that if all souls were identical, one with the universal *ātman*, it would not be possible to account for the different experiences of individual human beings and the different purposive actions of different bodies. We can add that in the Mīmāṃsā school there were different views about the ways in which the existence of the soul or self could be known. According to Kumārila the self was manifested to itself in self-consciousness, whereas for Prabhākara the existence of the permanent self was inferred, from the possibility of recollection, for example.

The arguments employed by the Vedic schools to prove the existence of a plurality of selves are interesting, and some of them are obviously similar to arguments which have been used in western philosophy. At the same time talk about proving the existence of the self can be misleading, unless some attempt is made to explain how the permanent self is conceived. We cannot, of course, give detailed descriptions of the psychological theories of the various schools. But it is important to understand that when the Nyāya, Vaiśesika, Sāṃkhya and Yoga philosophers talked about the final liberation of the self, they did not conceive the empirical self as the permanent factor which is liberated from the phenomenal world. According to the Nyāya-Vaiśesika doctrine the permanent self is an uncreated and eternal non-material entity to which consciousness, mind and memory accrue in association with the body. The liberated self is without memory, without feelings, and without what we would ordinarily think of as mind. Similarly, for the Sāṃkhya-Yoga philosophers mental powers and activities, such as feeling and remembering, are evolutes of *Prakṛti* or essentially dependent on them, and they cannot, therefore, survive after final liberation, which means liberation from *Prakṛti*. It is *purusha*, the transcendental self, which continues to exist at liberation. And though the active self is the result of the co-operation, in some rather mysterious way, of *purusha* and *Prakṛti*, *purusha*, considered in itself, is unchanging and does not act. It is the unobjectifiable self or subject, the condition of consciousness but itself transcending consciousness, in the sense, that is to say, in which consciousness entails a distinction between subject and object, knower and known.

These remarks may seem very obscure. But it seems to me that the general point of view to which I have referred is connected with two factors. One is the Indian philosophers' understanding of the dependence of psychical operations such as feeling and remembering on physical factors. In the Sāṁkhya philosophy, for example, most of what we might globally describe as mind is conceived as an evolute or product of self-developing matter. The other factor is belief in transmigration, which obviously militates against identification of the liberated self with the changing empirical ego. That is to say, the permanent self, which attains or can attain final liberation, must be distinguishable from the plurality of minds, each of which is linked to a particular terrestrial incarnation. And what can this permanent self be but the transcendental subject, corresponding to the transcendental ego of western philosophy? It may well remind us of Aristotle's active or agent intellect, though the comparison should not be pressed, inasmuch as the *purusha* of the Sāṁkhya system was not conceived as being in itself an active substance or entity.[1]

In view of the fact that the Sāṁkhya philosophers regarded not only the senses but also what we would ordinarily think of as mind as evolutes of *Prakṛti*, self-developing or evolving matter, it may be difficult at first to see why they should think it necessary to postulate the existence of *purusha*. One answer was that the development of Nature is for the sake of spirit or soul. Another, as we have seen, is that consciousness presupposes a subject which transcends objectification. But even if we are satisfied with such answers, we may still go on to ask why the Sāṁkhya school should postulate a plurality of spiritual selves. For how can we distinguish one *purusha* from another, when *purusha* transcends all distinguishing characteristics? This was a question which the philosophers of the Advaita Vedānta were quick to ask (Madhva also raised the same question.) They questioned not so much the Sāṁkhya view of the nature of the self (as pure consciousness, in which subject and object are one) as the compatibility of this view with the assertion that there is a plurality of selves.

According to Śaṁkara, the great philosopher of the Advaita Vedānta, the *existence* of the self is evident. If anyone expresses doubt, he thereby affirms his own existence. A man cannot seriously doubt that there is a self. But he may very well be ignorant of the self's nature. And it is with this topic that Śaṁkara concerns himself, not simply as a theoretical exercise but rather because in his view it is of supreme importance to man to achieve liberation from ignorance of his true self. In other words, liberation, the goal of life, and full realization of one's true or inner self are one and the same thing.

It hardly needs saying that Śaṁkara rejects materialist identification of the self with the body. I can objectify my body and must be other than it. The Buddhist theory of momentariness is also rejected as untenable. Experience of memory, for example, shows that there is a self which transcends changing states and can unify them in one consciousness. The individual self is thus a permanent subject, a subject which perceives and knows things, though it does not create them. There is a sense in which Śaṁkara is a realist. That is to say, on the level of experience on which it makes sense to speak of individual selves, we cannot maintain successfully that physical objects are simply the self's mental creations. The self is subject, but it is a 'witness', a knower rather than a creator.

The objection can be raised that consciousness is intermittent. In dreamless sleep the self is not conscious. Therefore it cannot properly be described as being essentially subject. In dreamless sleep the self either ceases to exist or, if it is a permanent reality, it is not a subject. Śaṁkara, however, regards the self as conscious even in dreamless sleep, though in this state subject and object are one. Descartes maintained that the soul was essentially a thinking subject. And Śaṁkara maintained that the self (*jiva*) is essentially subject. To do so he obviously has to postulate a form of consciousness which differs from the consciousness of waking life.

In waking experience the self is aware of its distinction not only from physical objects but also from other selves. In other words, on the level of phenomenal reality and of what most people take to be the only form of experience, there is a plurality of selves. According to Śaṁkara, however, the individual self is, in truth, an appearance of the one universal self. The many selves of phenomenal reality are all appearances of Brahman, and they are, therefore, one, inasmuch as they are all Brahman appearing. The psychophysical organism is an appearance of the Absolute, but it is important to bear in mind that the self, in itself so to speak, is real. It is the plurality of selves which is phenomenal, not the inner or true self, which is one with Brahman. This oneness with Brahman is always there, always an ontological fact. But it is by no means always understood or realized. To realize one's true self, one has to penetrate or strip away the veils of illusion or appearance. And if a person understands that he or she is one with Brahman and, therefore, one with all other selves, this truth will influence the person's attitude to others in the phenomenal world. It may indeed seem that it is not possible to grasp this alleged truth, inasmuch as all awareness is awareness of something, thus implying distinction. But Śaṁkara postulates a higher level of awareness or consciousness, in which subject and object are identical. In this sense of consciousness Brahman itself can be described as pure consciousness.

The philosophy of Śaṁkara, with its ideal of realizing complete union with the impersonal or suprapersonal Absolute, was obviously incapable of exercising a wide popular appeal; and, as has been noted in the chapter on religion, lines of thought appeared within the Vedānta school which were more in accordance with devotional religion. It would be incorrect, however, to suppose that the thinkers who represented this line of thought appealed simply to the demands and implications of devotional religion or even simply to the more theistic passages of the sacred texts. For example, Rāmānuja, the expounder of what is described as qualified non-dualism, argued that the theory of pure consciousness was really nonsense. That is to say, the subject-object distinction is essential to consciousness, and to talk about a consciousness in which there is no such distinction is to misuse language. It is all very well to postulate a higher type of perception by which the self perceives Brahman and its oneness with Brahman. The fact remains that perception involves a distinction between perceiver and perceived, and perception which is not perception of something, thus involving a distinction, is meaningless.

Rāmānuja's line of argument against Śaṁkara was not without weight. But his own qualified non-dualism itself gave rise to difficulties, inasmuch as he wished to hold at one and the same time that the self was distinct from God and yet that God was the one reality. It is not surprising that later on Madhva interpreted the famous Upanishadic statement 'that thou art' as referring to the self's likeness to God. In his view, the ignorance which needed to be overcome was not ignorance of the self's identity with Brahman but ignorance of the self's relationship to God, as essentially dependent upon God.

Perhaps there is too much space devoted to India. But the search for the true self, or the true nature of the self, was a conspicuous feature of Indian thought. The Vedic poems present a picture of a people who were far from regarding this world as an illusion or reducing the human person to what F. H. Bradley called a miserable metaphysical point. In the Vedic poems the word *ātman* was used in a variety of ways, to mean sometimes breath, sometimes life, sometimes the body, sometimes the soul or self. When it was used to mean the self, it meant, of course, the individual self. There is, however, a passage of the *Rig-Veda* in which we can find the idea of what we might describe as the cosmic self, a reality behind, so to speak, both the gods and the things of this world. In other words, for the reflective mind the Vedic texts offered points of departure for different lines of thought about the human being, ranging from materialism to the attempt to ascertain the relation between the human soul and the ultimate reality. It was this last mentioned line of thought which became prominent in the Upanishads, with their spiritualist interpretation of the self and their assertions about the relation between the human spirit and Brahman. The thinkers of the Vedic philosophical schools could thus find support for a variety of speculative theories in the ancient texts by focusing their attention on certain passages rather than others. The philosophers, however, did not simply assert but argued; and we have seen how a line of argument based on the subject-object distinction was a prominent feature of their thought (cf p. 82). Thus even in the case of the Sāṁkhya philosophy, in which operations which would generally be regarded as constituting mind were looked upon as evolutes of *Prakṛti*, and so of matter, the subject-object distinction was used in support of the inferred existence of *purusha*, spirit. This epistemological approach to speculation about the psychophysical constitution of man was, it seems to me, in accordance with the general tendency of the Hindu thinkers to emphasize the overcoming of ignorance as an essential feature of liberation. To be sure, in the case of some schools, such as Sāṁkhya and Nyāya, the religious approach gives the impression of being a later development or of something tacked on. In the Vedānta school, however, religious, metaphysical and epistemological approaches to philosophical anthropology were closely associated.

The Chinese Approach to Reflection on the Human Being

When we turn to Chinese thought about the human being, we find a predominantly ethical approach. Interest is centred on man as a moral agent and on the moral perfecting of his nature. Chinese thinkers do indeed pursue some psychological themes, but the context of their reflections is ethical. An obvious example is provided by discussion of the feelings and desires. As Mencius held that man was good by nature, and as feeling seems to belong to human nature, he naturally laid emphasis on feelings such as that of commiseration, with which, in his view, man was endowed by nature and which were clearly commendable. It is obvious, however, that from the moral point of view some feelings could be described as bad or undesirable, and under the Han dynasty we find Tung Chung-shu, in the second century BC, maintaining that feelings, associated with *yin*, were the source of evil. In this case, how could it be asserted, with Mencius, that man is good by nature, if, that is to say, feelings are rooted in human nature? The obvious solution was to maintain that the human being is potentially rather than actually good by nature, and that this potential goodness must be developed by education. Man's power of moral judgement and rectitude and firmness of will must be developed, so that mind may be able to control feeling and desire. Two questions arise, however. Are we justified in making such general judgements as that feelings are good or that, on the contrary, they are bad? Wang Ch'ung, in the first century AD suggested that such sweeping generalizations are unjustified. Secondly, it is all very well to talk about the mind controlling feelings, but cannot feeling be regarded as belonging to mind, as a mental phenomenon? According to Ch'eng I, who lived in the eleventh century and was one of the founding fathers of Neo-Confucianism, what man is originally endowed with is (human) nature, which, considered as master of the body, is called mind. Feelings are expressions of mind. That is to say, they are mental phenomena. Though, however, mind, considered in itself or abstractly, in the same in all, the expressions of mind, such as thoughts and feelings, are not. Here we have to take into account 'capacity', which differs in different people, different capacities being due to physical nature or the body, a precipitate, so to speak, of material force. This sort of idea was developed by Chu Hsi, the famous twelfth-century Neo-Confucianist, who made a distinction between the mind before it is aroused or becomes active and the mind after it has been aroused. Feelings are the mind after it has been aroused, and desire emanates from feeling. In the substance-function language, human nature, which is equivalent to mind, is substance, whereas feelings are function, the substance as active, that is to say, as responding to stimulus. Like Ch'eng I, Chu Hsi ascribed the difference between human beings to differences in material force, their material endowment. He did not intend to imply, however, that differences in material force determined a person's character in such a way that moral improvement was impossible or that the mind which acquired a firm grasp of moral principles could exercise no control over desire and action.

In Neo-Confucianism a distinction was made between principle (*li*) and material force (*ch'i*). Looked at from one point of view, principle resembled the Platonic Idea or Form. All principles, those actually exemplified and those only potentially exemplified, together formed the 'Great Ultimate'. There was no concrete thing in which a principle was not exemplified, but the exemplification was always united with material force. Conversely, material force never actually existed without principle. It was not, therefore, a substance on its own. To be sure, some Neo-Confucianists applied descriptive epithets which suggested that it was a substance. Thus it was described as being 'clear' or 'turbid', to explain the difference between intelligent and stupid people. Logically however, material force, conceived abstractly or apart from principle, should be analogous to Aristotle's 'first matter', except that *ch'i* was regarded as dynamic, as material force. In the human being the mind, as the potentiality of knowing all principles, was represented as principle, while the body was, of course, related to material force. If, therefore, we bear in mind the fact that, even though Chu Hsi insisted on the logical priority of principle, of the Great Ultimate, concrete substances were regarded as combinations, so to speak, of principle and material force, we can see that the Neo-Confucian representation of mind as principle did not imply that mind and body were two independent and juxtaposed substances. Together they formed one substance. It is doubtless arguable that there was in Neo-Confucianism a certain tendency to dualism. For example, Chu Hsi spoke as though the Great Ultimate were a metaphysical reality, and in the human being he made a distinction between the physical body, considered as an integration of 'turbid' material force,[2] and spirit, considered as the master of the body. Moreover, according to Chu Hsi, what integrates and disintegrates is material force, not principle. At death the body, together with the earthly aspect of the soul, returns to Earth, whereas the heavenly aspect of the soul and the vital force return to Heaven. Such statements, taken by themselves, seem to imply dualism. But Chu Hsi may have meant little more than that at death the body visibly disintegrates, whereas the mind and life, of which it cannot be properly said that they disintegrate, mysteriously vanish. The mind may be principle, but principle does not exist apart from material force. Further, Chu Hsi explicitly states that consciousness is possible only when mind is united with material force.

In can hardly be claimed that the Neo-Confucianist view of man as a unity of principle and material force, a view which in some respects reminds us of Aristotle's account of man, provides the sort of basis for a belief in personal immortality which is provided by Cartesian dualism. In China there was, of course, a widespread popular belief in the existence of the spirits of ancestors. In Taoism as a religion there was a preoccupation with immortality or, more precisely, with the hope of prolonging life indefinitely by a variety of practices. Further, Pure Land Buddhism doubtless owed much of its popularity to its promise of entry into paradise to those who had faith in the saving grace of the Eternal Buddha, and it adapted itself to Chinese traditions by praying that the spirits of ancestors might enjoy the happiness of paradise. To represent the Chinese people as a whole as having no belief in an after life would be a gross exaggeration. As far, however, as Confucianist philosophers were concerned, they were remarkably unconcerned with the topic. For one thing, they were concerned primarily with moral and social reform in this life and regarded speculation about any other life as an undesirable and irrelevant distraction. For another thing, they did not believe that questions about a possible after life could be answered. Both attitudes found expression in sayings attributed to Confucius himself. Certain philosophers, such as Wang Ch'ung in the first century AD, flatly denied immortality, on the ground that there was nothing to survive. The general Confucianist attitude, however, was to abstain from pronouncements on the matter and to lay emphasis on the idea of immortality of influence, by good example or by writing. In respect of continued influence Confucius and Mencius were very much alive.

One might expect that the Taoist philosophers, with their talk about entering into harmony with the universe, would expound some theory of survival. It must be remembered, however, that the Taoist Absolute was really the universe, considered as one. The universe was regarded as in a state of constant transformation (in its self-expression, that is to say; the One in itself, as substance, did not change, but as function, as manifested in the myriad things, it did); and birth and death belonged to this process. According to the Taoist sage Chuang Tzu, the wise man simply accepted death as a natural phenomenon, this acceptance being part of what was meant by being in harmony with nature or the universe. The *Tao* was not in itself a visible object, with shape or form or determinate characteristics. Nor was the mind of man a visible and tangible object. In this sense it was spiritual. But, according to the *Chuang Tzu*, when the body disintegrates, mind goes with it. It is not surprising that when the adherents of religious Taoism sought immortality, it was immortality in this world which they sought. In spite of its mystical utterances there was a marked naturalistic tendency in Taoism.

This was not true of Buddhism. As has already been suggested, the doctrine of no-self or the phenomenalistic analysis of the self was hardly a promising basis for the doctrines of transmigration and of the transcending of the succession of lives through the attainment of Nirvāna. But this was a difficulty of which Chinese Buddhists were aware, and they tended to reintroduce the idea of a permanent soul. We certainly cannot say that Buddhism was unconcerned with life after death. This would certainly not be true of Buddhism as a religion. This, however, was one of the features of Buddhism to which its Neo-Confucianist critics took exception. According to Ch'eng I, for example, the Buddhists were motivated by love of life and fear of death, a motivation which expressed an undesirable self-love. Neo-Confucianist criticism of Buddhism was doubtless sometimes unfair, but it expressed a conviction that Buddhism, originally a foreign importation, was alien to Chinese traditions and ways of thought and tended to divert attention from man's social obligations, whether family or political, by directing it to the attainment of Nirvāna.

Though Buddhism officially rejected the theory of *ātman* and substituted a phenomenalistic analysis of the self, there is a sense in which it shared the Indian emphasis on the true self, the self which is capable of attaining enlightenment and liberation. This is clear enough not only in the more popular religious Buddhism in China but also in Ch'an (Zen in Japan) Buddhism, which aimed at realization of the one Buddha-mind or Buddha-nature, already present in all sentient beings. In Confucianism, however, which was for centuries the official state philosophy, emphasis was placed on the moral agent, conceived as the human being in society. Confucianism certainly distinguished between different aspects of or factors in the human being. It cannot be described as materialist. But it was predominantly this-worldly, in the sense that it focused attention not on Nirvāna but on moral self-cultivation and the fulfilment of social obligations.

Medieval Christendom and Islam
It is hardly necessary to say that the Chinese philosophers were aware that human beings share some characteristics with other things, while they also possess their own peculiar characteristics. Sometimes emphasis was placed on what was common to all things. The Taoist sages, for example, emphasized the universal presence of the *Tao*, while the T'ien-t'ai and Ch'an Buddhists insisted on the presence of the Buddha-nature in all sentient things. For the matter of that, we have seen how the Neo-Confucianists regarded all concrete things as exemplifying both principle and material force. At the same time, efforts were made to differentiate between what we might describe as different levels of being. This was sometimes done in physiological and psychological terms, by distinguishing, for instance, between different grades of material force, unrefined and refined, and between different aspects of soul, earthly and heavenly. Special emphasis, however, was laid on man as a moral agent, or the human mind's power to recognize moral principles and ideals and to direct action in accordance with these

principles and ideals. Thus according to Tung Chung-Shu in the second century BC human beings alone can practise human-heartedness and righteousness, a characteristic which shows their superiority to every other creature. As Chu Hsi was to say, the moral mind is not different from the human mind. But it was the mind in its moral aspect and function on which the Confucianists laid most store as a distinguishing characteristic of the human being.

In Greek philosophy we can find a variety of approaches. Plato laid emphasis on man's power to recognize moral ideals, though he combined with this an emphasis on man's intellectual powers. With Aristotle we find a biological approach, in the sense that he distinguished between living and non-living things and then between different levels of life, between the basic different kinds of *psyche*. In his treatment of things possessing life emphasis was placed on the ascending degrees of cognitive life. It is not, of course, intended to imply that Aristotle neglected man's moral life. This was obviously not the case. In the *De Anima*, however, in which he dealt specifically with the psychophysical constitution of the human being, strong emphasis was placed on man's intellectual life as a distinguishing characteristic. It was man as knowing, as a cognitive agent, who was placed in the centre of the picture. This emphasis was clearly in accordance with the picture of the highest life for man as given in Aristotle's *Ethics*.

The Aristotelian psychology, as we doubtless all know, was influential in the philosophy of the Middle Ages, both in medieval Christendom and in Islamic thought. This meant that, whatever some spiritual writers may have implied, philosophers such as St Thomas Aquinas regarded the human being not as a juxtaposition of two substances, soul and body, but as one substance, the soul conceived as the 'form' or entelechy of the one living, sensing, feeling, thinking, willing organism. To be sure, there was controversy about whether the agent intellect of the third book of Aristotle's *De Anima* should be regarded as a function of the human soul, as Aquinas conceived it, or as a separate Intelligence, the lowest in the hierarchy of separate Intelligences, as Avicenna, for instance, regarded it. But this does not alter the fact that the medieval philosophers thought of the human being as one substance, in which there are distinguishable basic components, rather than in terms of a dualism such as was to be defended later on by Descartes.

In the Middle Ages, however, there was a religious faith to be taken account of, not only in Christendom but also in Islam. For example, as a Christian theologian, Aquinas believed that man was *capax Dei*, capable of union with God, not simply through his own efforts but through co-operation with divine grace. In the general sense of seeing the human being as orientated to union with the ultimate reality Aquinas was at one with the Vedānta philosophers in India and with Plotinus in the ancient world. There were also differences between them, of course. But we cannot discuss them here. The point is that Aquinas, in his attempt to accommodate Aristotelian psychology to the Christian faith, transformed Aristotle's view of the highest activity open to man (I refer to the picture of theoretical activity in the *Ethics*) into the supernatural vision of God as the goal of human life.

This conception of the end or goal of human life was obviously connected with belief in immortality. What Aristotle himself thought about personal immortality remains obscure, a point which John Duns Scotus was to emphasize. But Aquinas, as an orthodox Christian, believed in it. As, however, he took seriously the Aristotelian view of the human person as one substance, he maintained that the disembodied soul was not, strictly speaking, a person. It seemed to follow that in a well run theistic universe the resurrection of the body could be expected, even if we cannot know how it takes place. Belief in bodily resurrection was clearly foreign to the mind of Aristotle, but it was part of orthodox Christianity.

It was also a feature of Muslim belief, being clearly implied in the Koran. The Neoplatonizing Aristotelians, such as Avicenna (d. 1037), while finding room in their psychological theories both for the possibility of prophetic revelation and for personal immortality, did not show much belief in bodily resurrection. According to Avicenna, the pronoun 'I' refers to the soul, not the body, a view which is more Neoplatonist than Aristotelian. Averroes, however, the eminent twelfth-century commentator on Aristotle, held that as matter was the principle of individuation, there was no means of distinguishing between disembodied souls or minds. It may seem, therefore, that he should have rejected the idea of personal immortality. And he has sometimes been so interpreted. In point of fact he affirmed his belief in bodily resurrection, in accordance with Muslim faith, though it seems pretty clear that he conceived it in terms of the soul informing an astral or pneumatic body rather than in terms of a literal revivification of the body which perished at death.

We can say, therefore, that both in medieval Christendom and Islam psychological theory inherited from the past had to come to terms with already existing religious beliefs. It is true that more effort was spent on systematic harmonization in Christendom than in Islam, inasmuch as most of the leading Christian philosophers were theologians, whereas the Muslim thinkers who relied heavily on Aristotelianism and Neo-platonism were apt to regard Muslim doctrines as pictorial or imaginative ways of expressing the truth. We must add, however, that in the Islamic world psychological theory became increasingly associated with Muslim spirituality and theosophy, centring round man's relationship with and orientation to God. Thus in Sufi thought a good deal of attention was devoted to classification of the successive stages or 'stations' in the soul's spiritual ascent. (The relatively permanent 'stations', attainable by human effort, were distinguished from transient 'states', which were due simply to divine favour.)

In spite of the existence of different approaches, emphases and ideas, it is obviously reasonable to claim that in one respect psychological theory in India, China, ancient Greece, medieval Christendom and Islam had a common feature, namely that it preceded the rise of the particular sciences as separate disciplines. This is not meant to imply that no attention was paid to empirical observation. This was certainly not the case. What I mean is that psychological theory was regarded as an integral part of philosophy and was pursued in the context of a world-view. Indeed, even in the West after the Middle Ages psychology was regarded as part of philosophy long after physical science had gone its own way. It is only in relatively recent times that various psychological disciplines have arisen which regard themselves as independent of philosophy.

In View of the Development of Psychology, has the Philosopher anything to say about Human Nature?
If we look at the article on psychology in the *Encyclopaedia Britannica* (volume 18, 1973), we find the statement that whereas psychology began as part of philosophy, in the late nineteenth century it became a separate experimental science. Obviously, this statement should not be understood as denying the empirical fact that a number of psychological disciplines or sub-disciplines have arisen, such as abnormal, comparative, experimental, industrial, physiological and social psychology, which claim to be branches of science rather than of philosophy. It may well be the case that some psychological theories have been put forward as scientific theories when it is none too clear that the claim can be substantiated. I am thinking of theories which it is difficult to test empirically, inasmuch as their proponents would probably not have been prepared to admit that any event or phenomenon would count against the theory in question. A theory of this kind may be illuminating, but its claim to be an empirical hypothesis is at any rate

disputable. But this is not a topic which need detain us. The question which I wish to ask is this. Given the rise of psychological disciplines which are classified as belonging to science rather than to philosophy, what, if anything, remains for the philosopher to do in this area of thought?

One thing which philosophers can do, and, of course, actually do, is to examine the psychological theories of past philosophers. If they confine themselves simply to exposition and interpretation, they are acting as historians of philosophy. But let us assume that they discuss the theories in question and adopt some attitude towards them, a critical or evaluative attitude.[3] What are their criteria for judging? One obvious criterion is internal consistency or coherence. For example, a philosopher might argue that the Buddhist theory of momentariness, in its application to the soul, could not be reconciled with belief in transmigration. A positive evaluation of consistency or coherence would clearly be presupposed; but the philosopher's criticism of Buddhist theory would not, by itself, commit him to any definite alternative theory. He would be claiming that if the Buddhist thinker valued consistency or coherence, he could not accept both the theory of momentariness and belief in transmigration. But if the critic confined himself to drawing attention to what he believed to be an example of inconsistency, he would not thereby commit himself to claiming that the Buddhist should embrace one particular thesis and reject the other. Let us suppose, however, that a philosopher criticizes Hume's phenomenalistic analysis of the self on the ground that Hume forgot that it was he who was looking into his mind and seeing a succession of psychical phenomena. The critic is not denying the truth of the statement that we have different successive thoughts, desires, and so on. He is arguing that Hume overlooked something, namely the function of the self as subject. To substantiate his claim he would presumably appeal to phenomenological analysis of consciousness. And it seems to me that the structure of consciousness, as revealed in that analysis, is unaffected by the development of physiological psychology, industrial psychology, and so on. After all, such disciplines presuppose consciousness.

Let us turn for a few moments to the approach to psychology through examination of ordinary language. In order to be able to make the point briefly, any consideration of questions which can be raised in regard to the concept of ordinary language is omitted. Further, it is assumed that examination of ordinary language can be of real use, inasmuch as it reminds us of ideas of the human being which reflect man's experience of himself and which have been expressed in concrete utterances, not, that is to say, in the form of abstract theory.

In my opinion, ordinary language tends to support what we might describe as an Aristotelian view of the human being rather than the theory that the human being consists of two distinct substances. We say, for example, 'I went for a walk', rather than 'I took my body for a walk', as though the body were a separate entity, such as a dog. 'I went for a walk' suggests the belief that the body is part of the human person. Similarly, we use such expressions as 'he hit me' rather than 'he hit my body'. We also use such phrases as 'I think', 'I believe', 'I want'. Taken together, these kinds of expressions suggest the idea of one living, moving, sensing, thinking, willing organism.

At the same time there are statements in ordinary language which might be interpreted in a different sense. For example, I might say, 'I have left my body to a teaching hospital'. Again, it would be quite natural to say, 'he bruised my arm' or 'he lost his leg'. Nor would it be very odd to say 'well, he had a pleasant smile, but I could not tell what he was thinking'.

It is not my intention to suggest that statements such as 'he hit me' and 'he bruised my arm' are irreconcilable. If one takes into account the whole context and also alternative ways of putting things in ordinary language (such as 'he hit me on the arm' instead of 'he hit my arm'), it is doubtless possible to form a more or less unified and coherent view of the human being. The philosophers' process of interpretation, however, is obviously guided by a general view of the human being which is already present in his mind. There are ambiguities in ordinary language, and we can hardly make a selection among possible meanings without a regulative idea. To express the matter in a tautological way, a philosopher's interpretation of ordinary language is a philosophical interpretation. It may, of course, be an interpretation which makes sense of a diversity of ways of speaking and paints a coherent picture; but it is none the less a philosophical construction. Gilbert Ryle's *Concept of Mind* (London, 1949) was obviously a philosophical work. Whether we agree or not with all that he says is irrelevant to this point. In other words, one of the things which the philosopher can do in the psychological area is certainly to reflect on the implications of ordinary language. This activity is not without value, for the expression of man's experience of himself in concrete ways can hardly be devoid of significance.

The foregoing remarks may give the impression that I regard ordinary language not only as something fixed but also as being pretty well equivalent to current English. This, however, is not the case.

Obviously, a philosopher is likely to reflect on the version of ordinary language with which he is personally well acquainted. Indeed, he is wise to do so. At the same time there is clearly room in principle for a comparative study of ordinary language as found in different cultures. And it might be found that the implicitly expressed views of the human being differed somewhat. Another point to be made is that ordinary language may very well embody beliefs and theories which are open to criticism. But this is generally recognized. And I do not propose to pursue the point, though the relevant comparative investigation would be of considerable interest.

However this may be, it does not follow from what I have said that the philosopher must confine himself to reflection on ordinary language, paying no attention to the findings of, for example, physiological or experimental psychology. For one thing, it is possible, I suppose, to develop a philosophy of the sciences relevant to psychology, which would be analogous to philosophy of natural science. For another thing, there are questions which arise in connection with science and which the philosopher can perfectly well consider. For example, though brain transplants would obviously be far more difficult than heart transplants, we can hardly say in advance that they are absolutely impossible. If such an operation did turn out to be possible, it might very well give rise to problems relating to personal identity. And I do not see why the philosopher should not consider the implications of this hypothetical case.

Further, the philosopher could develop a general view of the human being which would take account of the findings of the various relevant sciences, and he could indicate ways in which he thought that these findings affected the view expressed implicitly in ordinary language. In other words, there is room for a synoptic view of the human being, a philosophical anthropology, which would take into account not only phenomenology, so far as it is relevant, and the implications of ordinary language but also the findings of the relevant scientific disciplines. At the same time the empirical sciences are limited, by the nature of the case, in what they can tell us about man. There are other aspects of the human being which are of importance and relevance for any general view, his capacity to recognize moral ideals, for example, and the tendency, expressed in various religions, to relate himself to a metaphenomenal reality. In other words, though much in the psychological theories of cultures such as India and China may seem to us to be pre-scientific and outmoded, we should not shut our eyes to the possibility that the general approaches of philosophers in other cultures represent real aspects or features of the human being which should be taken into account in any overall view. The human being is not only what empirical science represents him as being. He is also, for example, the moral agent who featured so prominently in the philosophy of imperial China. It may be said that consideration of these other aspects of the human being belong elsewhere than in psychology. That may be, if psychology is understood in a pretty restricted sense. But perhaps a broader view of man is possible and desirable, without, however, questioning the value of specialized disciplines. Consideration of the philosophies of other cultures can help to correct a certain myopia.

6

Some Ideas of History in
Different Cultures

Introductory Remarks
In this chapter we are concerned with some general views of human
history as found in the philosophies of different cultures. In other
words, we are concerned with what is sometimes described as speculative philosophy of history rather than with critical philosophy of history.
Speculative philosophers of history develop general views or interpretations of human history as such, for example, as a succession of cycles
or as a continuous goal-directed process. The critical philosopher of
history is primarily concerned with problems arising out of reflection
on historiography, on the work of the historian. If, for example, we
assume that the historian offers explanations of historical events, what
is the nature of this explanation? Again, in what sense, if any, can
historiography be objective? Critical philosophy of history is thus
analogous to philosophy of science, whereas speculative philosophy of
history is analogous to speculative cosmology or philosophy of nature.
Further, critical philosophy of history presupposes serious historical
studies, as distinct from chronicling or the mere keeping of records, and
it is a relatively modern western development, whereas speculative
philosophy of history is much more ancient. To be sure, any detailed
speculative philosophy of history presupposes some knowledge of
historical data.[1] But a general idea of the course of history can rest on
other grounds than reflection on the work of historians. For instance,
an interpretation of human history as a succession of cycles might rest
on the assumption that the universe constitutes one harmony, and that
as day and night and the seasons succeed one another in regular cycles,
so must human history exemplify a cyclical pattern.

As every human being exists in an historical situation, one might
perhaps expect that when philosophical thought develops in a given
culture, it will always include reflection on human history. We have,
however, to distinguish between a general idea of history and the
sustained attempt to show how the validity of this idea is supported by
an examination of particular historical phenomena. An attempt of this

kind presupposes a real interest in human history; and there may be factors which militate against the awakening of this interest. This was notably the case in India. Generally speaking, the minds of the Indian philosophers were orientated to the concepts of enlightenment and liberation, when liberation meant release from the phenomenal world, the world of time, change and rebirth. Even in the pluralist Vedic schools the phenomenal world was regarded as something from which liberation was desirable. In the Advaita Vedānta the world of becoming was seen as the appearance of one unchanging ultimate reality, Brahman. And the minds of the Buddhist thinkers were set on the attainment of Nirvāna. The Indian philosophers had indeed the idea of history as a succession of cycles, corresponding to cosmological cycles; but their general attitude to the phenomenal world was not such as to encourage a lively interest in or emphasis on human history. In the West we can find an analogous attitude in the thought of Plotinus, who was more interested in the 'flight of the alone to the Alone' (*Enneads*, 771b.) than in political events, which he obviously regarded as surface phenomena.

It is doubtless true that the theme of Indian lack of interest in this world can be exaggerated. The epic poems hardly give the picture of a society which was unconcerned with terrestrial affairs. True, the *Gītā* expounded the ideal of acting and fulfilling social duties in a spirit of detachment, but it none the less preached action, even military action, as a duty. And the *Māhabhārata*, of which the *Gītā* formed a part, not only contained rules of conduct for householders and kings but also gave an imaginative account of the way in which political society and kingship arose, in response, that is to say, to the need for protection. Further, though society without any political authority was not regarded as a practical possibility, in early Indian political thought the state was regarded as subject to the law which obtained in the universe at large. Again, though the Indians did not show the same devotion as the Chinese to the compiling of records, there are some records of rulers and states in the *Purānas* and in Buddhist literature. In addition, some writers composed what might be described as manuals for princes. Notable among such productions is the *Artha-Śāstra*, attributed to Kautilya, minister of the Emperor Chandragupta (321–296 BC), in which the author discussed a variety of topics relating to political life.

Though, however, in India before the Muslim conquest there was undoubtedly some political theory, this is not quite the same thing as philosophy of history. In any case the fact remains that the philosophers of the Hindu schools were interested in psychological and epistemological themes relating to the realization of the true self rather than in human history. They had indeed the general idea of history as a succession of cycles. For example, in the Sāṁkhya-Yoga school *Prakṛti*, the formless material element, was regarded as developing itself, in some ill-defined way, for the sake of spirit or *purusha*, the process taking the form of successive movements of development or evolution and of re-absorption. But, as stated above, there is a difference between a general idea of history and a sustained attempt to show how this general idea is verified by reference to historical events. It is, of course, only natural that the modern movement in India to liberation from alien rule should have been accompanied by a growth in national self-consciousness and in interest in Indian history. But we are concerned here with the classical traditions of Indian philosophy. And given the general attitude and predominant interests of the philosophers, we would hardly expect that there would be much to say about Indian philosophy of history in this chapter. The philosophers were much more concerned with ideas than with history.

Views of History in Chinese Thought

It has often been asserted that in contrast with the Indians the Chinese had a lively interest in history, as shown by their enthusiasm for compiling historical records. One of the so-called Confucian Classics was the *Book (or Classic) of Documents*, generally known in the West as the *Book of History*. This collection of documents relating or purporting to relate to ancient times doubtless includes later additions or forgeries, but its recognition as a basic work illustrates Chinese interest in the preservation of historical records. Another early work, traditionally ascribed to Confucius, was the *Spring and Autumn Annals*. Neither work was confined to what we would normally recognize as historiography. But they contained historical material.

The Chinese were understandably proud of their ancient civilization. Indeed, they came to look on China as pretty well co-terminous with the civilized world. The sense of national unity, however, obviously required time to develop. And it was under the Han dynasty that an attempt was made to write a complete history of China. (Under the Han dynasty the unity achieved for a relatively brief period under the Ch'in dynasty was consolidated.) Ssu-ma T'an, who died in 110 BC, began the work which is known as *Records of the Historian* and which was continued and completed by his son, Ssu-ma Ch'ien. (Father and son successively held the post of Grand Historian.) It dealt with the history of the Chinese nation from the time of the legendary

Emperor Yao onwards. Another notable work was the *History of the Former Han Dynasty*. Compiled principally by Pan Ku, it dealt with the period from about 200 BC to AD 22. Further historical works were compiled during the T'ang and Sung dynasties, the most notable being probably the *Great Mirror*, compiled by Ssu-ma Kuang and his associates in the eleventh century.

Though the Chinese thinkers were conscious of the continuity of Chinese civilization, they were also, of course, aware of historical change, of the alternation of periods of consolidation and disunity, of harmony and disharmony, of a process of change which for many centuries they conceived as cyclical, as analogous to the waxing and waning of the moon and the alternation of the seasons.

The mind of the Chinese thinkers tended to be dominated by the ideal of harmony. This ideal was present, of course, in Taoism, with its idea of harmony between the individual human being and nature, the universe of which the human being is an expression. It was also present in Confucianism, with its ideal of harmony in the family, in the local community, in the state, and in the universe at large. For example, there should be harmony in the individual between the rational and affective factors in human nature; there should be harmony between the individual and the societies to which he or she belongs; there should be harmony between the will and actions of the rulers and the mandate of Heaven; and in the world at large there should be harmony between Heaven, Earth and Man, between the macrocosm and the microcosm.

This ideal harmony should, of course, find expression in human history, in the development of human society. But it is not necessarily realized in this way. There was a tendency to locate the great harmony in the beginning or in very early times. For example, in the *Book of History* it is asserted that social harmony existed in the reign of the legendary Emperor Yao in the third millenium BC. This social harmony could, however, be disturbed, by injustice for instance. And it came to be popularly believed that if a ruler seriously disturbed social harmony or prevented its development, Heaven showed its displeasure by portents of various kinds. To be sure, this idea of mutual influence between man and his environment did not pass unchallenged. Thus Wang Ch'ung, a naturalistically-minded philosopher of the first century AD, attacked what he regarded as superstitious accretions to Confucianism and rejected the notion that the misdoings of rulers were responsible for natural calamities and portents. In his view, eclipses of the sun and moon had nothing to do with the policies of governments. There was no good reason to suppose that a calamity such as an earthquake was due to human sins or that it was a heavenly rebuke to an unjust or oppressive ruler. Generally speaking, however, the idea of a universal harmony was a conspicuous feature of Chinese philosophy, and there was a close connection between this idea and interpretations of human history.

As for the theory of historical cycles, this was presented by certain writers in ways which were clearly linked with the theory of the unity of man and nature. In ancient Chinese cosmology, as was noted in chapter three, order in the world was regarded as the result of the interplay of two forces or principles, *yin* and *yang*, the former being passive, relatively weak and destructive, while the latter was active, strong and constructive. From these two forces there proceeded the five agents or elements, earth, wood, metal, fire and water, each of which was associated with a certain colour. The five agents were regarded as predominating in turn, and the period of predominance of each of these was correlated with an historical period. Thus in the second century BC, under the Han dynasty, Tung Chung-Shu correlated the successive predominance of each of the five agents with an historical period, a set of five such periods representing a cycle. Again, in the eleventh century, Shao Yung, a Neo-Confucianist, worked out an elaborate mathematical scheme in which an historical cycle, lasting for thousands of years, was represented as consisting of twelve epochs, the earlier epochs being correlated with the rising predominance of *yang*, while the later epochs were correlated with the rising predominance of *yin*. There is obviously no point in considering further details of this, to us at any rate, rather fantastic theory. But the theory is none the less of some interest as expressing, even in a bizarre form, the idea of the interrelation of all things in the universe. It may shed no real light on human history, but it at any rate illustrates the Chinese search for synthesis, which was a prominent feature of Neo-Confucianism.

It is worth remarking that with the Chinese thinkers reflection on human history was conspicuously motivated, as one might expect, by practical considerations. These could, of course, be ethical. Confucius himself was given to appealing to the moral examples of sage-emperors and wise rulers. In other words, history could be and was used to inculcate moral lessons. Again, knowledge of the succession of periods and cycles was supposed to be useful to rulers and their advisers. Such knowledge could be used for divination and prediction; and those who worked out schemes of cycles and periods thought of themselves as performing a useful service to the state.

Another point to which it is worth drawing attention is this. We tend to think of Confucianism as extremely conservative, in the sense that it canonized, as it were, certain social and political structures, as though they were valid for all time. And this idea is doubtless verified, at any rate when Confucianism had become the official state philosophy. There were, however, exceptions. Thus, in the seventeenth century, Wang Fu-chih, who attacked Chu Hsi's theory of the Great Ultimate, in which all 'principles' (*li*) are united and who insisted that the universe consists only of constantly changing concrete things, drew an important conclusion in regard to human history. As human history, as well as nature, is constantly changing, we can safely conclude the institutions which are suitable in one historical situation may be quite unsuitable in another situation. According to Wang Fu-chih, Confucius was well aware that society evolves and abstained from presenting any detailed schemes for social organization.

The interpretation of history as consisting of successive cycles was the prevailing theory for centuries. An evolutionary view, as distinct from a theory of cycles, came to the fore in connection with the movement for social and political reform in the last decades of imperial China. A notable exponent of the evolutionary view was K'ang Yu-wei (1858–1927), who tried to persuade the Emperor to initiate a policy of reform but who found his plans thwarted by the formidable dowager Empress. His idea of historical progress was probably inspired, in large part at least, by western thought; but he liked to father it on Confucius, whom he regarded as a reformer. In brief, K'ang Yu-wei distinguished three successive ages, the age of disorder, the age of rising peace and the age of great peace or of the great unity. He retained the theory of cycles to the extent that he represented each of these ages as itself comprising what we might describe as minor versions of the periods of disorder, rising peace and great peace; but the total process was regarded as exemplifying overall progress. The age of great peace lay in the future, and in it the division into national states would be transcended, racial discrimination would disappear, private property too, and equality of men and women would be achieved. The onward progressive movement, however, would never reach definitive completion in the sense that no further enrichment of human life would be possible.

After the formation of the Chinese Republic, K'ang Yu-wei adopted a rather different attitude and pressed, unsuccessfully, for recognition of Confucianism as the state religion and even for restoration of the imperial throne. But this change of attitude does not alter the fact that his philosophy of history was both optimistic and universalistic. In modern China a Marxist-inspired interpretation of history has taken the place of older theories. But this is, in its own way, also optimistic and universalistic. It will be interesting to see what becomes of Marxian universalism in its confrontation with nationalistic pride and aspirations.

Cyclical and Non-Cyclical Theories of History
We have noted that interpretations of history as a succession of cycles were common in ancient India and China. They can also be found in Greek philosophy, with the majority of Stoics, for example. It is, however, a mistake to talk about 'the cyclical theory of history', as though there were only one such theory. Suppose, for example, that it is held that there is a succession of worlds, each of which is born, develops, disintegrates and perishes, being succeeded by the birth of another world. And suppose that human history as we know it is repeated in each world. A theory of this kind can be found, for instance, in Nietzsche's hypothesis of the Eternal Recurrence, when he suggested that in infinite time all events would eventually be repeated an infinite number of times. We must obviously distinguish between this type of theory and the theory according to which there are successive cycles within the history in which we are actually living. We must also distinguish between the concept of cycles as involving the repetition in successive cycles of the same or, more precisely, similar events and the concept of cycles as involving the repetition not of particular events but of general patterns or structures.

Such distinctions are relevant to the contention which one sometimes encounters, that the theory of cycles and the interpretation of history as one goal-directed or teleological process are sharply opposed and mutually exclusive. Attention has often been drawn, justifiably of course, to the influence of theistic belief on the interpretation of history. If we believe that the world was created by a personal God for a purpose and that the divine plan is fulfilled in and through human history, we can hardly be indifferent to history. Further, it has been maintained, we must look on human history as one goal-directed process, a view which is sharply opposed to a cyclical theory of history. The theological conception of history as a teleological process can indeed undergo various degrees of secularization, ranging, for example, from Hegel's philosophy of history to dialectical materialism. Whatever form it may take, it is none the less opposed to the ancient theory of historical cycles.

It seems to me that this contention stands in need of qualification in the light of the kind of distinctions referred to above. The claim that historical events are repeated in successive world-cycles is clearly incompatible with the implications of Christian doctrine. It was presumably against this sort of view that St Augustine was objecting when he remarked in his *De Civitate Dei* (*On the City of God*) that Christ, having died once, never dies again. If, however, the theory of cycles is taken to mean simply that a general recurrent pattern of development is discernible in the rise and fall of civilizations, this is not in any way incompatible with theistic belief in general or with Christian doctrine in particular. It is possible to believe that divine providence works in and through the cycles, and, if one wishes, that in spite of the recurrent pattern there is overall progress. As an example of a philosopher who tried to combine a theory of cycles with rejection of the idea of the necessary repetition of similar particular events, we can refer to Gianbattista Vico in the first half of the eighteenth century. In the second half of the eighteenth century Herder, too, tried to combine the idea of cultural cycles with recognition of possible progress towards the realization of man's potentialities.

Needless to say, it is not intended to maintain that there is no sharp difference between the claim that historical events are repeated and the claim that there is no repetition in history. Again, there is clearly a difference between the statement that there is a discernible recurrent pattern in the rise and fall of civilizations or cultures and the statement that no such recurrent pattern is discernible. The point is simply that when we are considering actual philosophies of history, we have to distinguish carefully between the variety of forms which cyclical and non-cyclical theories can take.

Ibn Khaldūn

When one turns to Islam, one's thought is apt to centre at once on the remarkable fourteenth-century thinker Ibn Khaldūn. To look to Islam in its earlier days for ideas about history may seem pointless. Scholars, however, have argued, and not unreasonably, that Mohammed made a powerful contribution to broadening the conception of history which existed previously among the Arab tribes to whom he addressed his message. Obviously, Mohammed was not a philosopher, nor was he given to theoretical speculation. The scholars in question do not, however, claim that he was. Their point is this. Among the Arab tribes to whom Mohammed's message was immediately addressed there was indeed an historical consciousness, transmitted orally by storytellers and poets; but it was the historical consciousness of a clan, of a group bound together by blood-ties in virtue of descent or of alleged descent from a common ancestor. The groups were constantly engaged in feuds and bloodshed, but each had its orally transmitted memories of its origins and of the past exploits of its leaders. In the Koran, however, Mohammed went back to creation and to common ancestors of the human race who were not Arabs. He was interested in the first place in converting Arab tribes to monotheism, but his vision extended from creation to the day of judgement, his God was the creator of the world and of the whole human race, and his message was conceived as possessing universal significance. To be sure, his general theological vision of history was derived from Judaeo-Christian sources, though he himself contributed to its being associated with a militant Arabism. At the same time the broad vision was certainly there, providing a foundation for a world-religion which, in the course of time, came to be accepted by peoples who were not of Arab stock.

Muslim historiography, as distinct from orally transmitted memories of the past, had to await the foundation of the Arab empire. It naturally centred round Islam, but in the annals composed under the Abbassid dynasty, which ruled from 762 at Baghdad, there were references to other cultures, such as those of Greece and India. Prominent among such works was the *Annals* of Al-Tabari (d. 923), which started from creation. The work was abridged and continued by Ibn Al-Athir (d. 1234). In this historical literature little effort was made to explore causal connections or to draw general conclusions about social evolution. It was left to Ibn Khaldūn to develop a philosophy of history.

Born at Tunis, Ibn Khaldūn lived for a time in Muslim Spain. Returning to Africa, he eventually became a professor of jurisprudence and, for a short period, chief judge at Cairo, where he died in 1406. His main work was a history of the world, but he is best known for the *Muquaddimah*, consisting of the original introduction to and first book of the history. In it Ibn Khaldūn tried to exhibit what he regarded as the inner meaning of history. That is to say, he was not content with narrating past political events and the rise and fall of dynasties but wanted to make clear the causes of events. He thought of himself as founding a new science, the science of human civilization and social organization. It is natural, therefore, that he should have been compared with Vico, the eighteenth-century author of *La scienza nuova* (*The New Science*).

There is no good reason to suppose that Ibn Khaldūn's professions of belief in the operation of divine providence in history were insincere. He certainly believed that in some sense God is the Lord of human history, as of all else. And, as a pious Muslim, he allowed for prophetic revelation. When, however, he was dealing with the causes of historical events and with factors affecting ethnic differences and the rise of civilizations, he showed a markedly empirical bent of mind. For example, he laid emphasis on the influence on human beings of climate, geographical situations and economic factors. He believed that as God has created human beings such as they are, with the necessity for forming societies if they are to live and protect themselves and satisfy their developing needs, God can be said to will social organization and the growth of civilization. But in considering the development of any particular society or civilization, he fixed his attention on empirical causes and influential factors, even if, understandably, he allowed for a special divine impulse, so to speak, in the foundation of Islam.

Some of Ibn Khaldūn's ideas can, of course, be found in previous writers. He is chiefly remarkable, however, for having developed a general theory of the rise, development and decay of civilizations. His examples are naturally taken very largely from the history of tribes in northern Africa, from the rise of Arab power and from the fates of peoples who succumbed to Islamic conquest. But his interpretation of human history was conceived as having a far wider applicability than his examples might suggest. In other words, he was concerned with ascertaining historical laws.

A prominent idea in Ibn Khaldūn's interpretation of history is the concept of solidarity. In the case of a social group, such as a nomadic tribe, which co-operates in satisfying the basic needs of life, the feeling of solidarity is strong, and the leader does not stand apart from the members of the group but is one with them. To satisfy further needs, however, and to lead a more settled and peaceful life, urban organization is required. This urban life is the basis of civilization, in the sense that it is presupposed by the development of literature, art and the sciences. At first the original solidarity is preserved, and social cohesion is represented and maintained by the monarchy or ruling dynasty. In the course of time, however, as civilization advances, the citizens become soft and self-seeking, while the ruler tends to monopolize power, to exploit his privileges, and to hold himself aloof from his subjects. Solidarity and fortitude progressively diminish, and finally the society falls victim to conquest or absorption by another power. This process is constantly repeated, not in the sense that individual events are repeated, but in the sense that the rise and fall of societies and civilizations exemplify a common recurrent pattern. Thus, according to Ibn Khaldūn, a dynasty generally passes through five stages, ranging from the original successful appropriation of authority to eventual overthrow. But the precise forms taken by the various stages depend on particular conditions.

In what Ibn Khaldūn has to say about solidarity and fortitude he is obviously expressing a measure of sympathy with the vigorous, though primitive, life of peoples such as the Berbers. At the same time he insists that God has given mankind the power of thought and the power to acquire and increase knowledge, as well as the ability to develop crafts and to improve the material quality of life. Civilization is required for the realization of man's potentialities, and, in the opinion of Ibn Khaldūn, the larger the society, the higher the level of civilization which it can attain. At the same time urban civilization carries with it seeds of its own decay, and the society in question eventually gives way to a more vigorous society. Ibn Khaldūn doubtless thought of the Arab conquests, such as the conquest of the Sasanian Empire, as exemplifying this process.

Historiography did not, of course, cease to exist in the Islamic world after the time of Ibn Khaldūn, but it tended to be local in character, treating, that is to say, of the history, or phases of the history, of a particular Muslim people or state, such as Persia or the Turkish Empire. As far as philosophy of history is concerned, we can safely say that Ibn Khaldūn stands without a rival in the Islamic world.

Presuppositions of Speculative Philosophy of History
In view of the extensive material it would be foolish to attempt to recapitulate here the development of philosophy of history in western thought. Instead let us consider some general observations relating to the subject.

Some writers seem to give the impression of thinking that speculative philosophy of history, as distinct from critical philosophy of history or meta-historiography, depends on theological or metaphysical assumptions. If they mean simply that speculative philosophy of history can depend, and sometimes has depended, on such assumptions, their contention is obviously correct. For example, St Augustine's interpretation of history in his *De Civitate Dei* clearly presupposes a number of theological beliefs, such as belief in the existence of a personal divine creator who brought the world into existence for a purpose and whose providence operates in history, even if in ways which are generally obscure to us unless God chooses to reveal them. In fact, Augustine's view of human history can be described as a theology of history, in the sense that he looks at history in the light of Christian belief. It is a Christian vision of history. Again, though Hegel certainly tries to show that his view of history as a rational teleological process was empirically verifiable, the influence of his metaphysics, of his theory of reality or of the Absolute, is clear enough. As has already been remarked, his philosophy of history is an integral part of his system of absolute idealism. If history is the self-realization of the Absolute as spirit, it must be a goal-directed purpose. In general, we can say that in any philosophy of history which exemplifies the conviction that human history has a determinate end or goal independently of the ends which human beings set before themselves, a goal which is progressively achieved even if human beings are unaware of it, theological or metaphysical presuppositions are present. And if we propose to treat as speculative philosophy of history only those philosophies in which such presuppositions are present, it then becomes true by definition that all speculative philosophy of history depends on theological or metaphysical assumptions.

If, however, we understand speculative philosophy of history as including any totalizing view of human history, any theory which takes universal history as its subject-matter and makes pronouncements about, for example, a common recurrent pattern of development in all civilizations or cultures, it is doubtful whether all such interpretations of history must make theological or metaphysical assumptions in the sense which seems to be intended. It would be possible, for example, for someone to maintain that in all past civilizations a common recurrent life-pattern is discernible as a matter of empirical fact, and that this pattern will probably, as a matter of empirical hypothesis, recur in the future. We might indeed wish to object against this sort of theory that it only too easily involves fitting the facts to a preconceived scheme and that other interpretations of history are possible; but this is another matter. The point is simply that the sort of view which has been mentioned can be proposed without any presupposition being made save that human history is intelligible.

Again, it might conceivably be held, not that human history must proceed in a certain direction, towards the attainment of an end determined by God or by the nature of reality, but that as a matter of empirical fact it has proceeded in a certain direction up to date. It would be possible, for example, to detach from its moorings in absolute idealism Hegel's thesis that we can discern in history the progressive realization of freedom. After all, Hegel tried to show, by an examination of history itself, that this thesis was true. And one might choose to treat this thesis as an empirical hypothesis, disregarding any metaphysical presuppositions. To be sure, the objection can always be raised that the truth of an hypothesis of this sort cannot be proved, inasmuch as the attempt to verify it empirically involves selecting for emphasis certain aspects of human history and shutting one's eyes to or treating as 'accidental' phenomena aspects which tend to falsify rather than to verify the thesis. The point, however, is simply that it is theoretically possible to claim that human history has in fact been proceeding in a certain direction without presupposing a certain set of theological beliefs or metaphysical theories. It is indeed true that if one were to express approval of the direction which history is thought to have been taking or if one welcomed it, one would be making or implying a judgement of value. But this is not quite the same thing as to make theological or metaphysical assumptions.

To avoid possible misunderstanding, it had better be made clear that while I do not accept the contention that speculative philosophy of history depends, by its very nature, on theological or metaphysical assumptions, I have no intention of condemning the policy of developing a general theory of history in the light of such assumptions. Needless to say, one can justifiably find fault with any attempt to conceal presuppositions or to make out that there are no such assumptions when in fact there are. But there is no reason, for example, why a Christian thinker should not explore the implications of his beliefs in regard to history. Nor is there any good reason why an absolute idealist should not develop an interpretation of history in the light of the philosophy which he accepts. The situation would be different if the development of such theories of history necessarily involved denial or distortion of historical facts. But I do not think that this is the case. If we consider, for instance, St Augustine's interpretation of history, we can see that he makes judgements about relative importance which are related to his Christian faith. Thus he evidently believes that the dialectic between what he calls the City of Jerusalem and the City of Babylon is of greater importance or ultimate significance than the rise and fall of empires and kingdoms. But this does not commit him to denying historical facts relating to the rise and fall of Assyria or Babylon or Rome. What he does is to exhibit what he believes to be the inner meaning of history, as seen in the light of Christian faith. Obviously, those who do not share Augustine's faith will not give a similar interpretation of history. But it does not follow that Augustine was engaged in a disreputable procedure. His presuppositions are clear enough. He does not attempt to conceal them.

The Claim that Speculative Philosophy of History has been succeeded by Social Science

It may be the case that nobody would seriously dispute the claim that speculative philosophy of history can in principle be pursued without one's committing oneself to theological or metaphysical assumptions, other than the presupposition that human history is intelligible. It might be argued, however, that speculative philosophy of history, if pursued in this way, has become a superfluity and that it has given way or is giving way or should give way to social science.

One might, I suppose, have a purely, or at any rate primarily, theoretical interest in pursuing speculative philosophy of history. One might wish simply to understand the process of history, by, for example, coming to know historical laws, if there are any, without any practical end in view. It is possible to be interested in knowledge for the sake of knowledge, in satisfying the intellectual curiosity which Aristotle believed to be the motivating factor in theoretical inquiry. It is also possible, however, for a theoretical interest to be accompanied, or even overshadowed, by a practical interest or motive. For example, while early Chinese philosophers were inclined to look to the past for moral examples, those who developed theories of recurrent cycles thought of themselves as fulfilling a task which would be of use to rulers and their advisers, for the purpose of prediction. For instance, in the eleventh century Ssu-ma Kuang compiled a history of China entitled *Comprehensive Mirror for Aid in Governing*. Again, in the present century, Oswald Spengler maintained that his theory of cycles made it possible to predict the future of western civilization. If we were aware of the life-course of civilizations, and if we could determine at which point in its life-course western civilization had arrived, we would be able to predict the next phase. Such knowledge might, I take it, enable us to delay the process for a while; but Spengler's analogy of the life of an organism suggests that prediction of the phases of waning powers and senility could not be completely falsified.

Reference has just been made to theories of historical cycles. There is, however, no necessary link between a practical interest in the ascertaining of historical laws and emphasis on recurrent cycles. There is indeed a passage in the *Dialectics of Nature* where Engels suggests that the development of the potentialities of matter proceeds through cycles. But Marxist theory of history, as usually presented, gives us a picture of a continuous dialectical advance from primitive society up to the attainment of the ideal human society. There is in a sense a recurrent pattern, the emergence, for example, of a new class which eventually replaces the previously dominant class. But in the ideal society economic classes, as defined by Marx, would disappear. And it would be clearly misleading to describe historical materialism as a cyclical theory of history, though Marxists are confident that they know the laws of history, at any rate better than other people do.

The basic idea is really this. We are all accustomed to the idea, going back to Francis Bacon, that we cannot control nature or make it serve our needs, unless we know and take account of the laws of nature. Intelligent and successful action presupposes knowledge. To take a modern example, man could not fly to the moon, if he was ignorant of or disregarded what we describe as the laws of nature. Similarly, it has been argued, if human beings wish to control social development and to mould society according to their ideals, it is essential that they should know the relevant laws. Whether there are such laws is a question which is not considered here. Nor shall we embark on a discussion of the bearing on freedom of the claim that there are historical laws. The point is simply that the idea of ascertaining historical laws for a practical purpose does not commit one to the idea that history consists of recurrent cycles, in so far, that is to say, as this second idea is opposed to the conception of human history as one continuous dialectical process. This proviso seems to be required, inasmuch as the idea of history being governed by laws clearly presupposes the claim that historical phenomena can be sufficiently similar to one another for it to be possible to subsume them under general laws.

So far we have been thinking of speculative philosophy of history. We recall, however, that Auguste Comte regarded study of the laws of social development as belonging to the new science of 'social physics' or sociology. And from one point of view at any rate Marx can be seen as concerned with establishing a science of history or of social dynamics which would take the place of what he regarded as unrealistic theories and which would form the basis for successful revolutionary activity. In other words, it can be argued that speculative philosophy of history, when separated from theological beliefs and from the sort of metaphysical doctrines expounded by Hegel, tends to undergo a process of transformation into social science or, more precisely, into the complex of social sciences. This process of transformation would not indeed affect the continued existence of speculative philosophy of history when pursued in the light of theological or metaphysical beliefs, provided, of course, that there continued to be people who accepted such beliefs and were interested in exploring their implications in regard to human history. (Among modern theologically inspired thinkers about history we can mention such names as Christopher Dawson, Martin D'Arcy, Reinhold Niebuhr, Urs von Balthasar, Romano Guardini, Teilhard de Chardin, and perhaps even Toynbee in his later years.) Apart, however, from this activity, speculative philosophy of history, it could be argued, is outmoded. We require nothing besides historiography, the social sciences, and critical philosophy of history, in the sense of meta-historiography.

Some Comments on this Claim

The point of view just outlined is likely to give rise to a protest in some minds. One great attraction of speculative philosophy of history is that it offers unified views of the history of mankind. If, however, one talks about its giving way to social science, one naturally gives the impression of this unity being shattered and of its being succeeded by fragmentation. For there is a plurality of social sciences, such as economics, anthropology, sociology, social psychology and political science. It may indeed be difficult to make precise distinctions between some of the disciplines which have arisen and assumed different names, such as cultural and social anthropology. But the various disciplines presumably correspond to different aspects of a common theme or to distinguishable specializations or focusings of attention. In any case, since the time of Auguste Comte there has certainly been a fragmentation of social science. Obviously, there can be no objection to this from the scientific point of view. Nobody objects to there being a plurality of natural sciences. Why should anyone object to there being a plurality of social sciences? But this is not the point at issue in the present context. The point is this. Given the perfectly legitimate development of a plurality of social disciplines, or sub-disciplines, any suggestion that speculative philosophy of history is giving way or should give way to the social sciences is likely to seem very unsatisfactory to those who are attracted to speculative philosophy of history precisely because of its ability to present a unified view of history. If anyone feels the attraction strongly, he or she will doubtless think that even if the social sciences have been taking over some of the ground which would previously have been thought to be the province of philosophy, there must remain room for a synthesis or unifying view, and that the construction of such a synthesis is desirable.

What would such a synthesis be like? It could hardly consist simply in a mapping out of social science, in the sense of an account of the relations between the various relevant disciplines in terms of their approaches and methods of procedure and of what the scholastics would call their formal objects. This is not meant to imply that a synthesis of this kind cannot be constructed. What I mean is that it would hardly satisfy the person who was looking for a unified view of history. It would have to be a synthesis which took into account the theories advanced in the various social sciences and any laws which they may have formulated and which, on this basis, would try to develop a general picture of man in his historical social development. It would, of course, be tentative, subject to revision; and specialists in any particular social science might reject it. But it would at any rate presuppose the social sciences in their development up to date and not exclude them.

The comment may be made that the sort of person represented as dissatisfied with the idea of speculative philosophy of history dissolving, so to speak, into historiography and the various social sciences is much more likely to find what he or she is looking for in Marxism than in the sort of synthesis to which reference is made above. We are in the present context excluding speculative philosophy of history which is closely linked with theological or idealist presuppositions. Marxism, it may be said, is free from such presuppositions. At the same time it lays claim to knowledge of the laws of social development, and it represents human history as moving towards an ideal goal. According to Karl Marx, it is man who makes history, though his freedom to act is, of course, limited by the historical situation in which he finds himself. Further, successful action requires respect for the laws both of nature and of social development. Knowledge of historical laws, however, enables man to see in what direction history is moving and to take appropriate action. Marxism, therefore, can be said to claim to reveal the secret of history and, by revealing the secret, to confer power. Does not this claim constitute one of Marxism's main attractions?

The answer to this question is doubtless 'yes'. It seems, however, that Marx's theory of history has two aspects. On the one hand, it appears to imply a view of history as a teleological process, a goal-directed process, which it is hard to reconcile with Marxian materialism. To be sure, there is no reason, on Marx's premises, why human beings should not act for ends. For he does not deny the existence of mind. His materialism commits him to asserting the priority of matter over mind or spirit, but not to denying the latter's existence. If, however, we look on the Marxist theory of history as implying that a certain goal will be reached and that human beings are instruments in the realization of a goal which will eventually be reached in any case, this view of history seems to be a hangover, as it were, from Hegel, without the Hegelian metaphysical premises which served as a justification for a teleological interpretation of history. On the other hand, we can look on Marx as attempting to establish a science of history through the recognition and formulation of historical laws. And if we regard this aspect of Marx's thought as the really significant one, we can see him as looking forward to the further development of the social sciences. Marx himself never wrote any extended treatment of the materialist conception of history. Apart from some study of what he called the Asiatic mode of production, he devoted his attention mainly to a critical analysis of capitalist or bourgeois society. And from one point of view at any rate we can regard his interpretation of history as an empirical hypothesis or a programme for research, an attempt to establish a science of history or at any rate a scientific approach to history.

Needless to say, we are well aware that Marx was committed to a revolutionary cause, and that any representation of him as having a purely theoretical interest in the formulation of historical laws would be quite inadequate. We are also, no doubt, aware that the whole situation has been complicated by the use made of Marx's ideas by those who claim to be his successors and the custodians of the truth, people who have transformed a stimulating and provocative, though certainly not infallible, hypothesis into a dogma. Such considerations, however, do not prevent one seeing in the thought of Marx himself a kind of transition between speculative philosophy of history and social science.

Critical Philosophy of History
As a generalization, it seems true to say that in speculative philosophy of history an attempt is made to reveal the inner meaning of human history, the pattern which is present under, so to speak, the series of events which are thought of as recorded by historians. This is especially clear, of course, in the case of speculative philosophy of history which is closely linked with theological or metaphysical presuppositions, as with St Augustine and Hegel. If someone does not accept such presuppositions and doubts whether history has any meaning beyond what historians themselves reveal or can reveal, he is likely to turn his attention to what has been described as critical philosophy of history, provided, that is to say, that he has any interest in the philosophy of history. In critical philosophy of history the direct object of reflection is not so much history itself as historiography. This is not meant to imply that no reference is made to history, in the sense of the phenomena about which historians write. It is that the problems considered are

primarily those which arise out of reflection on historiography. If hardly anything has been said in this chapter about critical philosophy of history, this is because, as has already been explained, it is a modern western phenomenon. We can indeed find remarks about the writing of history in the works of some Chinese historians and in Ibn Khaldūn; but critical philosophy of history as we know it in the so-called analytic movement presupposes the historiography of the nineteenth and twentieth centuries. Speculative philosophy of history, however, responding to man's desire to understand the movement of history in which he finds himself, is more widespread. And for this reason we have concentrated attention on it.

It by no means follows, however, that the present writer looks on critical philosophy of history with disfavour or attaches no value to it. Some of the problems considered may seem to be theoretical puzzles which make little practical difference to anyone. For example, a plausible case can be made out for rejecting the concept of historical objectivity, and it is difficult for the person who accepts this concept to find completely satisfactory answers to some of the questions raised. But whatever is said, we are obviously unlikely to relinquish our ordinary conviction that there is a difference between fiction and historiography, and we shall doubtless continue to employ the sort of evidence of which we are accustomed to make use to distinguish between more and less objective historiography. There are indeed other problems of such a kind that acceptance of a certain solution might conceivably affect historiography. For example, if historians were to accept the theory that their explanations of historical events are defective, inasmuch as they make tacit appeal to general laws which are left unstated, it is conceivable at any rate that they would alter the structure of their explanations. Considered together, however, the problems in critical philosophy of history can serve the very useful purpose of shaking the mind out of its accustomed grooves and assumptions, and on anyone who is interested in questions arising out of reflection on historiography they can exercise a fascinating attraction.

At the same time one can understand that to some minds critical philosophy of history may give the impression of philosophers fiddling while Rome burns. To be sure, speculative philosophy of history is not necessarily concerned with urging any programme for the active restructuring of society. Hegel was notoriously concerned with understanding the past or, if preferred, the present as the culmination of the past which it subsumes in itself. And Marx's statement that, whereas philosophers had hitherto tried simply to understand the world, the point was to change it is well enough known.[2] As for the theory of a common recurrent pattern being exemplified in the lives of all civilizations, this is perhaps more likely to foster an attitude of detachment than one of active commitment to an ideal cause. Critical philosophy of history, however, precisely because its point of departure is historiography rather than history itself,[3] may seem to be even further removed from substantive social and political issues. Whatever we may think of Marx's interpretation of history, it is at any rate orientated to action, to the restructuring of society, whereas the dispute between those who try to assimilate historical explanation to a model based on explanation in science and those who insist on the difference between historical and scientific explanation may seem to have little practical relevance and to be the sort of topic which ivory-tower philosophers like to discuss.

This sort of attitude is understandable. But it seems to be short-sighted, intolerant and narrow. Needless to say, there is nothing wrong with the attempt to analyse a given social or historical situation, with a view to overcoming social evils and restructuring society in accordance with ideals, provided that infallibility (the possession of final 'scientific' knowledge) is not claimed and that different views about what should be done are given a fair hearing. And there is nothing unreasonable in claiming, for example, that to establish and preserve peace in the world is more important, for the general welfare of humanity, than discussion of the question how study of the past can yield objective knowledge when the past by definition does not exist. To demand, however, that philosophers should confine their attention to themes relating to social reform is to show intolerance and narrow-mindedness. Further, if the demand is really equivalent to demanding that all philosophers should embrace and try to promote a certain social-political programme, it is, if successful, destructive of genuine philosophical reflection. In any case theoretical inquiry is a feature of man's cultural life, even if it has no immediate relation to social commitment.

Let us sum up with a reference to Father Martin D'Arcy, in whose memory the lectures underlying this book were given. In the introduction to his book *The Meaning and Matter of History. A Christian View*[4] he raised and discussed the possibility of Christianity making a contribution to the philosophy of history. He believed that it could, but he recognized that in a Christian interpretation of history 'appeal is made to doctrines, which are accepted on faith and lie, therefore, outside the domain of the historian'. What has been stated in this chapter will have made it clear both that I am in substantial agreement with this contention and that I see nothing objectionable in exploring the implications of any set of presuppositions in regard to history, provided that the presence of presuppositions is recognized. As for critical philosophy of history, anyone who knew Martin D'Arcy will be aware that he was not attracted by what has sometimes been described as 'Oxford philosophy'. In point of fact, however, he himself discussed certain problems in critical philosophy of history, such as the nature of historical explanation. He would certainly not have rejected critical philosophy of history as worthless, even if he was more attracted by speculative philosophy of history. Whether he would have accepted the suggestion that speculative philosophy of history, when cut adrift from theological or metaphysical assumptions, tends to transform itself with social science, we do not know. But if he had accepted it, he would probably have gone on to claim that some unifying synthesis, some unifying view of man in his social development, was desirable.

7

Recurrence, Advance, and Historical Relativism

The Concept of Recurrent Philosophical Problems

One sometimes comes across people who have the impression that philosophers are always discussing 'the same old problems'. If they are claiming that philosophical discussion is confined to problems which were raised at an early stage in the history of philosophical thought and which have reappeared at intervals ever since, the claim is unjustified. That this is the case can easily be shown. For example, problems in the philosophy of science did not arise until science had attained a certain degree of development. Again, the sort of problems treated in the critical philosophy of history presuppose the existence of serious historical studies. The question, for instance, of the nature of historical explanation arises out of reflection on writing which clearly embodies explanation of some sort, not out of a mere chronicling of events, in which no real explanation of events is attempted. It is thus untrue to say that no fresh problems emerge in the development of philosophical thought.

It would be possible, however, to admit the truth of what has just been said and at the same time to maintain that philosophers have spent a great deal of time discussing recurrent problems which never seem to be solved to everyone's satisfaction. In reply we might wish to point out that if a philosopher claims to have proved the truth of a certain theory or thesis, the fact that not everyone agrees with him does not show that his claim is unjustified. For we have to distinguish between proof and persuasion.[1] If you offer me a proof of the truth of p and I fail to be convinced, the fact that I am not persuaded does not, by itself, warrant the conclusion that your proof was bogus or defective. I might have failed to understand the proof. Or I might be so wedded to belief in the truth of not-p or of some theory with which p would be logically incompatible or hard to reconcile that I was not really open to serious consideration of truth-claims made on behalf of p. Though, however, it is perfectly correct to say that a distinction must be made between proof and persuasion, this does not really affect the question whether there are or are not recurrent philosophical problems. If a problem constantly recurs, this inevitably suggests that it has not in fact been solved, even perhaps that it cannot be solved, at any rate in the way or ways in which people have tried to solve it. Given, however, the distinction between proof and persuasion, it is conceivable that a problem might recur, even if in fact it had been solved in the past.

Prima facie there seem to be recurrent philosophical problems, which are sometimes described as the perennial problems of philosophy, a phrase which is usually intended, I suppose, in an honorific sense. Metaphysically minded people might mention the problem of the One and the Many, and they could point out how this theme was recurrently discussed not only in western philosophy, from Greek philosophers up to, say, Hegel and Bradley, but also in the philosophies of other cultures. For example, it was discussed by the Vedānta philosophers in India, by Taoist and Neo-Confucianist philosophers in China, by thinkers in Mahāyāna Buddhism, and by Islamic philosophers up to, for instance, Sabzawārī in the nineteenth century. Another obvious candidate for classification as a recurrent problem is the problem of God. And if it is said that interest in this particular problem is not a conspicuous feature of contemporary philosophy in this country, we can mention the problem of human freedom (in a psychological, not a political sense). This problem has recurred, it might be argued, on a good many occasions, and it is still discussed. Moreover, it was discussed in early Islamic thought, and it was at any rate touched on in Chinese thought, in the context of a discussion of fatalism. Again, the question whether values are simply relative or whether there are in some sense absolute values and a universal moral law might be described as a recurrent problem. It was raised in ancient Greece, and it is still raised today. Then there is the question of human survival. Interest in a given problem may not be equally spread throughout the philosophies of all cultures in which philosophical thought developed. But on the face of it the concept of a recurrent problem seems to have been exemplified.

In the foregoing paragraph the phrases '*prima facie*' and 'on the face of it' were used deliberately. For it is arguable that talk about the recurrent problems of philosophy is based on a superficial impression which cannot stand up to critical examination. Consider, for example, the so-called problem of the One and the Many. What precisely is the problem? Is it a question whether there is a One? If so, are we asking, for example, whether there is any good reason for asserting that the

Many depend ontologically on a One which transcends them? Or are we asking perhaps whether things are so interrelated that they form one developing system, the world considered as a totality? If, however, we presuppose that there is or must be one ultimate reality, how are we to interpret the problem of the One and the Many? Presumably it is a question of the relation of the Many to the One. The precise meaning of this question, however, depends on the nature of our presuppositions. If, for example, we presuppose that there is only one reality and that the Many are its appearances, we are faced with the task of giving an account, if we can, of the relation between appearance and reality. If, however, we assume that the Many are not appearances of the One but, as interrelated, constitute it, the question of the relation between appearance and reality does not arise in the same form. In other words, it is misleading to say that philosophers such as Parmenides, Plato, Plotinus, Aquinas, Spinoza, Hegel, Bradley, Avicenna, Mullā Sadrā, Sabzawārī, Śaṁkara, Madhva, Lao Tzu and Chu Hsi were all concerned with the recurrent problem of the One and the Many. For this implies that they were all concerned with exactly the same problem, whereas the problems with which they were actually concerned have to be seen in the light of their various beliefs and presuppositions, which were not all the same.

This point can be clarified by considering the problem of human freedom. We may be inclined to say that the early Islamic thinkers, such as the Mu'tazilites, and Immanuel Kant were both concerned with the recurrent problem of human freedom, thus implying that the problem was the same in both cases. But suppose that we spell out the problem in each case. The early Muslim thinkers were faced by a problem arising out of ways of speaking in the Koran. On the one hand the call to obey the divine commands and the doctrine of reward and punishment seemed to imply that man was free to obey or disobey. On the other hand the sacred text asserted, or seemed to assert, that all events, including human actions, were caused by God. The question, therefore, arose whether the two ways of speaking could be reconciled or whether one line of thought should be sacrificed to the other. When, therefore, the Mu'tazilites defended human freedom and their opponents challenged their orthodoxy, the context of the debate was theological. In the case of Kant, however, the context was much more that of the classical or Newtonian physics. If the world is a system of bodies in motion, a system governed by mechanical laws, can man be an exception? In what sense, if at all, can he be justifiably described as free? If, therefore, we spell out the problems in terms of their respective contexts, it may seem that we should speak of two distinct problems, rather than of one single recurrent problem.

Some writers seem to have pressed their criticism of the idea of recurrent problems to such an extent that the alleged recurrent problem breaks up into a number of distinct problems which do not even have a measure of similarity to one another. Indeed, if we accept certain accounts of the matter, it seems to follow that we cannot understand the problems of past philosophers, inasmuch as the problems of philosophers in other societies or cultures have to be seen, if they are to be understood, from a perspective which is not ours. When we think that we understand them, we are really constructing problems in terms of our own perspective and reading them into the past. And when we speak of similar problems being discussed by philosophers in different cultures, it is not so much that they are similar as that we make them similar.

It seems undoubtedly true that talk about recurrent problems is open to well-founded criticism, on the ground that it does not allow for differences which would become apparent if the problems, as posed at different times, were spelled out in terms of their respective contexts. At the same time it seems equally true that there can be family resemblances between problems. Thus problems relating to human freedom are similar in a way in which they are not similar to problems relating to scientific induction. We may wish to speak of distinct problems rather than of recurrent problems. As we have seen, reasons can be given to support this point of view. But it does not seem to be altogether indefensible to speak of a problem recurring in different contexts. For example, we might wish to defend the practice of speaking of the problem of human freedom as recurring in a theological context, in the context of the classical physics, in the context of depth psychology, and so on. It is indeed possible to object to this way of speaking; but it at any rate allows for the family resemblances or measure of similarity to which we have referred.

Has this question of recurrent problems any real importance? In my opinion, it has. As we have noted, some people have the impression that philosophers are always discussing the same old problems, with the implication that in spite of all their discussion they never make any progress. If, however, we once understand that a so-called recurrent problem takes different forms, we can more easily see that it has to be considered afresh. If we reject altogether the concept of recurrent problems and insist that a problem raised in one context is quite distinct from what may seem to be the same problem when raised in another context, it is perfectly obvious that fresh consideration is required. But even if we prefer to speak, for example, of the problem of freedom as recurring in different contexts, we can still see that a solution offered to the problem when raised in an earlier context is unlikely to be considered satisfactory when the problem arises in a different context. For the very fact that it arises in a different context demands reconsideration. If, for example, the problem of freedom is raised in the context of modern physiology and psychology, it is natural that it should be considered again. For there are new relevant factors to be taken into account.

Criteria of Advance in Philosophy

We cannot, therefore, justifiably deny that there is any progress or advance in the development of philosophical thought simply on the ground that philosophers are always discussing the same old problems and solving none of them. If, however, we wish to claim that there have in fact been advances, when the word 'advance' is being used in an evaluative and not in a purely temporal sense, the question arises, what are our criteria of advance?

If we believe with Hegel that human history as a whole is an advance towards an ideal goal, the self-manifestation of the Absolute as self-thinking thought or as the identity of thought and being, the historical development of philosophy must be part of this advance, a very important fact, if philosophical thought can be described as the Absolute thinking itself in and through the mind of man. The process is dialectical for Hegel, inasmuch as this is the way in which thought develops. But this means that there is a continuous dialectical advance, later philosophies being superior in specifiable ways to earlier philosophies, as Hegel tries to show in his lectures on the history of philosophy.

Hegel's interpretation of the history of philosophy has its attractions. For one thing, it encourages the philosopher to believe that he is contributing, even if only in a modest degree, to a progressive movement. It is, however, obviously open to the objection that it depends on certain metaphysical assumptions which govern selection and emphasis. There is no question of Hegel paying no attention to historical data or of his inventing the data. The point is that the interpretation of the data is regulated by metaphysical presuppositions. This does not, of course, prove that the presuppositions are false. But it does mean that Hegel's interpretation of the history of philosophy is an integral part of his absolute idealism. This is clear enough in his treatment of oriental philosophy. Indian philosophy, for example, is treated as a stage in a development of thought culminating, at any rate up to date, in absolute idealism. In fine, it is Hegel's own philosophical position which determines the criteria for judging advance or progress in his interpretation of the history of philosophy.

This sort of thing has often been said about Hegel. But the general idea obviously has a much wider application. Is it not the case, it may be asked, that if one does not simply describe the development of philosophical thought but makes evaluative judgements about advance or regression, one is always expressing one's own philosophical position or stance? Indeed, is not this necessarily the case? If a logical positivist were to write a history of European philosophy, he would doubtless include a treatment of absolute idealism, but he would certainly not represent it as the highest position reached up to date. He would regard the rejection of absolute idealism as an advance, thus expressing his own philosophical position. Similarly, if an adherent of the Advaita Vedānta wrote a history of Indian philosophy, his own position would certainly influence his judgement of the theories of, say, the Cārvāka or materialist school. Again, if in his account of Chinese philosophy a Neo-Confucianist did not simply describe Buddhist thought in China but made evaluative judgements, these judgements would reflect his own philosophical position. In fine, it might be claimed that there are no neutral criteria of advance, but that any set of criteria always reflects a certain philosophical position. Provided that this fact is recognized, we know where we are.

It seems that there are no purely neutral criteria, if by this we mean criteria of advance which do not presuppose any value-judgement whatsoever. If we use logical criteria for judging advance, we presuppose that logical thinking is preferable to disregarding logical norms. At the same time purely logical criteria come nearest to the idea of neutral criteria. And as philosophers generally intend to observe logical norms, we can take the implied value-judgement for granted. To put the matter in another way, respect for logic is common to philosophers, though some philosophers have denied the universal applicability of logical criteria (usually in talk about God), whereas by no means all philosophers are absolute idealists or logical positivists or Thomists or Marxists or disciples of Śaṁkara or Taoists or Confucianists or what not.

Application of purely logical criteria, it may be said, will not carry us very far in judging advances in philosophy. If we happen to regard the task of the philosopher as that of enunciating analytically true propositions, the situation is rather different. But if we do not hold this view, the utility of purely logical criteria for judging advance is limited. For example, if philosopher *A* produces a formally invalid argument to prove the truth of *p* and philosopher *B* then draws attention to the defect or defects in the argument, this can count as an advance. But *p* might none the less be true, even though *A* would have failed to prove its truth. At the same time we can certainly use logical criteria in identifying examples of advance. Moreover, as we are accustomed to think of philosophers as not merely stating theories or theses but as arguing in support of them, logical criteria have an obvious relevance and importance.

Further, it is hardly a controversial statement, if one claims that there have been advances in logical theory. In the West, Aristotelian logic certainly represented an advance on the preceding absence of a systematically developed formal logic. It is generally recognized that advances were made both by the Stoic logicians and by those of the late Middle Ages, and modern logical studies represent further progress. In India there were specifiable advances in the development of logic from the old Nyāya logic, through the work of Buddhist logicians such as Dignāga, to the new Nyāya logic as represented, for example, by Raghunātha Siromani in the sixteenth century.

Apart from formal logic, we can also find examples of advance in the treatment of what would often be described as recurrent problems. Consider, for example, the so-called problem of universals. In point of fact 'the problem' has various different aspects. We can ask logical, psychological, epistemological and ontological questions. And if we value precision, it constitutes an advance if the various approaches and questions are sorted out and stated more precisely. It is not necessary to go to the extreme of maintaining that all philosophical problems are expressions of logical confusion in order to recognize that there is such a thing as logical confusion and that clarification of issues constitutes an advance.

It may be said that all the examples of advance to which reference has been made are formal, in the sense that they belong either to formal logic or to logic in a more general sense. Let me add, therefore, that, in my opinion, the history of philosophy provides examples of what may be described as insight. It may well be that in a number of cases what this author would consider to be examples of insight would be considered by others to be examples of oversight or of blindness. At the same time my claim can be defended without introducing obviously controversial issues. Consider, for example, the philosophy of religion.

In the Middle Ages a certain amount of attention was paid to problems arising out of religious language, but in a limited field. In modern philosophy this theme received relatively little attention. (Some philosophers, such as Berkeley and Kant, made remarks about the matter. Hegel dealt with it in his own way. But in general, however, we can regard modern philosophy as taking up again, though with different presuppositions, a theme treated in the Middle Ages by thinkers such as St Thomas Aquinas.) Thus it was revived in the context of what has been described as the analytic movement, linguistic philosophy or what not. It seems that recent discussion of the topic has shown a greater degree of insight into the complexity of religious language, an insight which represents an advance. Again, it seems that what Marx has to say in his early writings about the dialectical relationship between man and his environment represents an advance, as Marx claimed that it did, over his materialist predecessors.

When, however, people complain about the lack of progress in philosophy, they may mean that they find no body of accumulating philosophical knowledge comparable to the growing body of scientific knowledge. In reply it is possible to point out with Whitehead that if the history of European philosophy is littered with discarded systems, so is the history of science littered with discarded hypotheses. This is doubtless true. But the critic of philosophy may still feel dissatisfied. He can refer, for example, to the obvious fact that more is known now about nuclear physics than was known a hundred years ago, or that in medical science the body of reliable knowledge is much greater than it was in the days of Paracelsus. Is there, he may ask, anything comparable in the field of philosophy? At a certain time most philosophers at any rate may assume that a given thesis has been finally established; for example, that we can make a sharp distinction between analytic and synthetic propositions or between judgements of value and statements of fact. But then we find even such apparently well established theses being subjected to questioning and criticism. What is more, there does not seem to be agreement among philosophers even about the nature and scope of their discipline. It is all very well to insist on the distinction between proof and persuasion. The distinction is indeed a real one. The difficulty, however, is to identify any philosophical truth which can safely be regarded as proved. And anyway, how does one define 'philosophical truth?' I do not think that I can give any answer which seems to me completely satisfactory.

This situation does not however prove that there is no such thing as advance in philosophy. To take an example mentioned above, if a logician questions the claim that there is a sharp distinction between analytic and synthetic propositions or between judgements of value and statements of fact, he does so for reasons, not for the fun of it. If his reasons are judged sufficient to overturn the thesis in question, this represents an advance. Again, if his reasons are judged insufficient to refute the thesis but are none the less recognized as representing considerations which should be taken into account in any statement of the thesis or as contributing to discussion, this too is an advance. In science an hypothesis may be generally accepted largely because nobody sees any good reason for questioning it. If such a reason is proposed and it is judged necessary to revise the hypothesis, we have an advance. Analogously, a philosophical thesis may be commonly accepted by a group of philosophers because it has been defended by some eminent thinkers and members of the group have seen no good reason to question it. If eventually good reasons are proposed for questioning the thesis, thought has advanced. In other words, the mere fact that a thesis has been widely accepted and is then subjected to questioning or criticism does not show that there is no advance in philosophical thought. On the contrary, it illustrates advance.

As for the complaint that in philosophy there is no accumulating body of knowledge comparable to the growing body of scientific knowledge, this may very well be based on a misunderstanding of the nature of philosophy. There are obviously physiological facts, relating to the brain, for example, which were not known in the time of Aristotle but which are known now. Philosophy, however, does not make empirical discoveries of a comparable nature. And anyone who expects it to do so does not understand its nature. Further, we have to remember that though philosophy can be constructive, it is radically critical by nature. In its critical aspects it is prepared to examine all assumptions. From time to time it directs a critical eye to representations of its own nature and scope. In the process of questioning the mind may come up against the unquestionable. If so, this is a gain, something has been ascertained. In any case radical criticism is one of the essential aspects of philosophical thought. And to turn this into a ground of complaint is equivalent to demanding that philosophy should not be philosophy but something else.

To say, however, that philosophy has a radically critical function is not equivalent to admitting that no advances are made. If, for example, philosopher *B* accepts premises made by philosopher *A* and then develops the implications of these premises more consistently and thoroughly than was done by *A*, this is clearly an advance. For it enables us to see more clearly what the premises imply, and we are thus enabled to form a better judgement about them. I have argued too that there can be fresh insights in philosophy. To be sure, there may be differences of opinion whether an alleged insight is what it is claimed to be. The proper procedure then is to consider the matter more closely, which is, after all, what philosophers are accustomed to do.

Judgements about Advance and Judgements of Value

The objection may be raised that though we certainly do make judgements about advance and regression, such judgements always express our own perspective. This can be a shared perspective, of course; it need not necessarily be a purely personal point of view. In fact, it is really only shared perspectives which we need consider. If I had a very idiosyncratic or peculiar philosophical position and then made evaluative judgements about past philosophies, judgements which clearly expressed this peculiar point of view and which I made without bothering what other people thought, the situation would be obvious to all attentive observers. But this situation would be unusual. For if I make evaluative judgements about past philosophies, I am presumably hoping for agreement. I assume that whatever differences of opinion there may be between myself and others, there is a sufficient measure of shared perspective to justify the hope that my judgements will meet with acceptance. In any society there is a shared perspective. Obviously, in a pluralistic society there is a variety of outlooks. But there is none the less a shared perspective, underlying the differences, if, that is to say, we are entitled to speak of 'a society' at all, a phrase which implies some measure of unity. It may be possible to express the shared perspective, to some extent at any rate, in terms of a set of presuppositions, as R. G. Collingwood suggested. But they have to be dug out, so to speak. They do not stare one in the face. For apart from a deliberate process of reflection, analysis and explicitation, they are implicit assumptions. We take them for granted. And they govern our judgements about the past. Any society looks at the past in terms of its own perspective. The same is true in the area of philosophy, inasmuch as philosophy does not pursue a purely isolated path of its own but forms an element in the culture of a society.

This sort of view is not of course a novelty. For example, Hegel asserted that 'philosophy is *its own time expressed in thought* (Preface to the *Philosophy of Right, Werke*, H. Glockner, VII, p. 35), and that no philosopher can transcend his own age. Taken by themselves at any rate, these assertions imply that any philosophy is relative to its own

time, to the contemporary cultural situation, and that it is from the
perspective of this situation that the past is judged. It must indeed be
remembered that for Hegel the truth contained in earlier philosophy
was subsumed in later philosophical thought, and that nothing of value
was lost by the wayside. It was not, therefore, a question of looking at
past thought as though it were a purely external object which we see
(or reconstruct) from our own different perspective. For Hegel,
contemporary philosophy *was* past philosophy, in a higher stage of
development. At the same time there was clearly a strong element of
historical relativism in his thought.

In his lectures on the history of philosophy, Hegel maintained that
the last philosophy of a period was the highest stage of the development
of philosophical thought in that period. And in his *Critique of the
Dialectical Reason* Sartre tells us that in any age there is only one living
philosophy, and that, within the age in question, it is impossible to
transcend the living philosophy, in the sense of advancing beyond it. If
one tries to do so, one falls back into a preceding and outmoded
philosophy. According to Sartre, Marxism is the one living philosophy of
our age, though it needs a rejuvenating infusion of existentialist
humanism. Obviously, his idea of a living philosophy expresses a
judgement of value. For if 'living' were understood as meaning simply
existing and developing, the analytic movement would have just as
much right as Marxism to be considered the living philosophy of our
time. Indeed, it would have more right, inasmuch as Marxism
originated in the nineteenth century and, on Sartre's own admission,
has become ossified, at any rate in the Soviet Union. The point,
however, is simply that a theory of historical perspectivism or
relativism does not necessarily entail the view either that we can divide
history into neatly separated periods, in each of which we can identify a
last or final philosophy, or that in any age there is one, and one only,
living philosophy. In the twentieth century there are a number of
philosophical currents of thought, and we can of course judge other
philosophies, whether past or present, from within one of them. But as
already suggested, it might be argued that in spite of obvious
differences of opinion there is, to some extent at least, a shared
perspective, a common set of presuppositions, which govern our
judgements about the past, and so about advance or regression.

It does not follow that we ought not to make value-judgements about
advances in philosophical thought. Moreover, such judgements have
validity, given certain presuppositions. Perhaps this can be illustrated
in the following way. A westerner might criticize Indian philosophy,

especially the Advaita Vedānta, on the ground that it encouraged an inward-looking attitude and thus discouraged emphasis on social and political thought. Given the westerner's presuppositions and scale of values, the criticism would seem to be valid. If, however, we presuppose that enlightenment and liberation, in the sense envisaged by Śaṁkara, are of supreme importance, our judgement about Indian philosophy will be a different one. Again, given the traditional Chinese evaluation of the importance of social relationships, family and political, Neo-Confucianist criticism of Buddhism as socially harmful is at any rate partially valid. If, however, we share the common Buddhist view of the goal of life and of the role of monasticism in facilitating its attainment, we shall obviously make a different judgement about Buddhism in China. Analogously, there is no reason why we should not judge advances in philosophy from our twentieth-century perspective. It is important, however, to recognize that our interpretation and evaluation of past philosophy are not absolute, but relative to our own perspective. As Hegel said, we cannot transcend our own time. But we can at least recognize that we cannot do so.

Historical Relativism

A statement such as 'we cannot transcend our own time' may sound impressive, but how should it be understood? There is indeed a sense in which the statement is obviously true. For example, a human being is born into a certain historical situation. He or she cannot transcend this situation in the sense of being an external spectator of all history. For we are within history, not outside it. Further, the life of the human being is not conterminous with history. If I have been born in the twentieth century and am living as a citizen of the United Kingdom, I cannot at the same time be a citizen of ancient Athens or of imperial China under the Han dynasty. Even if I am a believer in transmigration and think that I was once a warrior in ancient India or a monkey swinging from tree to tree, I am neither of these things now. I can no more be living now in ancient India than I can be living now in the future world of the third millenium AD.

It will be objected that the statement that we cannot transcend our own time is not intended to express simply obvious truths of this kind. It has to be understood in a more sophisticated way. It may mean, for example, that we conceive the past from the perspective of the present, and that we interpret and evaluate past philosophies from the standpoint of the present. Complete objective neutrality is a myth.

This is a difficult thesis to deal with. For it is not quite clear what it involves or is supposed to imply. It is doubtless true that if we are asked what we think to be the most important or significant elements in the thought of Plato, we are likely to answer in terms of what we think to be of lasting importance or of what we believe to have significance for philosophical thought today. This is both natural and proper. At the same time are we incapable of recognizing that Plato may have ascribed, or did ascribe, an importance to elements in his thought which we, in view of changed circumstances of one sort or another, would not ascribe to them? And what applies to Plato can be said equally of Śaṁkara or of Chu Hsi or of the Japanese philosopher Dōgen. Analogously, if I wish to pass moral judgements about historical figures or about the customs of past societies, I naturally express my own moral convictions, which, incidentally, may or may not agree with the prevailing moral outlook of the society in which I live. What else can I do, if I am making a moral judgement at all? It does not necessarily follow, however, that I am incapable of understanding the moral outlook and convictions of a past society.

In other words, there is a sense in which we can transcend our time. We cannot, of course, share the perspective of the European Middle Ages in a sense which would imply that we were medievals, living in, say, the thirteenth century. But it is not impossible for us to understand, to a greater or lesser degree, how the medievals looked at the world and society. Their perspective finds expression in their literature and thought, their art and architecture. To be sure, puzzles can be proposed, based, for example, on the fact that the past, by definition, no longer exists and, therefore, cannot be looked at, and on the fact that it is we who interpret existing literature, monuments and works of art as evidence of the past. Though, however, such puzzles form fascinating themes for consideration in the critical philosophy of history, few people seriously doubt that there can be different degrees of understanding of the past. This applies, of course, not only to the western past but also to other cultures. Though it may be very difficult for a modern westerner to understand the ways of thought expressed in, say, the *Tao te Ching* (or *Lao Tzu*) or the *Chuang Tzu*, we all assume in practice that different degrees of understanding are possible, and that in this sense we can transcend our time. It may be said that our assumption is unwarranted, and that any appeal to common sense is naïve. But the assumption is not an arbitrary one. It is based on experience of actual work done, in the exploration of medieval thought, for example.

The twentieth-century European or American is doubtless different in many ways from the citizen of Periclean Athens or from the Japanese in the time of Prince Shōtoku. (Prince Shōtoku Taishi, who was Regent from 592 to 622, was an influential figure in the spread of Buddhism in Japan. He wrote commentaries on three Buddhist texts.) But we are all human beings, with certain needs, and there is an element of continuity. It is perfectly natural that we should tend to interpret the past in the light of its relation to or significance for the present. At the same time it would seem to be an exaggeration if it were suggested that an interpretation of the past is nothing but a projection of ourselves and our own society and world. And to the extent that we can understand a past society or a past system of thought on its own terms, we can be said to transcend our time.

It may be said that this account of historical relativism is a caricature. The relativist is not committed to denying that there is any sense in which it is true to say that some people have a better understanding than others of the philosophical thought of another age or society or culture. If two people look at a landscape from the top of a mountain, they can be said, refinements apart, to share the same perspective. But this does not alter the fact that one may see more clearly than the other or be better able to interpret what lies before him. Analogously, the evidence for the thought of the early Taoist sages exists in the present and is seen from a twentieth-century perspective. But there are accepted criteria for interpreting such evidence; and one person may be better qualified than another to employ these criteria and interpret the significance of the evidence. Again, the relativist is not necessarily committed to maintaining that there is only one kind of perspective. He might very well admit that there can be such a thing as a common human perspective, within the general framework of which there is a variety of perspectives, personal, social and cultural. What he would hold presumably is that we cannot escape from all perspectives and take a point of view which is not perspectival.

However this may be, it seems desirable to attempt to move away from a sharp polarization. That is to say, if we ask why people have expounded a relativist position and why other people have objected sharply against it, we may see that they both have points to make and that the extremes on either side are untenable. On the one hand, it is obviously true that we cannot look at the philosophies of the past from any other position in history than our own, not in any literal sense. On the other hand, we are quite capable of recognizing our own tendency to interpret past thought in terms of our own interests and values, and we can endeavour to understand how a given philosopher

conceived his own work and what significance it had for his contemporaries. If it is said that we can never be absolutely certain that we
have interpreted correctly the actual mind of Plato or Confucius or any
other past philosopher, this seems quite true. It does not follow,
however, that all interpretations are purely arbitrary impositions and
on the same level. There are limits to the meaning which can
reasonably be given to any piece of literature. A further point to
remember is that significance must be significance for someone, and
that it is, therefore, variable and not something fixed once and for all.
What the philosophy of Plato meant for a contemporary thinker is not
necessarily quite the same as what it means for us. But both meanings
or significances can be real. It does not make much sense to ask, what is
the significance, the one real meaning? If we once assume that there
must be one, and only one, real meaning, we shall soon find ourselves
claiming that we cannot know it, and that any significance which we
ascribe to the philosophical literature of the past is a purely subjective
projection. In a sense, of course, it is a projection; but, as already
stated, there is no good reason to suppose that all interpretations are on
the same level, which they would be if they were all arbitrary
impositions. Whether we emphasize the significance which we believe
that a past philosophy has for us today or whether we try to determine,
as best we can, the significance which it had for its author or for his
contemporaries obviously depends on our interests and purpose. In any
case the significance is relative, relative to us, relative to the
philosopher in question or relative to his contemporaries. To say this,
however, is not to say that anything goes.

The Historical Conditioning of World-Views
Let us now turn to a brief consideration of Hegel's statement that a
philosophy is its own time expressed in thought. Let us take the statement by itself, and interpret it as implying that any philosophy is
historically conditioned in such a way that there cannot be a
perennially true philosophical system which simply needs to be handed
on to successive generations as the definitive truth. Hegel himself
asserted the existence of a perennial philosophy, but by this he meant
the development or onward march of philosophical thought through
the centuries, in and through distinct systems with their contingent and
historically conditioned elements. Obviously, I am using the phrase
'perennial philosophy' in a rather different sense. So let us forget about
Hegel and simply consider the claim that any philosophical system is

historically conditioned in a sense which would exclude its being perennially true, true for all time.

An historian of philosophy is likely to feel considerable sympathy with this point of view. Reference was made in the last paragraph to the idea of a philosophical system being handed on to successive generations as the definitive truth. The objection will at once be raised that indoctrination does not make one a philosopher. This is true. The reply might indeed be made that it would be a case of people seeing for themselves the force of the arguments and the truth of the conclusions, rather than of their being indoctrinated. But that there is or could be a philosophical system which would impose itself on all unprejudiced minds as the final and definitive truth is a claim about which the historian of philosophy is likely to remain sceptical. He might admit that the idea of a final system is an ideal goal; but it is improbable that he would feel any confidence that such a system could ever be constructed, on the ground that any actual system will be historically conditioned, reflecting its cultural milieu in specifiable ways.

Some people were either irritated or amused by the frequency with which the late Professor C. E. M. Joad used the words 'it all depends what you mean by . . .'. If asked, for example, what he thought of democracy, he was likely to say 'it all depends on what you mean by democracy'. This gambit can indeed be irritating, especially if one does not really know what one means. But Joad's attitude was perfectly reasonable. Thus in regard to the contention that there is not and cannot be any perennially true system of philosophy, we can hardly express an opinion, unless we know in what sense the phrase 'system of philosophy' is being used.

It would be in accordance with ordinary usage, I think, to describe a world-view or *Weltanschauung*, expounded by a philosopher, as a philosophical system. By a world-view I mean an interpretation of the world which tries to co-ordinate in one overall picture different aspects of the world and of human experience, including, for example, the scientific view of the world and man's aesthetic, ethical, religious, social and political life. In other words, I envisage the philosopher as presupposing science, morals, art, religion, social and political life and as trying to create a synthesis, a general view in which the inter-relations between the various elements are exhibited. For various reasons, this sort of enterprise is not fashionable nowadays. But we need not bother about this aspect of the situation. The question is, whether there can be a perennially valid world-view of this kind, or whether every such world-view is historically conditioned.

If we are talking about a comprehensive world-view as a whole, it will certainly be historically conditioned in one way or another. To take an obvious example, if a philosopher endeavours to integrate man's political life into an overall synthesis, he will fix his attention on the political life and institutions of his time, whether it is a question of the Greek *polis*, the medieval institutions of the feudal state and the Church, or the post-medieval state. He can, of course, see the present in the light of the past; but he cannot integrate a future which does not yet exist. It is obvious to any serious student that in regard to social and political theory the philosophies of, say, Aristotle, St Thomas Aquinas, Hobbes, Hegel, the medieval Islamic thinker Al-Fārābi, and the Confucianists in China were all historically conditioned in ways which can be specified. Again, if a philosopher tries to integrate into a world-view the scientific knowledge or theories of his time, it is clear that his reflections will be historically conditioned, inasmuch as scientific knowledge grows and is not something which takes a final shape at any particular time. Even such a convinced Thomist as Jacques Maritain was obviously well aware of the fact that St Thomas's ideas on scientific matters were historically conditioned.

A philosopher's thought can also be historically conditioned in regard to his approach and the problems which he raises or selects for emphasis and discussion. For example, Kant's basic problems were determined to a large extent by various historical factors, such as the rationalist philosophies, empiricism and the development of the classical or Newtonian physics. Again, Hegel's problems were determined to some extent by the thought of predecessors and contemporaries. Indeed, it frequently happens that a philosopher's problems are, so to speak, set by other philosophers. He does not think in a void, but in a definite historical situation. Again, it hardly needs saying that Karl Marx's approach and problems presupposed and were influenced not only by the development of left-wing Hegelianism and of previous socialist thought but also by the contemporary social and economic situation in the industrialized countries.

In the first chapter attention was drawn to some general ways in which philosophy has been influenced by extra-philosophical factors or by the absence of a certain factor in a given situation. It was maintained, for example, that in the ancient world the nature of Greek and Roman religion and the absence of any commonly accepted authoritative source of religious and moral teaching contributed to the increasingly conspicuous function of philosophy as a guide to life. In regard to the Middle Ages, emphasis was laid on the influence of philosophical thought by the background of religious belief and by Christian theology. And attention was drawn to the variety of ways in which, in the post-medieval world, the development of the particular sciences has exercised an influence on philosophy. These points have already been discussed.

From what I have been saying it should be clear that I accept the contention that any comprehensive world-view will be historically conditioned, and that to the extent in which it is historically conditioned it can be described as relative to its time. At the same time it is important to bear in mind the fact that philosophers can make statements, the truth of which transcends any transient historical situation. There is no reason, for example, why Aristotle should not have made statements about the voluntary and the involuntary, which are not valid only in regard to the ancient Greeks. Again, though in any attempt to integrate man's social and political life into a general world-view a philosopher will naturally pay attention to the forms of political life which are familiar by experience to himself and his readers, he may very well make statements which hold good in regard to any society which we are likely to regard as a political society. Further, the logical validity of an argument does not depend on the passing historical situation in which it is proposed.

When treating of advance, the belief was expressed that there can be genuine insights in philosophy. Let me add the following point. In the case of a given insight we may perhaps be able to explain its occurrence at a certain time. For example, if it is true that there is now a greater insight into the complexity of religious language than there used to be, we can certainly offer reasons why this insight should have occurred in the context of the analytic movement, and why attention should have been paid to language in modern philosophy. It by no means follows, however, that the insight in question is valid only in relation to the historical situation in which it occurred.

To sum up the main line of thought hitherto: the fact that a comprehensive or would-be comprehensive world-view is historically conditioned in a variety of specifiable ways does not entail the conclusion that the truth of all the statements made by the philosopher in question is simply relative to his own time. For one thing, in his construction of a general philosophy he may very well apply to particular circumstances or situations principles which have a wider validity. To put the matter in another way, recognition of the historical conditioning of a philosophical world-view does not necessarily entail a relativist theory of truth. In textbooks of scholastic philosophy the authors were accustomed to include a refutation of relativism on the ground that it could not be stated without self-contradiction. Whether this refutation holds good or not seems to depend on whether a proposition can be self-referring. However this may be, it seems clear that there can be perennially true propositions, in the sense of propositions which are true whenever they are enunciated. The common-sense view, I suppose, would be that the truth of a statement such as 'President Carter is talking to President Brezhnev on a transatlantic phone' is relative to the existence of a certain state of affairs. If Carter were not talking to Brezhnev, the statement would be false. There are, however, propositions of a hypothetical or conditional nature which are true whenever uttered. A phenomenologist's claim that 'consciousness is always consciousness *of*' is one of them. This is presumably equivalent to 'if there is consciousness, it is consciousness *of*'.[2] In any case, if we are prepared to allow that there can be necessarily true propositions, we must also admit that some of them can be included in historically conditioned systems of philosophy. We ought not to jump from the premise that world-views are historically conditioned to the conclusion that every statement included in such a world-view is historically conditioned, in the sense that its truth is relative to a certain transient historical situation.

In this case the question arises whether it would not be possible to develop a perennially true philosophical system, consisting simply of necessarily true propositions. Presumably, the answer is 'yes', provided, of course, that it could be found possible to arrange the propositions in such a way that they formed a system. This condition would be fulfilled, if it could be shown, for example, that from one ultimate necessarily true proposition the others followed deductively in a certain order. Presumably, we would then have a perennially true system. Even if, however, such a system were possible and were actually developed, it seems that it would exemplify a rather narrow conception of philosophy. Rightly or wrongly, people expect from philosophers something more than the enunciation of analytically true propositions. At the same time I would not be prepared to assert that the construction of a perennially true system in the sense mentioned is impossible, though its relation to reality would be perhaps a controversial issue.

Understanding Cultures other than Our Own
We have maintained above that even if a past philosophy is historically conditioned in specifiable ways and is, to this extent, relative to its

time, the fact that we can specify those ways shows that we can have a genuine understanding of the philosophy in question and that we can, in this sense, transcend our own time, though there is also, of course, a sense in which we cannot do so. At the same time someone may comment in the following way. When distinguishing cultures, in an admittedly rather arbitrary way, we treated western culture as one developing whole. And from the philosophical point of view there is obviously a good deal to be said in favour of this policy. For a considerable amount of Greek thought was taken over and appropriated by medieval thinkers, and ways of thought and concepts employed in the ancient world and in the Middle Ages reappeared in post-medieval philosophy. To be sure, there were also differences, and we are not entitled to assume without more ado that because the same word, 'substance' for example, was used by successive thinkers, they all attached the same meaning to the word. In spite, however, of changes, differences and new developments, there is a real measure of continuity in western philosophy. And we would naturally expect that, in view of this continuity, we would be able to achieve some genuine understanding of the thought of earlier western philosophers. Even if we are not prepared to follow Whitehead in describing European philosophy as a series of footnotes to Plato, we can not only assess his significance for us today but also attempt, with some measure of success at least, to interpret him in his own terms and judge what he thought important. When, however, it is a question of cultures different from our own, with which the West has had little connection until relatively modern times, the situation is rather different. Ways of thought can differ sharply. For example, we may expect to find in Chinese philosophy features which we consider essential to philosophical thought and fail to find them. We can be mystified by the way in which Mahāyāna Buddhist thinkers talk about 'emptiness' and 'not-being'. And we can come across statements which seem to us frankly self-contradictory and unintelligible. If we try to translate oriental thought into western categories and concepts, we may fear, and with good reason, that we are distorting it. If we do not translate it into western ways of thought, we may despair of understanding. In other words, are there not ways of thought which are relative to different cultures and which cannot be understood by people of another culture?

It is doubtless true that there can be and are ways of thought which are relative to a given culture, in the sense that they are characteristic of it and not of some other culture. For example, in a book on early Chinese philosophy, Professor Donald J. Munro of the University of

Michigan draws attention to the fact that what the Chinese thinkers considered important were the behavioural implications of a statement or belief. Whereas, generally speaking, western philosophers have been concerned with the truth or falsity of statements and with proving their truth or falsity, the Chinese thinkers showed a 'regrettable lack of attention to the logical validity of a philosophical tenet' (*The Concept of Man in Early China*, p. ix). They were interested instead in the bearing of a statement or belief on human behaviour. Let us take it that Professor Munro is correct in what he says. It obviously follows that he has understood a feature of Chinese philosophical thought. He is warning the reader what to expect. We have indeed to guard against assuming that western tradition and customs and outlook necessarily constitute absolute standards of judgement. But if a way of thought, to speak perhaps rather absurdly, is really a way of thought at all, it is in principle understandable, whatever the practical difficulties may be. To think otherwise is equivalent to claiming that members of other cultures are so radically different from ourselves that use of a common descriptive term, such as human being, is unjustified. I trust that none of us accepts this contention.

8

Patterns and Laws in the History of Philosophy

Dempf's Theory of Three Stages

In the preface I stated my intention of saying something in the final chapter about the question whether a common recurrent pattern of development is discernible in the philosophies of those cultures in which philosophical thought is known to have developed. To avoid talking in a purely abstract way, it seems appropriate to proceed by outlining an actual claim that such a pattern can be found. My subsequent comments should make clear my own attitude to the general question.

In 1947 a German-speaking philosopher, Alois Dempf, published at Vienna a book entitled *Selbstkritik der Philosophie* (philosophy's criticism of itself), in which he represented philosophical thought as exemplifying a process of development in three successive stages, in the sense that these stages have recurred in the philosophy of each distinct culture which has had a philosophy. First of all, there is philosophy as cultural. That is to say, philosophical thought originally presupposes a cultural crisis and tries to overcome it by providing a moral justification of the traditional outlook and values. The thought of Confucius in China would be an example. Secondly, there is philosophy as cosmology. That is to say, there is an attempt to give to the moral justification of tradition the framework of a world-view, of the conception of an ordered universe. Thus Plato and Aristotle might be seen as placing Greek ethical life within a wider cosmological or metaphysical setting or framework. Thirdly, there is philosophy as anthropological or personalistic. The clash of world-views or cosmologies gives rise to relativism and scepticism, and this phase gives rise to the centring of philosophical reflection on man himself, the human person. Thus in modern western philosophy personalism and existentialism can be said to have centred round man, while Marxism obviously focuses attention on human history and society. Further, inasmuch as language and the concepts expressed in language are human phenomena, it can be said that in the so-called analytic movement, which avoids the old-style construction of world-views, there has been, in a real sense, a concentration of attention on man.

Obviously, Alois Dempf was aware of differences between philosophical traditions, which could not be accounted for simply in terms of this general scheme. He therefore produced a number of auxiliary hypotheses. For example, some differences could be accounted for in terms of sociological explanations. If, for instance, a cultural crisis took the form of a clash between an aristocratic and a priestly class and the latter prevailed, the result would be a theologically orientated style of philosophy. If, however, the clash was between aristocratic and bourgeois classes and the latter prevailed, the result would be a lay or secular style of philosophy. Dempf also offered psychological explanations of differences. For example, in the cosmological stage of thought he associated subjective idealism with the predominance of will, objective idealism with the predominance of intellect (*Vernunft*), naturalism with the predominance of imagination, and materialism with the predominance of calculating reason (*Verstand*). Again, in the anthropological or personalistic phase Dempf associated the predominance of ethics with will, that of a mystical orientation with emotion, and that of a metaphysical interpretation of man and his life with intellect. Allowance was also made, of course, for the influence on philosophy of such factors as religion and economic life.

The idea of a recurrent pattern or rhythm in the philosophies of different cultures is analogous to, for instance, Spengler's idea of a recurrent pattern in the lives of civilizations. Further, if the historical development of philosophy is conceived as regularly following a certain general pattern, and if differences between the philosophies of different cultures can be explained in terms of ascertainable causes, we can presumably formulate laws which enable us to predict. Dempf did in fact envisage such laws, and he assigned the task of formulating them to what he called 'the historical reason'.

At the same time Dempf did not wish to endorse determinism or a rigid theory of cycles. He recognized what he described as 'the constructive reason', which can show, for example, the one-sidedness of a given philosophical theory or position. In this case there is presumably no necessity for the theory to recur. Indeed, Dempf saw philosophy as becoming increasingly more self-critical and self-limiting, and he seems to have regarded personalistic philosophy not simply as the final stage in the philosophical thought of a culture but also as constituting an advance in an evaluative sense. This attempt to combine a theory of cycles with recognition of the possibility of overall progress recalls to mind the philosophies of history of Vico and Herder.

Let us now consider some points concerning the applicability of Dempf's three-stage scheme. It is desirable to emphasize the fact that the scheme is being used simply as an example of theories of recurrent patterns in the history of philosophical thought, with a view to making a general point about such theories. In the book mentioned above Dempf identifies thirteen cultural epochs in which philosophy has exhibited what he describes as a normal pattern of development. For example, in Indian thought he identifies four cultural periods, while Greek philosophy, philosophy in the Hellenistic-Roman world, Christian philosophy in the ancient world, medieval philosophy, the philosophy of the Renaissance and post-Renaissance thought are all listed as distinct units. If we were concerned specifically with exegesis of Dempf's theory as such and with commenting on it, we should obviously have to take this classification of cultural periods into account. But whatever its merits or demerits may be, I intend to exclude it. This may in a sense be unfair to Alois Dempf. However, as already indicated, I am simply using the three-stage scheme as a point of departure for making a general point about theories of this kind.

Comments on this Theory

A point in favour of the three-stage scheme suggested by Dempf is that while, on the one hand, it is not obviously unfalsifiable, it is not, on the other hand, so clearly linked to the development of philosophical thought in one particular culture that it would be surprising to find it exemplified in all cultures in which philosophy developed. Suppose that I claimed to have made the discovery that all philosophies exemplify a pattern of challenge and response. You might feel inclined to comment that so far from being a new discovery, universal exemplification of this pattern could be stated in advance, in view of the nature of philosophy.[1] For if we leave out 'philosophizing' which consists in repeating the arguments and theories of some outstanding thinker, must not philosophy, by its very nature, be a response to a challenge of some sort? It might, however, be argued that Dempf's three-stage scheme is not in fact exemplified in the philosophy of this or that culture. There is at any rate the real possibility of argument. At the same time it is certainly not immediately obvious that the scheme applies only to the philosophy of one particular culture or has been based simply on reflection on one particular philosophical tradition. It seems, therefore, that we can reasonably treat the scheme as an empirical hypothesis which may be confirmed or disconfirmed by examination of the historical data.

A plausible case can be made in support of Dempf's thesis. But it is also possible to make a reasonable case against its universal applicability. And it is very difficult, perhaps even impossible, to settle the issue in any definitive manner. This is indeed the point, namely that if we leave out of account both theories which, by the nature of the case, must be verified and those which we can justifiably see at once as highly unlikely to be universally verified and concentrate on theories which might or might not be universally verified, we are unlikely to be able to decide in a definitive manner whether they are in fact universally verified. One main reason for this state of affairs is that a great deal depends on what elements in the philosophy of a culture one chooses to emphasize. By emphasizing certain elements we may be able to work out a persuasive case for claiming that a pattern is exemplified. But it may also be possible, without perversity, to emphasize other elements and to make out a persuasive case for claiming that the pattern is not exemplified. This is not to suggest that reflection on comparative philosophy with a view to ascertaining whether a common recurrent pattern of development is discernible should not be pursued. And it is obviously true that the defender of one view may be convinced that he has made a better case in support of his view than the case presented by the defender of another view. At the same time I can understand someone maintaining that the topic is unmanageable, or that we can come to no definite commonly accepted conclusion, and that it is preferable to confine one's attention to questions which can be more easily answered.

Having stated this general point of view, let me add some illustrations. For the reason mentioned above we had better forget the name of Alois Dempf and remember simply the three-stage scheme, philosophy as cultural, philosophy as cosmology, and philosophy as anthropological or personalistic.

Let us suppose, for the sake of argument, that China can reasonably be regarded as a unit when it is a question of distinguishing between cultures.[2] It is certainly not unreasonable to claim that the background of early Chinese philosophy was formed by a cultural or at any rate a social crisis, the progressive disintegration of the feudal system and a state of increasing turmoil and unrest. We can see Confucius as transmitting the old cultural heritage and as interpreting and defending it in the light of his own ethical ideas. The early Taoist sages can also be seen as trying to show man how he should live in a world of unrest and insecurity, though their conception of the ideal human life obviously differed from that of Confucius and his followers. Again, the Legalists were concerned with promoting adoption of the political and social measures which they believed to be necessary if the evils of contemporary society were to be overcome. As for a cosmological phase, we could refer to the process of development within Confucianism which culminated in Neo-Confucianism, a movement which incorporated within itself elements from Buddhist and Taoist thought. What about an anthropological or personalistic phase? In Buddhism we might see this as represented by the tendency, conspicuous in Ch'an Buddhism, to emphasize personal experience at the expense of concentration on scriptural exegesis and on theoretical speculation. Possibly we might also appeal to what might be described as a 'back to Confucius' movement under the Ch'ing or Manchu dynasty. Further, if we extend our idea of Chinese culture to include recent developments, we could obviously appeal to the man-centred philosophy which has taken the place of Confucianism as the official ideology of China.

At the same time it is also possible to argue against the applicability of the three-stage scheme to philosophy in China. We might, for example, emphasize the fact that cosmological speculation goes back to very ancient times in China, represented by the *yin-yang* theory, not to speak of the Taoist theory of the One. It is indeed much more natural to emphasize the ethical aspects of early Chinese thought than the cosmological elements. But in this case we might wish to maintain that Chinese thought was always, in a certain sense, anthropological, namely in the sense that it stressed the primacy of the ethical. Even in Neo-Confucianism the idea of the practical orientation of thought was not abandoned, even if certain thinkers emphasized objective inquiry into the 'principles' of things.

A defender of the three-stage scheme could, of course, cope with such objections. He could point out, for example, that the theory in question does not postulate abandonment of ethical in favour of cosmological thought but maintains rather that cosmological thought was developed to give a framework for a set of values or for an idea of how human life should be lived. But I have no intention of claiming that the three-stage theory, as applied to China, is indefensible. On the contrary, it can be presented in a persuasive manner. What I suggest is that its advocate selects for emphasis certain features of Chinese thought, though it is possible to make out a reasonable case for emphasizing other elements.

Turning to India, we can doubtless find a cultural crisis, if we look for one. We can refer, for example, to the early invasions and the clash between the beliefs and attitudes of the invaders and those of the indigenous peoples, though this is admittedly a theme in which much remains obscure. We can also see in the development of the Vedic schools a reaction to a crisis produced by the birth and growth of Buddhism and Jainism. We can then go on to note that in Vedic schools such as Sāṁkhya cosmological theories were advanced which formed a background for a way of life. Finally, it could be argued that in the philosophies of Rāmānuja and Madhva in the Vedānta school we can see a personalistic reaction against the Advaita Vedānta of Śaṁkara.

In a real sense, however, most Indian philosophy was anthropological, in the sense, that is to say, that it was orientated to human enlightenment and liberation. This is true even of Śaṁkara's system. Attention can indeed be drawn to Buddhism, with its relative silence in regard to metaphysical problems, as an example of thought which concentrated on man and his destiny or goal in life. But we can hardly use early Buddhism to show that the final phase of Indian thought was personalistic. (Even though Buddhist thinkers commonly rejected the idea of a permanent substantial self, Buddhism was essentially a way of life for human beings.) For the origins of Buddhism preceded, not followed, the development of the Hindu Vedic schools. Further, if we divide Indian thought into cultural periods and make the first period terminate with the spread of Buddhism, we lay ourselves open to the suggestion that we have fitted an identification of cultural periods to a preconceived view of the successive stages of the development of philosophy. (Dempf divided 'old Indian philosophy' (up to about 300 BC) from 'middle Indian philosophy', 'neo-Buddhist philosophy' and 'Hindu philosophy' from about AD 600.)

As for Islam, serious objections can be made to the policy of treating the Islamic world as one cultural unit. If, however, for the sake of argument, we agree to treat it as a unity, it is doubtless possible to make out a plausible case for the applicability of the three-stage scheme. Thus we can reasonably see a cultural crisis in the exposure of the Arab peoples to other ways of thought and to external criticism of their Muslim beliefs, a crisis which gave rise to the beginnings of philosophical thought in a theological context. I am thinking, for example, of the Mu'tazilite theologians who discussed some philosophical themes, such as the question of human freedom; and of the thought of Al-Kindī in the first half of the ninth century, thought which was directed to the defence of Muslim beliefs but which contributed to providing early Islam with a philosophical terminology. In the philosophies of leading Muslim philosophers of the Middle Ages, such as Avicenna, we might see a cosmological phase of thought, largely of Neoplatonist inspiration. And it might be argued that a succeeding anthropological or personalistic phase of thought was represented in one way by Ibn Khaldūn in his philosophy of history and in another way by the Sufi and illuminationist traditions in Persia.

It is possible, however, to emphasize other aspects of Islamic thought, which would tell in favour of a rather different picture. For example, though in Sufi philosophy or theosophy and in cognate lines of thought emphasis was certainly laid on the human soul's ascent to God, some people might prefer to stress other aspects of Islamic philosophy in Persia, such as the development of the metaphysics of existence from Suhrawardī in the twelfth century to Sabzawārī in the nineteenth century. It is not meant to imply that these thinkers were indifferent to religious mysticism. It is simply that one might choose, without being guilty of any obvious perversity, to stress the metaphysical and cosmological aspects of their thought and to see them as providing a metaphysical background for esoteric Muslim religion rather than to see them as representing an anthropological or personalistic phase of thought, in the sense in which this phase of thought can be regarded as a reaction to the clash of world-views.

In the foregoing paragraphs the cultures of China, India and Islam have been treated as units. When we think of western thought, it is probably true to say that we mentally divide it up into periods, such as Greek and medieval philosophy. It is difficult to avoid the impression that degrees of ignorance and knowledge have something to do with the matter. Consider China. Most of us are probably not well acquainted with Chinese philosophy, apart from some general knowledge of a world-famous figure such as Confucius. It may not, therefore, occur to us to question the propriety of treating Chinese philosophy as a unit, especially if we are aware of the way in which the Chinese were inclined to regard their country as having continued to be for centuries pretty well conterminous with the civilized world, and also of the fact that in the course of its history China came to enter into a state of relative petrifaction. In the case of Islam, however, we may very well question the propriety of treating Islamic culture as one unit. And when we direct our attention to the West, of which most of us know much more than of China, India or Islam, we probably think at once in terms of traditional divisions. After all, we are well aware that medieval society differed in specifiable ways from Greek society, and that the post-Renaissance western world differed in important respects from the medieval world. It may, therefore, appear that if we wish to try out the three-stage scheme on western philosophy, it should be applied in turn to each of the periods which we are accustomed to distinguish, to see whether it fits, rather than to western thought as a whole. A further consideration is that while it is obviously questionable whether we can regard western thought (or, for the matter of that, Chinese, Indian and Islamic thought), as a completed totality, we can at any rate treat the philosophy of the ancient world and that of the Middle Ages as completed wholes, even if there is, for example, considerable difficulty in deciding when the medieval period began and ended.

It would hardly be possible in this chapter to try out the three-stage scheme on western thought considered as a whole and on each of the periods into which the thought might be divided. We must be content with a few observations which will serve to illustrate the general point.

Let us consider for a few moments early Greek philosophy. It has been traditionally represented as predominantly or primarily cosmological in character, as concerned with the nature of the world in which we find ourselves. It may very well appear to have presupposed not a cultural crisis but the establishment of a relatively stable urban civilization in the Greek cities of Ionia and southern Italy, a milieu which permitted the free expression of a spirit of objective inquiry, of that curiosity of which Aristotle speaks. In other words, reflection on early Greek thought may seem to indicate that the contention that the beginning of philosophy in any culture presupposes a cultural crisis which it tries to resolve is falsified. Whether we think in terms of western philosophy as a whole or of Greek philosophy as a separate unit obviously makes no difference in this case.

It might also be argued, however, that it was precisely the growth of Greek urban civilization which constituted the crisis, in the sense that it provided a more sophisticated milieu in which traditional beliefs and myths were subjected to questioning. In other words, it can be argued that the early Greek philosophers did try to overcome a cultural crisis, in so far, that is to say, as their thought was orientated to replacing myth by reasoned philosophical reflection. It is true that the cosmological aspects of early Greek philosophy may seem to make this interpretation appear artificial and forced. But there were, of course, other aspects, social, ethical and religious. If we were prepared to write off the early Greek philosophers as primitive scientists and to regard Socrates as the first real philosopher of Greece, we could indeed identify the crisis with the fifth-century enlightenment at Athens and so confirm the applicability of the three-stage theory. This is not, however, a procedure which commends itself to me at any rate. It seems that the pre-Socratics are best described as philosophers. Even so, a case could still be made out for claiming that early Greek philosophy did in fact represent or embody a response to a cultural crisis.

One other example must suffice. If we treat medieval philosophy as a separate unit and if we wish to argue that in its final phase it was anthropological or personalistic in character, there are several features of late medieval thought to which we can refer. We might refer, for example, to complaints, made at the time, of the aridity of academic studies and of their remoteness from what the critics believed to be important for man, and we could emphasize the development of speculative mysticism as represented by writers such as Eckhart and Gerson. For the matter of that, we might even claim that the logical studies, the prominence of which was partly responsible for the impression of aridity, themselves represented a man-centred phase of thought, inasmuch as it was human thinking which was being studied. To be sure, criticism by fourteenth-century thinkers of the metaphysical arguments and theories of their predecessors was sometimes closely linked with the contention that the purity of Christian faith had been contaminated by Graeco-Islamic metaphysics.[3] It might thus be argued that the critical movement was concerned with Christian doctrines, not with the human person. Indirectly, however, it was concerned with man. For one of the objections to the kind of metaphysics expounded by, say, Avicenna was that it in effect represented the universe as a system permeated by necessity, a view which would obviously have implications in regard to the human being.

It is also possible, however, to argue that what is sometimes described as speculative mysticism was more theology than philosophy. What Gerson, for example, demanded was that in theological studies more emphasis should be placed on the Christian life, or man's ascent to God, that, in other words, ascetical and mystical theology should be given a much more prominent position, and that attention should be paid to the whole man, not simply to his intellectual understanding of formulae of belief. This attitude did indeed show a concern with man and his Christian vocation, but, it might be argued, it was primarily a matter of theological studies. As for logical studies, these were indeed concerned with human, not divine thought; but we should not forget that there was a movement towards the greater formalization of logic and its separation from psychological considerations. Further, some might wish to lay greater emphasis than has usually been done on the theory of impetus which gained prominence in the fourteenth century and which could have resulted in a mechanistic view of the world, the idea, that is to say, of impetus or energy, originally imparted by the Creator, being transmitted from body to body.

The Theory of a Common Pattern and Formulation of a General Law

The observations above are not intended to imply that the three-stage theory is untenable. As already stated, a persuasive case can be made out to support it. For example, if we choose to regard Greek philosophy as representing a distinct cultural unit, we can persuasively argue that Socrates tried, by means of a clarification of concepts relating to moral values, to overcome the crisis culminating in the intellectual ferment in fifth-century Athens, that Plato and Aristotle contributed to providing a cosmological or metaphysical framework for Greek ethical life, and that in later Greek thought philosophy tended to become more and more a way of life, a teacher of how the individual human being should live his or her life and attain interior peace, the emphasis being variously placed, sometimes, for instance, on ethics, at other times on mystical religion. Similarly, a reasonable case can be presented to support the view that philosophy in western Christendom during the Middle Ages exemplified the three-stage theory. And I have no wish to deny that plausible arguments can be given for its exemplification in non-western cultures.

At the same time it is obvious that before we can inquire whether a common pattern of development is discernible in the philosophies of different cultures, we have first to identify the cultures. And it seems unlikely that we shall be able to do this in a form which is immune from reasonable criticism. It has been further argued that even if we take it that our identification of cultures is satisfactory, the validity of the thesis that a common recurrent pattern of development is discernible in them depends to a considerable extent on what features of a philosophical tradition we select for emphasis, and that different judgements in this matter are probably possible, without, that is to say, making obviously perverse judgements.

It may be said that all this is really much ado about nothing. After all, every empirical hypothesis is revisable in principle. What does it matter if different views are possible? There can be rather different interpretations of the thought of an individual philosopher such as Plato or Kant. It is, therefore, only natural to expect that it will be possible to paint rather different pictures of the development of philosophy in a given culture. If the possibility of somewhat different interpretations of an individual philosopher's thought is not considered to be a good reason for abandoning attempts to interpret his thought, why should the possibility of painting rather different pictures of the philosophies of distinct cultures be considered a cogent reason for not pursuing inquiry into the presence or absence of a recurrent pattern of development in the philosophies of these cultures? There are sure to be differences, if the cultures are really distinct. And we can try to exhibit them. But it is also a matter of legitimate interest to inquire whether there is a common element, a common pattern of development which is discernible in spite of the differences.

This line of argument is not only understandable but also valid, as far as it goes. It is based, however, on a misunderstanding. As has already been said, I have no intention of condemning inquiry into the presence or absence of a common pattern of development in the philosophies of different cultures. It seems to be a topic of considerable interest. At the same time it is doubtful whether the inquiry is likely to result in what could properly be described as knowledge of a law which would enable us to predict the future of philosophy. If we set about interpreting Plato or Kant or Hegel, it is improbable that we are concerned with prediction. We are concerned with exegesis, and probably also with evaluation. If, however, we set about inquiring whether a recurrent pattern of development is discernible in the philosophies of all distinct cultures, we may very well have in mind discovery of a law of the development of philosophical thought, a law which has predictive force. But even if we decide that in past cultures the development of philosophy has generally exemplified some very broad common pattern, it is doubtful whether this would constitute a sufficient basis for drawing the conclusion that the pattern must be exemplified in the future. In the past nations have been inclined to settle differences, sometimes important and sometimes not so important, by war. Can we assume that there is a law such that the same pattern of behaviour will be followed in the future? Let us hope not.

The Concept of a Law

It might, however, be argued that while it may be difficult to show that there is one general law governing the development of philosophical thought, a law analogous to Auguste Comte's law of the three stages governing the history of mankind, it may very well be possible to formulate more particular laws relating to the development of philosophical thought. There may be, for example, particular recurrent sequences which permit the formulation of empirically based laws and which have predictive force.

Obviously, if we intend to discuss the question whether reflection on the historical development of philosophical thought permits the formulation of laws, it is desirable to have a clear idea of what is to count as a law. As we are not concerned either with moral precepts or with law in the sense of the positive law of the state, we have to look to science for a paradigm. We then encounter the difficulty that practising scientists tend to manage well enough without bothering their heads with the problem of stating explicitly the necessary and sufficient conditions for p to count as a law, while among philosophers of science there can be disagreement. It may seem that if we wish to discuss the subject of laws relating to the historical development of philosophical thought, we should look to social science for a paradigm rather than to physical science. But as physical science developed before social science, the social sciences have tended to look to physical science for a paradigm, even if they soon became aware that they had to make do with something less than the standard of a strictly universal law. (This is not intended to imply that physical science employs simply the concept of a strictly universal law, which is not the case.)

It seems to be agreed that for a statement to count as a law it must not be a tautology and that it must restrict the field of possibility, in the sense of being falsifiable in principle. We can, therefore, exclude tautologies, also definitions, of course. Further, for a statement to count as a law it must have the note of universality. Statements about particular things or persons and statements relating to particular times must be excluded. A statement such as 'President Brezhnev is now standing on the Lenin mausoleum in Moscow to watch a march past' obviously cannot count as a law. At the same time we have to allow not only for strictly universal but also for statistical laws. This seems to be required by reflection on modern physical science as well as on the social sciences.

What are we to say in regard to truth? If we are prepared to assert that truth and falsity are not predicable of laws, the question does not arise. If we are not prepared to adopt this position, are we to say that for p to count as a law it must be true? It seems to me that to claim that p is a law is at any rate to claim that it is true. And if p is subsequently falsified, we would be inclined, I suppose, to say that though it was alleged to be a law, it had been shown not to be a law after all. This seems to imply that for p to be a law it must be true. The difficulty arises, however, that if every empirical law is revisable in principle, it cannot be conclusively verified in a sense which would exclude revisability in principle. Perhaps we can make a distinction between lawlike statements and laws, using 'laws' to mean lawlike statements the truth of which is sufficiently established for them to be recognized as laws by the scientific community, even if they are still revisable in principle. After all, we generally understand by scientific laws lawlike statements which are recognized as laws, even if we do not exclude the possibility of their having to be revised.

It seems, however, that scientists would not accept any and every empirical generalization as qualifying for description as a law. And the question arises, what are the criteria for distinguishing between laws and empirical generalizations which cannot reasonably be regarded as laws? The view has been put forward that scientists would not recognize as a law any universal generalization which could not be seen as having a function within the framework of a scientific theory, as related to other statements within the theory.[4] This may be the case; but an experimental law can presumably be recognized as such before it has been actually integrated into the framework of a scientific theory.

What we have been saying seems to be of limited applicability in the field of history of philosophy. However, if we are looking for laws in this field, we can at any rate exclude tautologies and definitions and singular statements and consider only universal generalizations of the type 'all A's are B's,.[5] Such statements obviously have predictive force. If we are going to make any further progress with our discussion, we have to give to the word 'law' a fairly wide range of meaning. We are all accustomed to hearing references to Parkinson's law. And I once read a novel in which one of the characters enunciated what he described, if I remember correctly, as 'Apple's law', to the effect that bad news drives out good. Inasmuch as we can doubtless imagine cases in which good news was sufficiently startling and important to prevail, in the minds of hearers, over an item of bad news, this so-called law was presumably intended to express a tendency. Reference to 'Apple's law' may indeed seem to be an irrelevant piece of facetiousness. But some writers are prepared to speak of laws, or at any rate of 'quasi laws', which assert tendencies, such as psychological tendencies, which are fulfilled under conditions which remain unspecified. The point is simply that even if it would be desirable in theory to give one clear and sharply defined universal meaning to the word 'law', common practice hardly squares with this ideal. As we have noted, however, there are limits to what we can describe as laws.

Generalizations from the History of Philosophy

Let us now refer to a thesis proposed by Étienne Gilson. He maintained that if a philosopher lays down certain premises but does not work out their implications consistently or thoroughly, another philosopher or other philosophers will eventually do so. We can doubtless all think of some examples of the sort of thing which he had in mind. Aristotle drew the conclusions, or what he believed to be the conclusions, from the Platonic theory of Ideas or Forms, with a view to showing the untenability of the theory. Again, Hume has often been represented as drawing conclusions from empiricist premises stated by Locke, which Locke himself had not drawn. And the German philosopher Fichte believed that Kant had failed to draw the proper conclusion from his own premises when he refused, in spite of urging by Fichte, to eliminate the thing in itself. Further, no very extensive hunt through articles in contemporary philosophical periodicals is required to come across examples of a philosopher pointing out what he believes to be the implications of a colleague's statements.

There is no great difficulty in imagining cases in which the implications of statements made by a philosopher would not be worked out thoroughly and consistently. Even if we allow for the possibility of the thought of a good many little known philosophers having been treated in modern doctoral theses and learned monographs, there have doubtless been philosophers whose writings have been neglected. Again, a change in the direction of philosophical thought, in the prevailing fashion, might lead to theories being passed over in silence. Given certain conditions, however, we might claim that reflection on the history of philosophy shows that there is a tendency for the implications of premises stated by philosophers to be worked out, when the philosophers themselves have neglected to do so. And if we are prepared to regard as a law, or at any rate as a 'quasi law', the general statement of a tendency which will be fulfilled under unspecified conditions, we could, I suppose, regard Gilson's thesis as a law or lawlike statement.

Let us consider another example. If we consider the way in which early Greek philosophy developed after Parmenides, the way in which the monism of Spinoza was followed by the monadology of Leibniz, the transition from the absolute idealism of Bradley and Bosanquet to the pluralism of G. E. Moore and Bertrand Russell, and the way in which, in the Vedānta School, the non-dualism of Śaṁkara was followed by the qualified non-dualism of Rāmānuja and then by the so-called 'dualism' or pluralism of Madhva, we may conclude that there is a recurrent sequence of such a kind as to justify our claiming that assertion of monism is followed by the assertion or reassertion of pluralism. (Reference here to monism is obviously to substantive monism, not to attributive monism (the doctrine that all things are of one kind, say material). The latter is quite compatible with monism. For there can be a plurality of things of one kind.) In other words, we might claim that there is an historically confirmed law that assertion of monism is followed by an assertion of pluralism. (I have heard it suggested by a philosopher that this is a tautology. But I fail to see that this is the case.)

One further example. In Greek philosophy the pre-Socratic cosmologies were followed by the sceptical questioning of the fifth century BC, and the speculative thought of Plato and Aristotle was followed by the scepticism which prevailed in the Platonic Academy until the revival of dogmatism. In the Middle Ages we find fourteenth-century thinkers criticizing metaphysical arguments advanced by their predecessors and restricting the scope of what could be known by philosophical reasoning. In the post-medieval world the succession of materialist systems was followed by Kant's questioning and rejection of rationalist metaphysics, while the metaphysical speculation of post-Kantian German idealism was followed by the 'back to Kant' movement. In Great Britain the synthesizing constructions of the idealists were succeeded by the analytic movement in its various forms. In China, when Confucianism came to develop cosmological and metaphysical speculation, this was interspersed from time to time by naturalistic and materialist lines of thought. We may thus be inclined to formulate the generalization that a metaphysical phase of thought is followed by a critical and questioning phase of thought, a generalization which permits us to predict that if a metaphysical phase of thought were to occur in the future, it would be followed by a critical phase of thought. There are indeed some inconvenient facts to take into consideration. For example, while there was apparently a sceptical line of thought in Indian philosophy, it preceded rather than followed the consolidation and development of the Vedic schools. But no doubt we could cope with such facts, if we wanted to do so.

It is doubtless arguable that in view of the differences between philosophies we should not speak of recurrent sequences in the historical development of philosophical thought. But let us assume that such sequences are in fact discernible. In this case we can formulate empirically based generalizations which have at any rate some predictive force, in the sense that they permit prediction that if *A* occurs, *B* will eventually occur. If, therefore, we are prepared to describe such generalizations as laws, it follows that we can formulate some laws relating to the history of philosophy.

Are Such Generalizations of Interest to the Philosopher?

The question arises, however, whether such laws or generalizations, 'universals of fact', are of any interest to the philosopher. True, a phrase such as 'being of interest' is relative, in the sense that it invites the question 'to whom?' If someone believes that history in general is governed by laws and that future historical events are predictable in principle, it may, of course, be of interest to him to discover laws relating to the development of philosophical thought, inasmuch as the history of philosophy is part of history in general. It can obviously be argued, however, that the historian of philosophy is interested not so much in monism as such as in particular systems, the philosophies of, say, Parmenides, Spinoza, Bradley and Śaṁkara. Just as the political and social historian is primarily interested in the American or French or Russian Revolution rather than in revolution as such, so is the historian of philosophy primarily interested in particular philosophies, as individual entities, and in the relations between them.

The reply can be made that the political and social historian generally confines his attention to a particular country or area or period, and that it goes without saying that an historian of the United States, for example, is interested in the American Revolution rather than in the French or Russian Revolution. But the universal historian or the philosopher of history may very well be interested in comparing revolutionary situations and their outcomes, and he might go on to try to formulate a law or laws based on his analysis. Similarly, the historian of early Greek philosophy is obviously interested in the philosophy of Parmenides rather than in that of Spinoza or Śaṁkara. But the student of comparative philosophy or the philosopher of the history of philosophy can obviously distinguish between types of philosophy, monism, pluralism, idealism of various kinds, materialism and so on, and there is no reason at all why he should not be interested in formulating generalizations on the basis of reflection on these types and the connections between them, generalizations which have some predictive force, even if a limited one. We should not talk about things being of interest, unless we are prepared to say to what class or classes of people we claim that they are interesting.

However this may be, it is difficult to conceive of a philosopher being interested in recurrent sequences as such. Let us assume that assertion of monism has in fact been regularly followed, sooner or later, by assertion or reassertion of pluralism. In this case assertion of pluralism has presumably been followed, sooner or later, by assertion or reassertion of monism. If, therefore, a recurrent sequence is the only factor to take into account, one might just as well predict that if pluralism occurs in the future, monism will also recur (other things being equal) as that if monism recurs, pluralism will also recur. If a philosopher is prepared to predict that if monism recurs, pluralism will also recur but is not prepared to predict that recurrence of pluralism would be followed by recurrence of monism, this is obviously because he regards monism as false and pluralism as true. A convinced monist would, of course, adopt a different position. In both cases prediction expresses a critical evaluation of philosophical theories. And if the philosophers in question were to formulate lawlike statements, these statements would reflect their respective evaluations.

There are indeed other possibilities. For example, someone might predict the recurrence of monism not because he believed that monism was true but because he thought that monism had a basis in psychology and that it was probable that there would continue to be people who, for psychological reasons, would be satisfied only with a monistic world view. But we cannot consider all possibilities here.

It is not intended to suggest that advertence to recurrent sequences in the history of philosophy would have no part to play in the reasoning of the philosophers whom we have imagined. For example, one might note cases in which assertion of monism has been followed, sooner or later, by reassertion of pluralism, seek for an explanation in the natures of these two types of philosophy, and then formulate a lawlike statement. Advertence to a recurrent sequence would then have a part to play in the process of reasoning. But the resulting lawlike statement would not be merely a generalization based simply on this advertence. It would be the fruit of the search for explanation, of a critical evaluation of the relevant types of philosophy. If, therefore, a convinced pluralist were to assert that recurrence of monism in the future would be followed by a reassertion of pluralism, he would really be claiming that monism was of such a kind that, given the fulfilment of certain conditions, such as the continuance of philosophical reflection, its assertion would sooner or later provoke or cause a reassertion of pluralism. If he formulated this point of view in a lawlike statement, we could regard the statement as part of or dependent on a philosophical theory.

In a work published in 1963 I suggested that we could hardly expect anything else in the future but 'a dialectical movement, a recurrence of certain fundamental tendencies and attitudes in different historical shapes' (*A History of Philosophy*, VII, pp. 440–1, London, 1963). By 'different historical shapes' I meant, of course, different philosophies. As for the tendencies, I was thinking of the tendency to raise metaphysical problems and to take them seriously and the tendency to believe that discussion of such problems is profitless and a waste of time. My prediction that expressions of these tendencies would recur was certainly partly based on reflection on historical data or phenomena. Referring to the dialectic between the two tendencies, I asserted that 'this is what we have had hitherto, in spite of well-intentioned efforts to bring the process to a close', and I cited two or three historical examples of the metaphysical tendency. Obviously, I could have mentioned a number of examples of both tendencies. At the same time I explicitly related the two tendencies in question to two aspects of the human being. In other words, my prediction that the dialectic between the two tendencies would continue was not simply the result of advertence to recurrent sequences in the history of philosophy. It was also the expression of a theory of man, of a philosophical anthropology. Indeed, it could be argued that I interpreted the historical data in the light of this theory. And if I had explicitly formulated a lawlike statement relating to the two tendencies, it would have reflected this theory. Other philosophers might reject the theory, interpret the significance of the historical data in a different way, and make a different prediction. It does not follow that there could be no discussion. The discussion, however, would presumably centre round the critical evaluation of certain philosophical theories. It is this, I have suggested, which is of real interest to philosophers. The question of laws is secondary.

The Covering Law Theory of Historical Explanation and the History of Philosophy

Why, however, should anyone even raise the question of laws in this context? The historian in the ordinary sense may report the formulation of laws. Thus the historian of England in the relevant period may report the formulation of Boyle's law and of Newton's universal of gravitation. But he does not usually spend time trying to formulate historical laws. He concentrates on telling his story. Similarly, the historian of philosophy obviously tries to show the connections between philosophies and movements which he believes to have been connected;

but he is not generally accustomed to concern himself with formulating laws relating to the development of philosophical thought, nor with prediction. He tells his own intelligible story, just as the political historian does. As he is doubtless something of a philosopher himself, he may include some critical evaluation of theories or arguments. But this is not the same thing as formulating laws. Is not this whole question of laws relating to the history of philosophy a contrived or artificial problem, which has little practical relevance?

There are several ways in which this question of laws might arise. For example, if we believed that there are historical laws and that history in general pursues a predictable course, it would be natural to assume that it is possible to discover laws relating to the development of philosophical thought, inasmuch as this development is part of history in general. If, however, we believe that human history is not governed by laws, we are likely to regard the question whether there are laws relating to the development of philosophical thought as superfluous, unless indeed some special reason can be given for raising the question in regard to this particular area.

The question might indeed arise, not because of any presuppositions about history in general, but as a result of advertence to recurrent sequences in the history of philosophy. To be sure, there is no recurrence or repetition in a literal sense. And if we press the statement that each thing is what it is and not something else, we may be inclined to claim that any talk about recurrence is unjustifiable. If, however, we are prepared to admit that one can discern similarities sufficient to justify talk about recurrent sequences, there is nothing very odd in raising the question whether reflection on such sequences enables us to formulate any laws or lawlike statements. This is the approach which has been adopted in this chapter.

There is, however, another possible approach, to which there has hitherto been no allusion. Some philosophers have maintained that there is only one model of explanation, deductive explanation, and that if historiography is a science, this model must be exemplified in historical explanation. That is to say, historical events are explained by showing that they follow from a set of premises which includes a general law or laws. (Obviously, an historical event cannot be deduced from a general law alone. The premises must also include statements relating to particular events.) As historians rarely refer explicitly to laws in their explanations of events, defenders of what is known as the covering law theory of historical explanation have maintained that what historians actually provide are usually sketches of explanations.

They appeal tacitly to laws, but the laws need to be made explicit if the sketches are to be filled out.

This is, of course, a very summary statement of the covering law theory, in which a lot of relevant points have been omitted. For example, if the model of explanation is believed to be exemplified primarily in physical science, we have to allow for the distinction (as Professor Carl G. Hempel has done) between nomological and probabilistic explanation. In the second type of explanation the relevant laws are statistical. But the matter cannot be pursued here. The point is that if we accept the covering law theory of historical explanation, and if we regard hsitorians of philosophy as undertaking to explain the development of philosophical systems and movements, we seem to be committed to inquiring whether the historiography of philosophy exemplifies the alleged model of explanation and to trying to identify the laws which historians of philosophy include, whether explicitly or implicitly, among the premises of their explanations. It may be objected that to act in this way is to express a prejudice, the presupposition that explanation in physical science is the only type of explanation. The covering law theorist would presumably reply that it is simply a case of the model of explanation having been most clearly exemplified in physical science.

If someone were to require an example of a serious attempt to apply the covering law theory of historical explanation to the history of philosophy, I admit that I could not cite one. But the subject has been introduced simply to indicate a way in which the question of laws relating to the development of philosophical thought could be raised. As for the substantive issue, let us now consider this briefly.

Given sufficient ingenuity, defenders of the covering law theory can make out a plausible case for claiming that the theory is verified in political and social historiography, and no doubt they could do the same in regard to the history of philosophy. For example, it could be argued that historians of philosophy presuppose and tacitly appeal to a number of empirical generalizations. Suppose, for instance, that a philosopher who is commonly recognized as an able and indeed outstanding thinker seems to have contradicted himself flatly and obviously, and that there is no good reason for claiming that he had simply changed his mind between making one statement and making the other. Before concluding that the philosopher was in fact guilty of a flagrant self-contradiction, the historian is likely to explore possibilities of reconciling the apparently conflicting statements. And the covering law theorist might argue that the historian tacitly appeals to the empirical generalization that thinkers of a certain calibre do not contradict themselves in ways which could hardly fail to be obvious to themselves. This is why the historian tries to dissolve the apparent contradiction, if he can find a reasonable way of doing so.

However this may be, the generalization in question surely expresses a conviction which the historian brings with him when he approaches his studies. In the course of life or experience we all form, even if not explicitly, certain generalizations which guide our expectations. And historians of philosophy are not exceptions. They do not approach these studies with empty minds. At the same time it is doubtful whether the presence of such generalizations or hypotheses are relevant to the theme which we have been discussing in this chapter. That is to say, generalizations or general impressions which the historian brings with him when he approaches his studies should not be confused with lawlike statements which he might wish to formulate as a result of his studies. We might also bear in mind the possibility that a statement to which the historian of philosophy is said to make tacit appeal may be entailed by our concept of philosophy.

Finally, the question of laws relating to the historical development of philosophical thought may be raised in the hope that if laws can be discovered, we shall be able to predict the future of philosophy. As indicated above, we cannot do much by way of prediction, beyond making certain conditional statements (of the 'if-then' type). Suppose that someone asks me what is coming next in philosophy. I might be prepared to state, in a very general way, in what direction philosophical thought is moving, much as I can say whether or not a nuclear war in the near future seems to me to be probable. But I do not know whether or not a nuclear war will eventually occur. Nor do I believe that there is any law which would enable me to make a reliable prophecy. Nor can I reveal the future of philosophy. Nor do I believe that any lawlike statements which reflection on the development of philosophical thought might justify me in making would enable me to have fore-knowledge of the future of philosophy. For one thing, there are many extra-philosophical factors which might affect the course of philo-sophical thought, factors which we are hardly in a position to foresee.

Epilogue

In the foregoing chapters certain conclusions, related to distinguishable questions, have been stated. For example, in the seventh chapter it has been argued that we can reasonably speak of advances in philosophy, in an evaluative sense of the word 'advance', even if we cannot think of criteria of advance which presuppose no value-judgement whatsoever. Advances can be of different kinds. For instance, Étienne Gilson argued, rightly in my opinion, that Abelard raised the standard of philosophical thinking in the Middle Ages. And it can reasonably be claimed that the modern analytic movement has done much to raise standards in clarity and precision of thought and language in modern western philosophy. Obviously, this claim presupposes that we value clarity and precision of thought. But what philosopher would be prepared to assert that he valued obscurity and imprecision of thought when clarity and precision were attainable? There can also, it has been argued, be advances in 'insight', and one or two examples were given. These examples were taken from western philosophy. But others could be found in the philosophies of other cultures. For instance, I would be prepared to argue that the tendency on the part of some Buddhist thinkers to reintroduce the concept of the person as that to which states should be ascribed expressed an insight into the difficulties raised by the theory of momentariness, by the reduction of the self to a succession of vanishing states.

It has also been argued that though philosophy has been influenced by a variety of non-philosophical factors, and though comprehensive world-views are inevitably historically conditioned in specifiable ways, to recognize this situation is not the same thing as to endorse a purely relativist theory of truth. If it were the same thing, then rejection of a purely relativist theory of truth would presumably entail refusal to admit a large number of what can properly be described as historical facts, a policy which is hardly to be recommended. The strength of cultural relativism is that it can appeal to a very great number of historical data. But it is not always very easy to make out precisely what cultural relativism is supposed to imply. It is one thing, for example, to maintain that the thought of Aristotle was historically conditioned in a variety of ways. It is another thing to maintain that no statement made by Aristotle was or could be true except relatively to his own time. It may be said that cultural relativism does not involve any such extravagant thesis. But if it is divorced from a purely relativist theory of truth, it becomes, in my opinion, innocuous.

In regard to the question whether or not a common recurrent pattern of development is discernible in the philosophies of different cultures, a question to which brief reference was made in the final chapter of this book, it is difficult to come to any definite conclusion. This may indeed seem to be a most unsatisfactory state of affairs. But there are good reasons for adopting this position. On the one hand, it is possible, for example, to make out a persuasive case for acceptance of the scheme proposed by Alois Dempf. On the other hand, it is possible to select for emphasis aspects of the historical development of philosophical thought which tell against Dempf's thesis. After all, it is a question of one common pattern of development recurring in the philosophies of all cultures which had a recognizable philosophical tradition. The area of thought to be covered is vast and complex. If there are rather different interpretations of Plato and Kant and Śaṁkara and other well-known individual philosophers, it is hardly a matter for surprise if there is also room for different interpretations in regard to a very much wider area, and if it is difficult to decide between these interpretations in any decisive manner.

If, however, the reader expects something more definite than this, I think it more probable that in the philosophies of different cultures we would find a complex pattern of similarities and dissimilarities than that we would find one overall common and recurrent pattern of development. Discussion of this topic requires a more extensive knowledge of the philosophies of different cultures than I would care to claim. And in any case it would not have been possible to discuss the matter properly in this book, unless it were devoted entirely to the subject and were much larger than it is. However, eagerness to find a common recurrent pattern of development in the philosophies of different cultures is probably connected with a desire to formulate laws which will enable us to predict. This is a project with which I do not feel any passionate concern. In the final chapter it was stated that while I am prepared to admit that some law-like statements can be made on the basis of reflection on the history of philosophy, I am doubtful about their predictive value. To predict, for example, that if monism were to recur, a pluralist reaction would follow, is hardly to throw much light on the actual course which philosophical thought will pursue.

In regard to philosophy in India, I would like to draw attention to the following 'conclusion' or reflection. It is a great mistake to think of all Indian philosophers as preoccupied with mystical self-identification with the Absolute. As we have seen, the majority of the Indian schools were pluralist, and even in the Vedānta school there was a reaction against monism. Further, the philosophers, including those of the Vedānta school, developed serious arguments to support their theories. This can be seen clearly enough in the area of epistemology or theory of knowledge. It is important that this aspect of Indian thought should be underlined. Tominaga Nakamoto (1715–46), a Japanese scholar and merchant who lived at Osaka, emphasized what he considered to be the Indian inclination to mysticism, a characteristic which he ascribed to geography and climate. And in the West there is certainly a tendency to associate the thought of India with that of gurus, rope-tricks, the practice of yoga, and mystical absorption in the One. Precisely because of this tendency it is necessary, when we are talking about philosophy, to insist that the Indian philosophers were serious thinkers, who knew perfectly well how to distinguish between good and bad arguments. To be sure, no account of Indian philosophy could be adequate, if it were to pass over any mention of the religious orientation of so much of Indian thought. Generally speaking, the philosophers of India looked on the human being as having a destiny which transcended the confines of this world of time and change. But it by no means follows that the systems of the schools were based simply on hunches and mystical intuitions, lacking any strong intellectual backbone. This was far from being the case.

When treating of China, we drew attention to a feature of Chinese philosophy which must indeed be obvious to any student of this subject, namely the prominent emphasis placed on the human being's life in this world. This is particularly evident in the case of Confucianism, in which stress was laid on man in his social relations. But even in Taoist philosophy, with its ideal of being at one with the universe or with nature, the emphasis was on man's free development in this world, not on a future life. Further, though Buddhism was indeed in a sense other-worldly, in Buddhist thought as it developed in China prominence was given to the attainment of enlightenment in this life and to the idea that the life of the enlightened person need not differ in any external way from the life of the unenlightened. In Ch'an Buddhism we can see an 'inculturated' Buddhism, a form of Buddhism which was more adapted to the Chinese mentality and outlook than the Buddhism which had been imported from India.

In his work *Ways of Thinking of Eastern Peoples*, Professor Hajime Nakamura speaks of the introspective nature of classical Indian philosophy (as shown, for example, in the development of reflective psychology and theory of knowledge) and its metaphysical-religious orientation, traits which he contrasts with emphasis on the perception of the concrete and the practical and anthropocentric character of Chinese thought, as well as with the Japanese tendency to see the human being in terms of membership of a limited society. Other writers have referred to what they believe to be the emphasis placed in the West on the individual as an autonomous agent, an emphasis which they have contrasted with Chinese and Japanese stress on social relationships and with Indian emphasis on the universal self at the expense of the individual self.

Generalizations of this sort are apt to arouse in the mind various qualifications and reservations. For example, any picture of Indian philosophy as emphasizing the universal self at the expense of the individual self obviously reflects concentration of attention on the Advaita Vedānta, as though this were the only Indian philosophy. Again, any picture of western thought as emphasizing the individual at the expense of social relationships stands in need of a good deal of qualification. At the same time there certainly have been rather different views of the human being, rather different philosophical anthropologies. In one sense we obviously all know the answer to the question, what is man? That is to say, we can all point out human beings and distinguish them from elephants. Even those philosophers who deny that there is any such thing as human nature are as capable as the next man of distinguishing between the Africans in Africa and the lions in Africa. When, however, it is a case of answering the question in terms of an explicit account of man's nature and potentialities and his place in the world, there can be and have been rather different accounts, in which the emphasis is differently placed. Here, it seems, there is room for open-minded discussion between East and West. Different peoples have their different traditions, customs, religious beliefs and social and political institutions. But they all consist of human beings. And the question, what is man? is important for them all. In this book we have referred several times to the need for a philosophical anthropology. Obviously, it is not intended to imply that there have been no philosophical anthropologies up to date. For there certainly have been and are such anthropologies. There is room, however, for collaboration between eastern and western thinkers in this matter. Some work has already been done on these lines. To take but one example, a conference between eastern and western philosophers resulted in a composite volume entitled *The Status of The Individual in East and West* (edited by C. A. Moore). But there is doubtless much more to be done by way of examining which apparently different views can be regarded as complementary, discussing points of divergence and trying to assess the principles on which a more synoptic view or theory might be developed.

Why is the expression a 'philosophical' anthropology used here? One reason has been mentioned in this book. In the West the human being has become the subject of a variety of disciplines which consider different aspects of the human being, physiological, psychological and social, and which are regarded as scientific disciplines. There is thus a certain fragmentation; and there is need for an overall view which goes beyond the limits of any particular scientific discipline. It is not intended to imply that there are no true statements which can be made about the human being antecedently (from a logical point of view) to the development of the particular sciences or, for the matter of that, to the comparative study of different philosophical traditions. At the same time it is essential that the findings of the sciences which relate to the human being should be taken into account in the development of a philosophical anthropology. They should not be ignored, on the ground that philosophy is something different from science. If this means that the philosophical anthropology will be to some extent provisional or subject to revision, in the way in which scientific hypotheses are in principle revisable, this is not sufficient reason for treating the scientific knowledge of the time as though it did not exist.

There are, however, aspects of man, of his experience and activities, which fall outside the scope of particular scientific disciplines, partly if not wholly. And reflection on different philosophical traditions can help to remind us of such factors, a reminder which is especially necessary if we are in any danger of believing in the omnicompetence of science or of subscribing to a narrow positivism. For one thing, the human being is a being in a world. Man has developed in time, in history, manifesting a succession of needs and of potentialities. And reflection on the nature and development of the human being leads on to reflection on his relations to reality in general, as known or knowable by us. Emphasis on the idea and desirability of philosophical anthropology should not be understood as equivalent to the suggestion that the philosopher should confine his or her attention to the human being simply as such and eschew all questions which would commonly be regarded as metaphysical. It is the human being, however, who raises such questions, in the light of human experience. The approach is from the side of man, and the problems which he raises reflect in some way or other his needs and potentialities. To put the matter in another way, all language-games, as was maintained in the fourth chapter, are expressions of human language, and all 'forms of life' (in the sense of the language-games theory) are forms of human life. It is natural, therefore, to start with the human being, the questioner.

Inter-cultural dialogue on the subject of the human being is regarded here as being simply one factor which is capable of contributing, on the level of philosophical thought, to furthering mutual understanding between peoples belonging to different cultures, and so to the development of a pluralistic world-society. In regard to the desirability of such a society, as distinct from an imperialism writ large or a world-wide totalitarianism, the present writer finds himself in agreement with Bertrand Russell. As for the possibility of mutual understanding between peoples with different cultural traditions, something has already been said about this theme, which need not be repeated here. It may, however, be as well to make it clear that I am not blind to the difficulties. I give what may seem to be a rather extreme example. Some years ago I had a conversation with a Japanese Buddhist university professor who asked me why, in my opinion, western philosophers were, for the most part, wedded to the idea that being is prior to not-being, and why they lay so much stress on the principle of non-contradiction. Being myself wedded to the idea that not-being (in a literal sense) generates nothing (does not generate anything, that is to say), and being accustomed to think that the presence of contradictions in one's thought is not something to rejoice over enthusiastically, I was somewhat nonplussed. Surmising, however, that the good professor was thinking of the Absolute, described as Emptiness or the Void, I made some distinctions which seemed to me appropriate. My friend's reply, though expressed much more politely, amounted to saying, 'there you go again, trying to iron out apparent contradictions. It is precisely this mentality which I am challenging'. In a situation such as this one may feel that an insurmountable barrier to understanding has been encountered. But this is not, I think, the case. Apart from the fact that it is a salutary experience to hear one's own way of thought called in question, any way of thought, if it is a way of thought at all, is intelligible in principle. The strange is not necessarily unintelligible. The Japanese professor evidently assumed that explanatory reasons could be given for what he took to be common presuppositions of western philosophers. And it should also be assumed that explanatory reasons can be given for points of view which we may find strange. It does not follow that if we can discover the reasons, we shall then agree with the point of view in question. But understanding and agreement are not the same thing. It may happen that a statement made by an oriental philosopher, if translated literally into English, sounds pretty well nonsensical. But we have to ask why it is made and examine the background. What is required is dialogue in depth.

It is open to anyone to comment that the Japanese professor evidently had in mind Buddhist theories which probably mean little to the bulk of the Japanese population nowadays, and that it is a mistake to imagine that one is promoting understanding among peoples by trying to understand philosophies, the influence of which is diminishing or even rapidly disappearing. While, however, it is undoubtedly true that we can hardly do much to promote understanding among peoples if we take it for granted that they presuppose doctrines or theories which have lost their hold on their minds, we should recall the point made in the preface to this book, that though systems come and go it may very well be possible to see in the philosophical tradition of a culture the expression of ways of thought which persist and which outlive their more or less transient embodiments. To gain a clear view of these persistent elements seems to be a main task of the comparative study of philosophy. Obviously, fulfilment of this task would not, by itself, produce peace and harmony in the world. But it can contribute, even if only to a very limited degree, to mutual understanding. For all we know, what K'ang Yu-wei called the Age of Great Peace may never be attained in history. But this possibility is no sufficient reason for making no efforts to attain it. And philosophers can, in various ways, make a modest contribution. It is not a question of demanding that every philosopher should have this end in view. Rather is it a question of seeing certain lines of philosophical (or meta-philosophical) reflection within a wider context.

Finally, it was stated at the end of the preface to this book that 'East is East and West is West' is a tautology. A verbal tautology, however, can be used to assert or imply something, something substantial. Imagine someone who is used to dogs but has recently acquired a cat. And suppose that he or she is so foolish as to expect the cat to behave in a manner appropriate to a dog, by eating, for example, food which is suitable for a dog but not for a cat. If one were to say to the person 'dogs are dogs and cats are cats', this might be a way of reminding him or her that dogs and cats are different species and that one should not expect them to behave in the same way. As for 'East is East and West is West', this might be a way of saying or implying that there are two different ways of thought, eastern and western. If so, the implication would be highly questionable, not to say downright untrue. In the philosophical field we can find ideas and lines of thought in an Oriental culture which bear more resemblance to analogous ideas or lines of thought in western philosophy than they do to some other lines of thought in the Oriental culture in question. For example, there is more affinity between materialism in India and western materialism than there is between Indian materialism and the philosophy of the Advaita Vedānta. Again, there is more affinity between the philosophies of Nāgārjuna and Śaṁkara on the one hand and the philosophies of Plotinus and Bradley on the other than there is between either group and materialism, whether western or eastern. This complex pattern of affinities, of similarities and dissimilarities, forms a basis for inter-cultural dialogue, which would be lacking if there were two monolithic ways of thinking, eastern and western, alien to one another and in mutual opposition. It may be said that, given the diversity of thought in both West and East, there is plenty of scope for discussion or dialogue without introducing the idea of inter-cultural dialogue. This is doubtless true. At the same time recognizable affinities between lines of thought in East and West can co-exist not only with differences in context or background but also with specifiable differences between the lines of thought in question. So there is not only ample scope for but also a need for inter-cultural dialogue, not with a view to producing a kind of patchwork syncretism but with a view, in the first instance, to mutual understanding, an understanding which may bring to the notice of both sides points of view or factors to which they have paid insufficient attention. The need is not, of course, all on one side. When Professor Fung Yu-lan was urging the reconstruction of Neo-Confucianism, he drew attention to the need for western logical analysis. When Nishida Kitarō (1870–1945), who is generally considered to have been the leading Japanese philosopher since the opening to the West, was engaged in rethinking the Buddhist philosophy of 'Emptiness' or 'the Void', he turned to western philosophy, from Plato up to modern phenomenology, for ideas relating to method. In the West examples of direct influence by eastern thought are indeed relatively few. The philosophy of Schopenhauer is probably the most conspicuous example. Apart, however, from direct influence, there are some recognizable affinities. Thus an affinity has been seen between the thought of Martin

Heidegger and Taoism. And it has even been argued that there is an affinity between some of Wittgenstein's ideas and Zen Buddhism. It is indeed understandable that this last contention has provoked a counter-argument, which may very well be valid. But the point is that if the East can learn from the West, as it undoubtedly can, we cannot exclude the possibility that the West may have something to learn from the thought of other cultures. In regard to philosophical anthropology, we may tend to think that western ideas must prevail throughout the world, inasmuch as it is in the West that the particular sciences relating to man have developed. Though, however, we cannot set limits in advance to the progress of any particular science within its own field, it by no means follows that any particular science, or even all the particular sciences together, can give us a comprehensive and adequate interpretation of the human being. And inter-cultural dialogue can serve the very useful purpose of bringing a diversity of aspects to the attention of participants, to the enrichment of the thought of all. It may seem that the present writer has 'a bee in his bonnet' on the subject of philosophical anthropology. But when we talk about the future of the world, we are presumably talking about the future of man, of the human being. How we think about man is not a trivial matter. All efforts at social engineering, all attacks on social engineering, pre-suppose ideas of man, even if these ideas are not made fully explicit. Further, such ideas can have world-wide repercussions. There is need, therefore, for inter-cultural dialogue, in which philosophers can and should play a part.

Obviously, I am presupposing judgements of value, about what is desirable. What is actually going to happen, we do not know. The human race, for all we know, may blot itself out or be reduced to a very primitive condition. Or we may fall victim to some world-wide tyranny. Neither possibility is, in my judgement, desirable. What is desirable is the progressive formation of a world-wide pluralistic society, in which respect would be held for different cultural traditions. It may seem absurd to suggest that the comparative study of philosophy can contribute in any measure to the attainment of this goal. It sometimes seems absurd to the present writer. The fact remains, however, that the goal can be attained only through the co-operation of many elements. And unless we despair of philosophy altogether or think that it is a game which has no social implications, we should be prepared to envisage philosophers as making some contribution, even if only a modest one, to the development of a truly human society.

There was a Chinese philosopher, Wang Yuo-wei (1877–1927), who abandoned philosophy for literature at the age of thirty, on the ground that the theories which he found attractive were incredible, whereas the theories which he found credible were repugnant. This is understandable. But as Chinese thinkers were quick to see, philosophical thought can have practical implications, an aspect of the matter which they were inclined to emphasize or even over-emphasize. For good or for evil philosophy has effects. Philosophers differ in their opinions about what effects are desirable. This is all the more reason for open-minded discussion or dialogue. If value-judgements are involved, as they certainly are, this does not mean that profitable discussion is ruled out. For there can be rational discussion of judgements of value. It may indeed be possible to envisage cases in which people are so diametrically opposed in their basic judgements of value that they have either to break off discussion or have recourse to abuse. But I think that such a situation is most unlikely to arise in the sort of inter-cultural dialogue which I have in mind.

Notes

CHAPTER 1 (pp. 1–19)

1 As an example of a psychological study of a philosopher, we can mention *Nietzsche: The Story of a Human Philosopher* by H. A. Reyburn, with the collaboration of H. B. Hinderks and J. G. Taylor (London, 1948). More profound is Karl Jaspers' existentialist study, *Nietzsche: An Introduction to The Understanding of His Philosophical Activity*, translated by C. F. Wallraff and F. J. Schmitz (Tucson, Arizona, 1965).

2 'Chief' in view of its subject-matter, God's revelation of himself and his redemptive work; 'science' not simply in the sense of a source of knowledge but also in the sense that while the premises of theology were regarded as revealed truths, the method was represented as conforming to the Aristotelian concept of science. There was indeed some controversy about whether theology should be described as being primarily a theoretical or a practical science. But we cannot pursue this theme here.

3 In a 1929 manifesto of the Vienna Circle (ascribed to Hahn, Neurath and Carnap) the development of 'the scientific conception of the world' was connected with such factors as dissatisfaction with traditional theological beliefs and even the modern process of production with its increasing mechanization, which was said to leave progressively less room for metaphysics.

4 To speak precisely, this statement expresses an interpretation rather than a 'bare' or 'naked' fact. In comparison, however, with obviously divergent interpretations one can reasonably speak of an historical fact.

CHAPTER 2 (pp. 20–38)

1 The dates of Śaṃkara's birth and death, like so many other dates in Indian history up to relatively modern times, are uncertain. The earlier Upanishads were composed between 800 and 400 BC. The Buddha's dates are generally given as about 563–483 BC. Vardhamāna, the 'Great Hero' of Jainism, lived about 500 BC, but Jainism seems to have originated long before his time. Materialism was probably present at any rate from the sixth century BC. The Vedic philosophies became definite systems after the time of the Buddha, but their roots go back to an earlier period. Sāṃkhya is said to be the earliest Vedic philosophical system.

2 This statement has to be qualified. The holy or enlightened person was supposed to be able to perceive the atoms by means of non-sensory perception.

3 When talking of inferential knowledge, Kumārila, the Mīmāmsā philosopher, laid emphasis on the element of novelty. That is to say, he thought of inference as a source of fresh or additional knowledge.

4 I say 'it', as the concept of a personal God is, for Śaṁkara, an appearance of the Absolute. We can refer to Saguna-Brahman, the personal creator, as 'he'; but Saguna-Brahman is the appearance of the suprapersonal Nirguna-Brahman. If, therefore, we are talking about metaphenomenal reality, it seems preferable to use the pronoun 'it' rather than 'he'.

5 The Advaitins were inclined to speak as though the nature of the empirical world as appearance could be known by reasoning. Critics objected that we could not know this without knowing Brahman (Reality as opposed to Appearance), and that on Advaitin premises this was not possible.

6 What Śaṁkara has to say on this subject invites comparison with statements made by St. Augustine and Descartes.

7 Śaṁkara's doctrine of *ātman* invites comparison (contrast too perhaps) with the western theory of the pure or transcendental ego as found, for example, in the philosophy of Fichte.

8 The Dvaita Vedānta philosophers, such as Madhva, rejected the theory of degrees of truth and reality.

9 In the early Vedic period the prevailing concept seems to have been that of immortality, in the sense of the soul passing at death to the abode of the gods. Belief in rebirth, in a succession of terrestrial lives, was a later development. But it was accepted by all schools except the materialist school. The belief seems to have been grounded on, or at any rate clearly connected with, ethical ideas. What a person is depends on his or her actions in a previous life; and the effects of actions in any given life must work themselves out, until there are no longer any bad effects or demerits.

CHAPTER 3 (pp. 39–58)

1 More accurately, it was preoccupied with prolongation of life in this world and with means to achieve this end.

2 It is recorded that in the year 2 BC a Chinese official received instruction in Buddhism from a foreign traveller, perhaps from north-west India. In any case Buddhism was present in China in the first century AD.

3 The adoption of Confucianism as a state or official philosophy in 136 BC did not mean that other traditions were proscribed. Nor did it mean that Confucianism was regarded as a state religion. When a constitution was being drafted after the establishment of the republic in 1912, K'ang Yu-wei tried to have Confucianism recognized as the state religion, but his efforts were unsuccessful.

4 Perhaps one ought to say 'Marxism-Leninism-Maoism', but this is rather a mouthful.

5 Underlying the use of analogies we can see a view of the unity of the world.

6 'White' signifies a colour, 'horse' a nature. The statement was possibly a means of drawing attention to a distinction between a thing and its qualities. Such paradoxes may have been intended to indicate that spatial and temporal distinctions are relative, or perhaps even that they are unreal.

7 Fung Yu-lan eventually turned towards Marxism, under pressure if I am not mistaken. He then maintained that his previous thought, inspired by Neo-Confucianism, represented the twilight of the old Chinese philosophy.

8 The logicians of this school were indeed partly concerned with 'the rectification of names' (making names and actualities correspond), an idea which was given a moral and social application by Confucius and his disciples. But the members of the School of Names seem to have interested themselves only in the logical aspects of the idea.

9 Metal, wood, water, fire, and earth.

10 The period of disunity should not be imagined as involving a relapse into barbarism. Irrigation works were undertaken and commerce developed. We can also mention that what is known as the 'Warring States' period (about 403 until 222 BC), to distinguish it from the preceding 'spring and autumn' period, came after the death of Confucius.

11 The injunction in Ode 235 not to mind the ancestors has caused commentators some difficulty. It is assumed here that the original injunction was indeed not to mind the ancestors.

12 It might perhaps be suggested that the One was a projection of the ideal of social unity. But the character of early Taoist thought militates against any such interpretation.

13 By Fung Yu-lan, for example.

14 The word *jen* was used by Confucius sometimes to mean benevolence or love in particular and sometimes to mean virtue in general, the quality of 'humanity' or 'human-heartedness'.

15 Hsün Tzu can be said to have represented a naturalistic tendency in Confucianism. For him Heaven was more akin to nature than to a divine being. In fact he denied the existence of spiritual beings and human immortality.

16 For Confucius 'Heaven' retained something of the meaning of a personal supreme Lord. He can certainly not be described as irreligious. But he avoided talking about spiritual beings, the spirits of the ancestors and life after death.

17 Mo Tzu's dates cannot be determined with certainty. He seems to have been born before the death of Confucius, but at any rate he lived shortly after Confucius.

18 Somewhat oddly, the Mohists insisted on the existence of spiritual beings, while sharply criticizing the expense of rites in their honour. The Mohists accused the Confucianists of encouraging expensive rites and ceremonies, while not believing in the existence of the beings in whose honour the rites were offered.

19 *Tao*, the Way, is also used to signify that of which the Way is the Way.

20 The One is not *a* thing, this rather than that. In this sense it is nameless. It is, however, immanent in all things, even, as is stated in the *Chuang Tzu*, in excrement and urine. When in the *Lao Tzu* it is said that Heaven and Earth are not humane but regard all things as straw dogs, and that the sage too looks on people in the same way, this should not be taken as advocating inhumanity, in the sense of unkindness or cruelty. What is meant is that Heaven and Earth are not choosy, so to speak, and that the sage too sees all people as expressions of reality.

21 The term 'human nature' (*hsing*) could obviously be used in a broader sense, to include desire and feeling. As used in a narrower sense, it meant human nature as possessing the Confucian virtues, such as benevolence (see note 14), embryonically or potentially.

22 There were, however, some naturalistically-minded Confucianists who had little use for the idea of Heaven willing anything at all.

23 This idea was not a novelty. In the *Lao Tzu* the *Tao* was described as void or empty, while in the *Chuang Tzu* (e.g. Ch. 12) it is said that the *Tao* originates from non-being (though this is not the only way of speaking). Kuo Hsiang objected that being cannot originate from not-being.

24 In this talk about 'Mind' we can presumably see the influence of Mahāyāna Buddhism. As for consciousness, this arose only in conjunction with material force.

25 On this subject see p. 56.

26 I owe this distinction to Professor Fung Yu-lan. 'Buddhism in China' refers to Buddhism as imported from India, whereas 'Chinese Buddhism' means Buddhism as absorbed into the culture.

27 On this subject see the writings of Joseph Needham, such as *Science and Civilization in China, Vol. 2: History of Scientific Thought,* and *Clerks and Craftsmen in China and the West.*

28 The Chinese had mechanical clocks, though pretty cumbersome ones, before the Jesuit Matteo Ricci arrived in China, bringing clocks and other instruments, towards the end of the sixteenth century. Ricci died at Pekin in 1610.

CHAPTER 4 (pp. 59–76)

1 *Rig-Veda*, I, 164,46 (edited by K. F. Geldner, Harvard 1951).

2 Some of the texts classified as Upanishads were composed very much later. The *Vedānta* or 'end of the Veda' consists of the earlier texts.

3 *Early Buddhist Theory of Knowledge*, p. 170

4 The word 'Yogic' is here used in a general sense. In the course of time a distinct Yoga school emerged and developed (generally associated with the Sāṁkhya school), but the word 'Yogic' is sometimes used, as here, not in the restricted sense of the techniques employed by the Yoga school but in a wider sense, to cover inward-turning contemplation in general, the search for the ultimate reality within the self.

5 *Atman* is not 'appearance'. The individual empirical self is purely phenomenal, but not the inner, permanent self, *ātman*, which is one with Brahman.

6 For Spinoza, the Many are already, so to speak, modes of the one Substance. But they are not necessarily recognized as such. The theory of levels or degrees of knowledge is an important feature of Spinoza's philosophy.

7 Śaṁkara had not the slightest intention of destroying religion. He was a religious reformer and is said to have founded several monasteries. He did not wish to deprive people of their devotional religion. Still, Madhva could of course claim that acceptance of the idea of the supra-personal Absolute was not compatible with the right religious attitude, as he understood it.

8 Madhva was inclined to consign to hell those of whom he strongly disapproved. Among well-known Indian thinkers he seems to have been the only one to have embraced belief in unending punishment. Some writers have assumed that he borrowed the doctrine of hell from Christianity. This would have been possible, but possibility alone is not sufficient to warrant a categorical statement that A borrowed an idea from B.

9 It is worth noting that for Rāmānuja, and for Madhva later on, Māyā, sometimes translated as 'illusion', meant not illusion but the creative power of God. For neither thinker was the world unreal. Nor of course was Spinoza's *Natura Naturata* unreal.

10 Influential among the Indian intellectuals, that is. The Advaita Vedānta obviously had a limited appeal.

11 *Buddhism: Its Essence and Development*, p. 11.

12 Mahāyāna Buddhist thinkers were inclined to claim that their teaching expressed an esoteric doctrine imparted by the Buddha to chosen disciples at the close of his life, and that Hīnayāna Buddhism represented a stage on the way. The mere fact that they made such a claim indicates an awareness of the difference between their speculations and what others claimed to be the genuine doctrine of the Buddha.

13 It was maintained that those who attained Buddhahood were capable of remembering past lives.

14 There is a marked similarity between Zen insistence on the immanence of the Buddha-nature and Taoist doctrine. Zen's predecessor in China, Ch'an Buddhism, was influenced by Taoism.

15 'Meditation' is a misleading word. For it suggests the idea of discursive thinking, whereas *zazen* demanded the abandonment of discursive thinking. *Zazen* was regarded not so much as a preparation for enlightenment as being itself enlightenment.

16 Cf. chapters (*suras*) 14,16,45,61. It seems to me that the Koran clearly presupposes that man is free to obey or disobey. The Mu'tazilite theologians, however, who emphasized human freedom and the power of reason, were thought by their conservative colleagues to be guilty of contaminating religious orthodoxy.

17 At the time some Neoplatonist treatises were wrongly ascribed to Aristotle. Besides, there were the Neoplatonist commentators on Aristotle.

18 See *Averroes on the Harmony of Religion and Philosophy*, translated with introduction and notes, by G. F. Hourani. Incidentally, it is incorrect to attribute to Averroes, as some writers have done, the view that a proposition can be both true and false at the same time.

19 Al-Ghazālī, himself a philosopher, made a systematic attack on Al-Fārābi and Avicenna. Averroes wrote a reply; not that this prevented his coming under suspicion for his own views.

20 Some years ago the present writer had some conversation with a Muslim from Pakistan, who occupied a high position in the educational world and who thought in precisely this way.

21 Ch. 50.

22 Born in Spain, Ibn 'Arabī was present at the funeral of Averroes, after which he went eastwards. He died at Damascus.

23 Al-Fārābi found room for prophecy. But he regarded prophetic revelation as impressed on the prophet's imagination and thus as expressing itself in symbols which were suited for people in general and which could stimulate them to action.

24 This has happened of course in individual cases. But the reference above is to philosophical thought in general. It seems to me that the continued viability of Islam on the intellectual level depends largely on the rethinking of its religiously orientated philosophy. This was more or less the view advanced by Mohammed Iqbāl (1877–1938), a Muslim philosopher of Pakistan, in his *Reconstruction of Religious Thought in Islam* (London, 1951).

25 With some theologians there was a desire to free Christian faith and theology from what they regarded as the contamination of Graeco-Islamic metaphysics. Also operative, however, was a more rigorous idea of what constituted a proof, a logical demonstration. This can be seen, for instance, in the thought of Nicholas of Autrecourt. Some of his ideas can be labelled as 'empiricist', as far as content is concerned. But his approach was logical. Has this or that theory been proved, in any strict sense of 'proof'?

26 Are we to take it that while first-order language is not understandable by those who do not participate in the relevant form of life, talk about the second order language is understandable? It seems to me difficult to see how this can be the case. If, for example, the language of Christian theology is regarded as a second-order language, how can it be understood if the first-order language is not understood?

27 It may be said that I ought not to introduce the subject of beliefs at this point, on the ground, for example, that first-order religious language is the language of praise and prayer, not of beliefs. But prayer to God presumably implies belief that there is a God to pray to, unless indeed one chooses to interpret the relevant utterances as having a purely pragmatic function of stimulating human beings to act in certain ways which are considered desirable.

28 *Philosophical Investigations*, translated by G. E. M. Anscombe, Part I, 23 (2nd edition, Oxford 1972). In the actual context Wittgenstein clearly

thinks of language-games in terms of such diverse linguistic operations as asserting, commanding, etc. But the common practice of extending the concept to distinctions between, say, religious language, the language of morals, and the language of aesthetic experience does not seem to be an illegitimate extension of the concept.

29 When Neo-Confucianists criticized Buddhism adversely, it was precisely to alleged social ill-effects that they drew attention, primarily at any rate. In some religions much less is demanded by way of assent to beliefs than in other religions.

30 I certainly do not intend to imply that at any given time a final and definitive synthesis can be constructed, which can then be handed on from generation to generation, as though it were the last word. I do not think this. But serious attempts at synthesis seem to me to be demanded by the nature of understanding, which calls for synthesis as well as analysis.

CHAPTER 5 (pp. 77–98)

1 The view of *purusha* as inactive was one of the Sāmkhya theories attacked by Madhva, the Dvaita Vedānta philosopher.

2 The 'clear' or 'refined' part of material force was said to form the human being's 'vital force', which belonged to the heavenly part of the soul.

3 I do not mean to imply that the historian of philosophy is debarred from critical discussion and evaluation. Historians of philosophy are always philosophers in some degree and are obviously interested in questions of truth or falsity. To what extent they include critical discussion depends very largely on practical considerations, such as their purpose in writing.

CHAPTER 6 (pp. 99–119)

1 By using the term 'historical data' I do not intend to commit myself to the claim that there are 'naked' historical facts, devoid of any element of interpretation. We can, however, distinguish between a large-scale interpretation scheme and the material which is fitted into the scheme.

2 Marx did not blame philosophers for having tried to understand the world. What he insisted on was the practical orientation of knowledge, the so-called unity of theory and practice. To represent him as questioning the value of knowledge would be to misrepresent him.

3 The question can be raised, in what sense, if any, can we successfully distinguish between history and historiography? Consideration of this question pertains to critical philosophy of history.

4 New York, 1959. It is not clear why in this book Father D'Arcy chooses to regard the terms 'philosophy of history' and 'historicism' as having one and the same meaning.

CHAPTER 7 (pp. 120–140)

1 This point has, of course, been made by a number of writers, for example by Antony Flew in his work *An Introduction to Western Philosophy*, pp. 21–3 (London, 1971).

2 It may be said that this statement is necessarily true in virtue of the meanings attached to the symbols. This is doubtless the case. At the same time we are talking about consciousness (is there any), not about the word 'consciousness', considered, as Ockham would put it, as standing for itself.

CHAPTER 8 (pp. 141–161)

1 The phrase 'challenge and response' is obviously borrowed from Toynbee. But it is used simply to illustrate a point, not to attack Toynbee, who was obviously interested in identifying particular challenges, responses and failures to respond in the lives of particular civilizations.

2 In the book mentioned above Dempf understood 'Chinese philosophy' as not extending beyond the first century BC. In his opinion there was as yet insufficient scholarly material available for him to be able to deal adequately with later Chinese thought.

3 This view seems to have been an element in Ockham's thought. But there are other fourteenth-century philosophers, such as Nicholas of Autrecourt, whose criticism of previous metaphysical theories and arguments was obviously inspired by a strict idea of what constituted a demonstrative proof and by empiricist tendencies, rather than by concern with liberating Christian theology from alien influences.

4 This does not necessarily mean that a law must be deducible from a higher law, in the way in which Kepler's laws were deduced by Newton from his general laws of motion. For there may be laws which function, at any rate for the time being, as ultimate. As for the distinction between experimental laws and theories, some philosophers have maintained that theories include terms referring to unobservables, whereas experimental laws do not. Other philosophers have argued that this distinction between observables and unobservables is relative, and that it cannot be made precise.

5 Some philosophers have argued that if a 'law' expresses simply observed factual regularities ('universals of fact'), it cannot restrict possibility, inasmuch as it does not cover unrealized instances. There must, therefore, be an element of necessity in laws. Philosophers, however, who defend a Humean line of thought and are unwilling to recognize this element of necessity, try to show that even if laws express observed regularities, they can none the less cover unrealized instances and so restrict the field of possibility. This is another indication of an area of dispute in discussion of the concept of law.

Bibliography

This bibliography is confined to books available in English and, with one or two exceptions, to books dealing with Indian, Chinese and Islamic philosophy. It is not intended to be exhaustive. No articles are mentioned.

A. GENERAL WORKS IN COMPARATIVE PHILOSOPHY

Gilson, E., *The Unity of Philosophical Experience*. London, 1955. (Treats of western philosophy only.)

Hajime Nakamura, *Ways of Thinking of Eastern Peoples, India, China, Tibet, Japan*. Revised English translation, edited by P. P. Wiener. Honolulu, 1964. (A pioneer work, in which the author relates thought to language.)

Northrop, F. S. C., *The Meeting of East and West*. Princeton (N.J.), 1946.

Moore, C. A. (editor), *Philosophy: East and West*. Princeton (N.J.), 1941. *Essays in East-West Philosophy*. Honolulu, 1949. *Philosophy and Culture–East and West*. Honolulu, 1959. *The Status of the Individual in East and West*. Honolulu, 1968. (These volumes contain contributions to successive East-West Philosophers' Conferences at Honolulu.)

Radhakrishnan, S., *Eastern Religions and Western Thought*. Oxford, 1939. *A Guide to Oriental Classics*, edited by W. T. de Bary and A. T. Embree. New York and London, 1975.

B. INDIAN PHILOSOPHY

1. General Works

Bowes, P., *The Hindu Religious Tradition. A Philosophical Approach*. London, 1977.

Chatterjee, S. C. and Datta, D. M., *An Introduction to Indian Philosophy*. Calcutta, 1939.

Danto, A. C., *Mysticism and Morality: Oriental Thoughts and Moral Philosophy*. New York, 1972.

Dasgupta, S. N., *A History of Indian Philosophy*. 5 vols. Cambridge, 1951–5. (A standard work on the subject.)

Hiriyanna, M., *The Essentials of Indian Philosophy*. London, 1949. *Outlines of Indian Philosophy*. London, 1958 (4th impression). (Good introductions to the subject.)

Hopkins, E. W., *Ethics of India*. New Haven, 1924.

Matilal, B. K. *Epistemology, Logic and Grammar in Indian Philosophical Analysis*. The Hague and Paris, 1971.

Morgan, K. W. (editor), *The Religion of the Hindus*. New York, 1953.

Potter, K. H., *Presuppositions of India's Philosophies*. New York, 1963.

Radhakrishnan, S., *History of Indian Philosophy*. 2 vols. London, 1962. (By a distinguished Indian philosopher.)

Sinari, R. A., *The Structure of Indian Thought*. Springfield (Ill.), 1970.

Smart, N., *Doctrine and Argument in Indian Philosophy*. London, 1964.

Zaehner, R. C., *Hindu and Muslim Mysticism*. London, 1960. *Hinduism*. London, 1962 (paperback 1966).

Zimmer, H., *Philosophies of India*, edited by J. Campbell. New York, 1957.

2. General works, Primary Sources.

Sacred Books of the East, edited by Max Muller. 51 vols. Oxford, 1875–. Reprinted at Delhi, 1964. (Contains both Indian and Chinese works.)

A Source Book in Indian Philosophy, edited by S. Radhakrishnan and C. A. Moore. Princeton (N.J.), 1957. (Contains selections and bibliographies of primary sources.)

Sources of Indian Tradition, edited by W. T. de Bary. 2 vols. New York, 1964.

The Wisdom of China and India. See under Chinese Philosophy, 2.

3. Early Indian Thought and Religion

(i) PRIMARY SOURCES

Edgerton, F., *The Bhavagad Gītā, Translated and Interpreted*. 2 vols. Cambridge (Mass.), 1952.

Hume, R. E., *Thirteen Principal Upanishads*. Oxford, 1921.

Macnicol, N., *Hindu Scriptures*. London, 1938. (Selections from *Rig-Veda*, and Upanishads, and the whole of the *Gītā*.)

Mascaró, J., *The Upanishads*. Translation from the Sankskrit, with an Introduction. Penguin Books, 1965 and reprints. (A selection of sublimer passages from the religious point of view.) *The Bhagavad Gītā*. Translated from the Sanskrit with an Introduction. Penguin Books, 1962 and reprints.

Radhakrishnan, S., *The Principal Upanishads*. London, 1953.

(ii) SECONDARY SOURCES

Barua, B. M., *A History of Pre-Buddhistic Indian Philosophy*. Calcutta, 1921.

Gonda, J., *The Vision of the Vedic Poets*. The Hague, 1963. *Notes on Brahman*. Utrecht, 1950.

Keith, A. B., *The Religion and Philosophy of the Veda and Upanishads*. 2 vols. Harvard, 1925. (A standard work.)

Macdonell, A. A., *Vedic Mythology*. Strasbourg, 1897.

Mehta, P. D., *Early Indian Religious Thought*. London, 1956.
Renou, L., *Religions of Ancient India*. London, 1953.

4. Jainism
Jaini, J., *Outlines of Jainism*. Cambridge, 1940.
Padmarajiah, Y. J., *A Comparative Study of Jaina Theories of Reality and Knowledge*. Bombay, 1956.
Stevenson, M., *The Heart of Jainism*. Oxford, 1915.

5. Buddhism
(i) PRIMARY SOURCES
Sacred Books of the Buddhists. Published by the Pali Text Society, London, 1909–.
Conze, E. and others, *Buddhist Texts through the Ages*. Oxford, 1954.
Thomas, E. J., *Early Buddhist Scriptures*. London, 1935.
Dhammapada, translated from Pali, with introduction by J. Mascaró. Penguin Books, 1973.
Buddhist Wisdom Books: Diamond and Heart Sūtras, translated and explained by E. Conze. London, 1975 (1958).
Large Sūtra on Perfect Wisdom, translated from Sanskrit by E. Conze. Berkeley, Los Angeles and London, 1975.
The Lankāvatāra Sātra. A Mahāyāna Text. Translated from the Sanskrit by D. T. Suzuki. London, 1956 (1932).
(For some translations from the Chinese see under *Chinese Philosophy* below.)

(ii) SECONDARY SOURCES
Conze, E., *Buddhism: Its Essence and Development*. London, 1951. *Buddhist Thought in India: Three Phases of Buddhist Philosophy*. London, 1962. *Thirty Years of Buddhist Studies*. Selected Essays. Oxford, 1967. *Further Buddhist Studies*. Oxford, 1975. (Selected essays.)
Eliot, C., *Hinduism and Buddhism. An Historical Sketch*. London, 1954.
Hattori, M., *Dignāga, On Perception*. Cambridge (Mass.), 1968. (Both study and translation.)
Humphreys, C., *Buddhism*. Penguin Books, 1951.
Jayatilleke, K. N., *Early Buddhist Theory of Knowledge*. London, 1963. (A standard work.)
Keith, A. B., *Buddhist Philosophy in India and Ceylon*. Oxford, 1925.
Kalupahana, D., *Causality: The Central Philosophy of Buddhism*. Honolulu, 1975. *Buddhist Philosophy: A Historical Analysis*. Honolulu, 1976.
Morgan, K. W. (editor), *The Path of the Buddha. Buddhism Interpreted by Buddhists*. New York, 1956.
Mookerjee, S., *The Buddhist Philosophy of Universal Flux*. Calcutta, 1935.
Murti, T. R. V., *The Central Philosophy of Buddhism. A Study of the Mādhyamika System*. London, 1955.
Robinson, R. H., *Early Mādhyamika in India and China*. Madison, Milwaukee and London, 1967.

Saratchandra, E. R., *Buddhist Psychology of Perception*. Colombo, 1958.
Stcherbatsky, T. I., *Buddhist Logic*. 2 vols. Leningrad, 1930.
Thomas, E. J., *History of Buddhist Thought*. London, 1959.

6. Materialism

Chattopadhyaya, B., *Lokāyata. A Study in Ancient Indian Materialism*. New Delhi, 1959.
Riepe, D., *The Naturalistic Tradition in Indian Thought*. Seattle, 1961.
Shastri, D., *A Short History of Indian Materialism, Sensationalism and Hedonism*. Calcutta, 1930

7. Vedic Schools

(i) PRIMARY SOURCES
    (a) *Sāmkhya-Yoga*
Sharma, R. D., *The Sāmkhya-Kārikā*. Poona, 1933. (Sanskrit text with English translation and commentary of Gaudapādācārya.)
Woods, J. H., *The Yoga-System of Patañjali*. Cambridge (Mass.), 1914. (Includes two commentaries.)
    (b) *Nyāya-Vaiśesika*
Nyāyadarsāna: The Sūtras of Gautama and Bhāsya with Two Commentaries. Translated by Ganganātha Jha. Edited by Ganganātha Jha and D. S. Nyayapadhyaya. Poona, 1939.
    (c) *Vedānta*
The Brahma Sūtra: The Philosophy of Spiritual Life. Translated by S. Radhakrishnan. London, 1960.
A Source Book of Advaita Vedānta, Edited by E. Deutsch and J. A. van Buitenen. Honolulu, 1971.
The Vedānta Sūtras with the commentaries of Śamkara and Rāmānuja, translated by G. Thibaut, are included in *The Sacred Books of the East,* Oxford, 1890–6 and 1904.

(ii) SECONDARY SOURCES
Bhattacharyya, G. M., *Studies in Nyāya-Vaiśesika Theism*. Calcutta, 1947.
Bhattacharyya, K. C., *Studies in Vedantism*. Calcutta, 1909.
Carpenter, J. E., *Theism in Medieval India*. London, 1926.
Coster, G., *Yoga and Western Psychology. A Comparison*. London, 1934.
Dasgupta, S. N., *Yoga Philosophy in Relation to Other Systems of Indian Thought*. Calcutta, 1930.
Deutsch, E., *Advaita Vedānta: A Philosophical Reconstruction*. Honolulu, 1969.
Devanandan, P. D., *The Concept of Māyā*. London, 1951.
Eliade, M., *Yoga: Immortality and Freedom*. London, 1958.
Faddegon, B., *The Vaiśesika System*. Amsterdam, 1918.
Guénon, R., *Man and His Becoming according to the Vedānta*. London, 1945.
Keith, A. B., *The Sāmkhya System*. London, 1924 (2nd edition). (A standard work.)
    Indian Logic and Atomism. Oxford, 1921. (On Nyāya-Vaiśesika.)

Mahadevan, T. M. P., *Gaudapāda. A Study in Early Advaita*. Madras, 1960.
Raghavendrachar, V. H. N., *The Dvaita Philosophy and Its Place in the Vedānta*. Mysore, 1941.
Raju, P. I., *Thought and Reality: Hegelianism and Advaita*. London, 1932.
Sastri, K., *A Realistic Interpretation of Śankhara-Vedānta*. Calcutta, 1931.
Sharma, B. N. Y., *A History of the Dvaita School of Vedānta and Its Literature*. 2 vols. Bombay, 1960–2.
Shrivastava, S. N. L., *Saṁkhara and Bradley*. Delhi, 1968.
Srinivasachari, S. M., *Advaita and Viśistādvaita*. London, 1961.
Staal, J. F., *Advaita and Neo-Platonism. A Critical Study in Comparative Philosophy*. Madras, 1961.
Thadani, N. V., *The Mīmāmsā*. New Delhi, 1952.
Urquhart, W. J., *The Vedānta and Modern Thought*. London, 1928.
Vidyabhusana, S. C., *A History of Indian Logic*. Calcutta, 1921.

C. CHINESE PHILOSOPHY
(with some reference to Japanese philosophy)

1. General Works

Chi'u Chai., *The Story of Chinese Philosophy*. New York, 1961.
Creel, H. G., *Chinese Thought from Confucius to Mao Tse-tung*. Chicago, 1953. (Paperback, Secaucus, N.J., 1962).
Day, C. B., *The Philosophers of China, Classical and Contemporary*. Secaucus (N.J.), 1962.
Fung Yu-lan, *The Spirit of Chinese Philosophy*. Translated by E. R. Hughes. London, 1947. *A Short History of Chinese Philosophy*, edited by D. Bodde. New York, 1948. (An excellent introduction.) *A History of Chinese Philosophy*. 2 vols. Translated by D. Bodde. Princeton (N.J.), 1952–3. (A standard work.)
Hajime Nakamura, *A History of the Development of Japanese Thought*. 2 vols. Tokyo, 1967.
Hughes, E. R., *Chinese Philosophy in Classical Times*. London, 1954. (with K. Hughes). *Religion in China*. London, 1950.
Liang, Ch'i-ch'ao, *A History of Chinese Political Thought*. London, 1930
Liu, Wu-chi, *A Short History of Confucian Philosophy*. Baltimore (Md.), 1955.
Needham, J., *Science and Civilization in China*. 5 vols. Cambridge, 1956–76, especially Vol. 2, *History of Scientific Thought*, 1956. Also *Clerks and Craftsmen in China and the West*, Cambridge, 1970.
Wang, Kung-ksing, *The Chinese Mind*. New York, 1946.
Wright, A. F. (editor), *Studies in Chinese Thought*. Chicago, 1953.
Wright A. F., *Buddhism in China*. Stanford (Cal.), 1959.
Zürcher, E., *The Buddhist Conquest of China*. 2 vols. Leiden, 1959.

2. General Works: Primary Sources.

The Sacred Books of the East. See above under B, 2.

A Source Book in Chinese Philosophy, edited by Wing-tsit Chan. Princeton (N.J.), 1963. (A very useful book of excerpts from the writings of Chinese philosophers, with introductory and explanatory material.)

An Outline and An Annotated Bibliography of Chinese Philosophy, by Wing-tsit Chan. New Haven, 1965.

Sources of Chinese Tradition. 2 vols. Compiled by W. T. de Bary with Wing-tsit Chan and B. Watson. New York and London, 1960. (Selected readings from writers of early times up to Mao Tse-tung, illustrating philosophical, social and political thought and background. With explanatory material.)

Sources of Japanese Tradition, edited by Tsunoda Ryusoka, W. T. de Bary and D. Keene. New York, 1958.

Japanese Religion and Philosophy: A Guide to Japanese Reference and Research Materials. By D. Holzman, M. Yuhiko and others. Ann Arbor, 1959.

The Wisdom of China and India. Edited by Lin Yutang. New York, 1942. (Selections from *Rig-Veda,* Upanishads, The Epics, Buddhist Writings, *Lao Tzu, Chuang Tzu,* Confucius, and literary sources.)

3. Primary Sources. Early Philosophers

The Chinese Classics. Translated by J. Legge. 5 vols. Hong Kong, 1960.

The Analects of Confucius. Translated by A. Waley. London, 1938.

The Works of Mencius. Translated by W. A. C. H. Dobson. Toronto, 1963.

Mencius. Translated with an Introduction by D. C. Lau. Penguin Books, 1970 and reprints.

Mo Tzu: Basic Writings. Translated by B. Watson. New York, 1963.

Lao Tzu: Tao Te Ching. Translated with an Introduction by D. C. Lau. Penguin Books, 1963 and reprints.

The Way and Its Power: A Study of the Tao Te Ching and Its Place in Chinese Thought. By A. Waley. London, 1935. (Includes translation.)

Chuang Tzu. Translated by H. A. Giles. London, 1961.

Chuang Tzu. Basic Writings. Translated by B. Watson. New York, 1964.

The Book of Lieh Tzu. Translated by A. C. Graham. London, 1960 (reprint, 1973).

The Book of Lord Shang. A Classic of the Chinese School of Law. Translated by J. J. L. Duyvendak. San Francisco, 1974; London, 1978.

The I Ching or Book of Changes. Translated by C. F. Baynes. 2 vols. London, 1951.

Records of the Historian. Chapters from the Shih Chi of Ssu-ma Ch'ien. Translated by B. Watson. New York, 1969. (From a work compiled in the 2nd century AD, covering Chinese history from early times.)

Courtier and Commoner in Ancient China. Selections from the History of the Former Han by Pan Ku. Translated by B. Watson. New York, 1974.

4. Primary Sources. Neo-Confucianism

The Philosophy of Human Nature by Chu Hsi. Translated, with notes, by J. P. Bruce. London, 1922. (Selections from essays and letters.)

Reflections on Things at Hand. The Neo-Confucian Anthology compiled by Chu Hsi and Lu Tsu-Ch'ien. Translated by Wing-tsit Chan. New York, 1967.

The Philosophy of Wang Yang-ming. Translated from the Chinese by F. G. Henke. Introduction by J. H. Tufts. Second edition, New York, 1964.

5. Primary Sources: Buddhist.

The Lotus of the Wonderful Law. Translated from the Chinese by W. E. Soothill. Oxford, 1930. Reprint, London, 1975.

Scripture of the Lotus Blossom of the Fine Dharma. The Lotus Sūtra. Translated from the Chinese by L. Hurvitz. New York, 1976.

Hui-neng. The Platform Scripture. The Basic Classic of Zen Buddhism. Translated by Wing-tsit Chan. New York, 1963.

The Platform Sūtra of the Sixth Patriarch. Translated by P. B. Yampolsky. New York, 1978.

The Blue Cliff Record. Translated from the Chinese by T. and J. C. Cleary. Boulder (Colorado) and London, 1977.

The Threefold Lotus Sūtra. Translated by B. Kato and others. New York and Tokyo, 1975.

Zen Master Dōgen. An Introduction with Selected Writings. By Yūhō Yokoi, with the assistance of Daizen Victoria. New York and Tokyo, 1976.

6. Secondary Sources on Particular Themes

Benoit, H., *The Supreme Doctrine. Psychological Studies in Zen Thought.* New York, 1955.

Bruce, J. P., *Chu Hsi and His Masters.* London, 1923.

Chang, Carsun, *The Development of Neo-Confucian Thought.* 2 vols. New York, 1957–62.

Ching, J., *To Acquire Wisdom: The Way of Wang Yang-Ming.* New York, 1976.

Cooper, J. C., *Taoism. The Way of The Mystic.* Wellingborough, 1972.

Creel, H. G., *Confucius: The Man and the Myth.* New York, 1949. (As *Confucius and the Chinese Way,* paperback, New York, 1960.) *What is Taoism? And Other Studies in Chinese Cultural History.* Chicago and London, 1970.

De Bary, W. T., and others, *Self and Society in Ming Thought.* New York, 1970. (and the Conference on Seventeenth-Century Chinese Thought). *The Unfolding of Neo-Confucianism.* New York, 1975.

Dumoulin, H., *A History of Zen Buddhism.* Translated by P. Peachey. London, 1963.

Hee-Jin Kim, *Dōgen Kigen: Mystical Realist.* Tucson (Ariz.), 1975.

Hu Shih, *Development of Logical Method in Ancient China.* Shanghai, 1922.

Kaltenmark, M., *Lao Tzu and Taoism.* Stanford (Cal.), 1969.

Munro, D. J., *The Concept of Man in Early China.* Stanford (Cal), 1969.

Piovesana, G. K., *Recent Japanese Philosophical Thought, 1862–1962: A Survey*. Tokyo, 1963.

Rubin, V. A., *Individual and State in Ancient China*. New York, 1976.

Suzuki, D. T., *Studies in the Lankāvatāra Sutra*. London, 1930. *Essays in Zen Buddhism*. 3 vols. London, 1927–34. (Reprint 1970.) *An Introduction to Zen Buddhism*. London, 1949. (Reprint, 1960.) *Studies in Zen*. London, 1955.

Waley, A., *Three Ways of Thought in Ancient China*. London, 1939.

Watts, A. (with Chung-liang Huang), *Tao: The Watercourse Way*. London, 1976.

Welch, H., *The Parting of the Way, Lao Tzu and the Taoist Movement*. Boston (Mass.), 1957.

Wu-chi Liu, *Confucius, His Life and Time*. New York, 1955.

D. ISLAMIC PHILOSOPHY

1. General Works

Guillaume, A., *Islam*. Penguin Books, 1956.

Fakhry, M., *A History of Islamic Philosophy*. New York and London, 1971. (Good introduction.)

Nicholson, R. A., *The Mystics of Islam*. London and Boston, 1914. (reissued 1963). *Studies in Islamic Mysticism*. Cambridge, 1921.

Peters, F. E., *Aristotle and the Arabs. The Aristotelian Tradition in Islam*. New York and London, 1968.

Rahman, F., *Prophecy in Islam*. London, 1958.

Rescher, N., *Studies in Arabic Logic*. Pittsburgh, 1963.

Rosenthal, E. I. J., *Political Thought in Medieval Islam*. Cambridge, 1958.

Schuon, F., *Understanding Islam*. Translated by D. M. Matheson. London, 1963. *Dimensions of Islam*. Translated by P. Townsend. London, 1970. *Islam and the Perennial Philosophy*. Translated by J. P. Hobson. London, 1976. (These books are concerned more with the general religious background than with philosophical thought as such.)

Sharif, M. M. and others, *A History of Muslim Philosophy*. 2 vols. Wiesbaden, 1963–6. (This work contains more about Muslim thought in Persia than Fakhry's work does.)

Von Grünebaum, E., *Medieval Islam*. Chicago and London, 1961.

Walzer, R., *Greek into Arabic. Essays on Islamic Philosophy*. Oxford, 1962.

Watt, W. Montgomery, *Islamic Philosophy and Theology*. (*Islamic Surveys*, Vol. I). Edinburgh, 1962.

2. Primary Sources

(i) AL-FĀRĀBĪ

Al-Fārābī's Short Commentary on Aristotle's Prior Analytics. Translated by N. Rescher. Pittsburgh, 1963.

On the Philosophy of Plato. Translated by Muhsin Mahdi. New York, 1962.

On the Philosophy of Aristotle. Translated by Muhsin Mahdi. New York, 1962.
On Attaining Felicity. Translated by Muhsin Mahdi. New York, 1962.

(ii) AVICENNA

Avicenna on Theology. Translated by A. J. Arberry. London, 1951.
Avicenna's Psychology. Translated by F. Rahman. London, 1952.
The Metaphysica of Avicenna (Ibn Sīnā). Translated by Parviz Morewedge. London, 1973.

(iii) AL-GHAZĀLĪ

Al-Ghazālī Tahafut al-Falsifah (Incoherence of the Philosophers). Translated by S. A. Kamali. Lahore, 1958.

(iv) AVERROES

The Philosophy and Theology of Averroes. Translated by M. Jamil-Ur-Rehman. Baroda, 1921. (A translation of the *Decisive Treatise* and other writings.)
Tahafut al-Tahafut (Incoherence of the Incoherence). Translated by S. Van den Bergh. Oxford, 1954; London, 1978. (Averroes' reply to Al-Ghazālī.)
Averroes' Commentary on Plato's Republic. Translated by E. I. J. Rosenthal. Cambridge, 1956.
Averroes on the Harmony of Religion and Philosophy. Translated by G. F. Hourani. London, 1961.

(v) IBN KHALDŪN

The Muquaddimah: An Introduction to History. Translated by F. Rosenthal. 3 vols. New York, 1958; 2nd edition, Princeton (N.J.), 1967.

(vi) RŪMI

Discourses of Rumi. Translated by A. J. Arberry. London, 1961.

(vii) IBN 'ARABĪ

The Wisdom of the Prophets (Fusus al-Hikam). Translated (from a French translation of the Arabic) by A. Culme-Seymour. London (Beshara Publications), 1975.
'Whoso Knoweth Himself' (from the Treatise on Being). Translated by T. H. Weir. London (Beshara Publications), 1976.

3. Secondary Sources on Particular Philosophers and Themes

Abdel-Kader, A. H., *The Life, Personality and Writings of al-Junayd*. London, 1962.
Affifi, A. E., *The Mystical Philosophy of Muhyid Dín-Ibnul 'Arabī*. Cambridge, 1939.
Afran, S. M., *Avicenna: His Life and Works*. London, 1958.
Burckhardt, T., *An Introduction to Sufi Doctrine*. Translated by D. M. Matheson. Lahore, 1959.
Corbin, H., *Creative Imagination in the Sufism of Ibn 'Arabī*. Princeton (N.J.), 1969. (By a specialist in the thought of Ibn 'Arabī.)
Fakhry, M., *Islamic Occasionalism and Its Critique by Averroes and Aquinas*. London, 1958.
Husaini, S. A. R., *The Pantheistic Monism of Ibn Al-'Arabī*. Lahore, 1970.

Iqbāl, A., *The Life and Thought of Rūmi*. Lahore, 1956 (3rd revised edition, 1974). *Reconstruction of Religious Thought in Islam*. London, 1951. *Development of Metaphysics in Persia*. London, 1908.

Izutsu, T., *A Comparative Study of the Key Philosophical Concepts in Sufism and Taoism*. 2 vols. Tokyo, 1966–7. (The first volume is on Ibn 'Arabī.) *The Concept and Reality of Existence*. Tokyo, 1971. (Largely on Sabzawārī's metaphysics.)

Mahdi, Muhsin, *Ibn Khaldūn's Philosophy of History. A Study in the Philosophic Foundation of the Science of Culture*. New York and London, 1957 (paperback, Chicago, 1964).

Nasr, S. H., *Three Muslim Sages*. Cambridge (Mass.), 1963. (Treats of Avicenna, Suhrawardī and Ibn 'Arabī.) *An Introduction to Islamic Cosmological Doctrines. Conceptions of Nature and Methods Used for Its Study by Ikhwān al Safā, al-Bīrūnī, and Ibn Sīnā*. Cambridge (Mass.), 1964. *Ideals and Realities of Islam*. London, 1966. *Islamic Studies*. Beirut, 1967. *Science and Civilization in Islam*. Cambridge (Mass.), 1968; New York, 1970. *Sufi Essays*. London, 1972. (Books by a distinguished Iranian scholar.)

Nicholson, R. A., *The Metaphysics of Rūmi*. Lahore, 1959.

Rahman, F., *The Philosophy of Mullā Sadrā*. Albany, 1975.

Smith, M., *Al-Ghazālī, the Mystic*. London, 1949.

Watt, W. Montgomery, *Free Will and Predestination in Early Islam*. London, 1948. *Faith and Practice of Al-Ghazzali*. London, 1953.

Wickens, G. M. (editor), *Avicenna, Scientist and Philosopher: A Millenary Symposium*. London, 1952.

Chronological Table

INDIA

Vedic period *c.*1500 or earlier to *c.*500 BC	**Vedas, Brāhmaṇas,** early **Upanishads**	**Jainism** restored by Vardhamāna, *c.*599–527 BC	**Cārvāka** possibly from 6th cent. BC	**Buddhism** The Buddha *c.*563–*c.*483
Epic period to *c.*AD 200	MAHĀBHĀRATA (including *Gītā*)			Third Buddhist Council, 247 BC
Period of formation of the Vedic schools	1. SĀṂKYA (oldest probably) Īśvarakrishna 3rd or 5th cent. AD (disputed)			Distinction between Hīnayāna and Mahāyāna probably shortly before Christian era.
	2. YOGA Systematized by Patañjali, 2nd cent. AD			1. HĪNAYĀNA (i) Theravāda (Ceylon and S.E. Asia) Buddhagosa, 5th cent. AD
	3. VAIŚESIKA Kanāda, 1st cent. AD			(ii) *Sarvastivāda* Vaibhāsika an offshoot. (iii) *Sautrāntika*
	4. NYĀYA Aksapāda Gautama, 3rd cent. AD Udayana, 10th cent. Gaṅgeśa, 12th cent. Rhagunātha, 16th cent.			2. MAHĀYĀNA (i) *Mādhyamīka* Nāgārjuna, 2nd cent. AD (ii) *Yogācara* Asāṅga and Vasubandhu, 4th cent. AD Dignāga, 6th cent. Dharmakīrti, 7th cent.
	5. PURVA MĪMĀMSĀ Jaimini, 4th cent. BC? Śabara, *c.*AD 400 Kumārila, 8th cent. Prabhākara, 8th cent.			During period of Muslim conquests (11th and 12th centuries) Buddhism ceased to be a living force in India.
	6. VEDĀNTA Bādarāyana, *c.*2nd cent. BC (i) *Advaita* Gaudapāda, 8th cent. AD Śaṃkara, 788–820 (ii) (ii) *Viśistadvaita* Rāmānuja, *d.*1127. Vedānta Deśika, 13th cent. Nimbarka, 13th cent. (iii) *Dvaita* Madhva, 13th cent. Vallabha, 15th cent. Caitanya, 16th cent. Baladeva, 18th cent.			

CHINA

ISLAM

Confucianism
Confucius, c.551–479 BC
Mencius, c.370–289 BC
Hsün Tzu, c.298–238 BC

Official State philosophy,
136 BC
Tung Chung-shu, c. 179–
104 BC
Ssu-ma Ch'ien, c.145–c.90
BC
Han Yü, d.AD 824

NEO-CONFUCIANISM
Ch'eng Hao, 1032–1085.
Ch'eng I, 1033–1107.
Sung dynasty, 960–1279.
Chu Hsi, 1130–1200.
Ming dynasty, 1368–1644.
Wang Yang-ming, 1472–
1529.
Ch'ing or Manchu
dynasty, 1644–1912.
Wang Fu'chih, 1619–92.
Yen Yüan, 1635–1704.
K'ang Yu-wei,
1858–1927.

Taoism
Lao Tzu, 6th cent. BC
(Legendary)
Chuang Tzu, 4th cent. BC

NEO-TAOISM
Wang Pi, AD 226–49
Kuo Hsiang, d.AD 312

Other Early Schools

1. MOHISM
   Mo Tzu, c.479–438 BC
   (Mohism faded out
   about 200 BC)

2. SCHOOL OF NAMES
   Hui Shih, c.380–305
   BC

3. LEGALISM
   Han Fei, d.233 BC

4. YIN-YANG
   Tsou Yen, c.305–c.240
   BC

BUDDHISM
Introduced in 1st cent. AD

Some Schools
1. THREE-TREATISES
   4th–7th cents.
   Kumārajīva 344–413.
   Seng-chao, 384–414.

2. CONSCIOUSNESS-ONLY
   6th–9th centuries.
   Hsüan-tsang, 596–664.

3. T'IEN-T'AI
   Hui-ssu, 514–577.
   Chih-i, 538–597.
   Hui-wen, 550–577.

4. HUA-YEN
   Fa-tsang, 643–712.

5. CH'AN
   Bodhidharma, d.c.534.

   Shen-hsiu, c.605–706.
   Hui-neng, 638–713.
   Persecution of
   Buddhist monasticism,
   845.

Mohammed, c.AD 570–632
Al-Ash'ari, 873–935.
Al-Kindī, c.800–c.866.
Al-Fārābi, c.875–c.950.
Ibn Sīnā (Avicenna),
980–1037.
Al-Ghazālī, c.1058–1111.
Ibn Rushd (Averroes),
c.1126–1198.
Suhrawardī, 1155–1191.
Ibn 'Arabī, 1165–1240.
Rūmi, 1207–1273.
Ibn Khaldūn, 1332–1406.
Mullā Sadrā, 1571–1640.
Sabzawārī, 1797–1878.

Index

(In certain entries principal references are in heavy type. A small *n* indicates that a reference is to a note. When several notes with the same number occur on a given page, the chapter number is added in brackets.)